Better Homes and Gardens®

CLASSIC AMERICAN RECIPES

© 1982 by Meredith Corporation, Des Moines, Iowa.
All Rights Reserved. Printed in the United States of America.
First Edition. First Printing.
Library of Congress Catalog Card Number: 81-67548
ISBN: 0-696-00795-9

On the cover: (clockwise from back left) Mother Ann's Birthday Cake garnished with peach preserves, California Cooler, Whole Wheat Bread, New Orleans Café au Lait, Fresh Fruit Salad, Short'nin' Bread, Steak Sandwiches, and Green Beans Amandine. (See Index for recipe pages.)

Our seal assures you that every recipe in *Classic American Recipes* is endorsed by the Better Homes and Gardens Test Kitchen. Each recipe is tested for family appeal, practicality, and deliciousness.

Better Homes and Gardens® Books
Editor: Gerald M. Knox
Art Director: Ernest Shelton
Managing Editor: David A. Kirchner

Food and Nutrition Editor: Doris Eby
Department Head—Cook Books:
Sharyl Heiken
Senior Food Editor: Elizabeth Woolever
Senior Associate Food Editors:
Sandra Granseth,
Rosemary C. Hutchinson
Associate Food Editors:
Jill Burmeister, Julia Martinusen,
Diana McMillen, Alethea Sparks,
Marcia Stanley, Diane Yanney
Recipe Development Editor:
Marion Viall
Test Kitchen Director: Sharon Stilwell
Test Kitchen Home Economists:
Jean Brekke, Kay Cargill,
Marilyn Cornelius, Maryellyn Krantz,
Marge Steenson

Associate Art Directors (Creative):
Linda Ford, Neoma Alt West
Associate Art Director (Managing):
Randall Yontz
Copy and Production Editors:
Nancy Nowiszewski, Lamont Olson,
Mary Helen Schiltz, David A. Walsh
Assistant Art Directors:
Faith Berven, Harijs Priekulis
Graphic Designers: Mike Burns,
Alisann Dixon, Mike Eagleton,
Lynda Haupert, Deb Miner,
Lyne Neymeyer, Trish Church-Podlasek,
Bill Shaw, D. Greg Thompson

Editor in Chief: Neil Kuehnl
Group Editorial Services Director:
Duane Gregg
Executive Art Director: William J. Yates

General Manager: Fred Stines
Director of Publishing:
Robert B. Nelson
Director of Retail Marketing:
Jamie Martin
Director of Direct Marketing:
Arthur Heydendael

Classic American Recipes
Editors: Jill Burmeister,
Diana McMillen
Copy and Production Editors:
Lamont Olson, Mary Helen Schiltz
Graphic Designer:
D. Greg Thompson

CONTENTS

6 INTRODUCTION

8 THE EAST

30 THE SOUTH

52 THE MIDWEST

66 THE SOUTHWEST

82 THE WEST

96 ALL-AMERICAN RECIPES

162 AMERICA CELEBRATES

186 INDEX

Clockwise from upper left:
(See Index for recipe pages.)
**Strawberry Shortcake,
Whole Wheat Batter Rolls,
Broiled Scrod
with Lemon Butter,
Chess Tarts,
Ramos Gin Fizz,
Lemonade,
Fig Bread,
Muffuletta,
Chocolate Chip Cookies,
and Glazed Carrots.**

CLASSIC AMERICAN RECIPES

The American cuisine reflects a medley of cultures found in the United States today. It's a blend of food heritages from the New World's original settlers, the immigrants who left their homeland to come to America, and our native Americans — all offering an array of food possibilities.

Classic American Recipes mirrors the ingenuity behind the development of American foods. Spurred by borrowed ideas, advanced food production techniques, and the available resources, a diverse cuisine has evolved.

Each region within the country has a food style all its own. Separate chapters on the five regions — the East, the South, the Midwest, the Southwest, and the West — include dishes unique to these areas.

American mobility and the mass communication system of today have resulted in many foods becoming national favorites rather than distinctly regional fare. The sixth chapter offers a selection of these all-American foods.

The book concludes with special recipes most often served by Americans during holidays and celebrations.

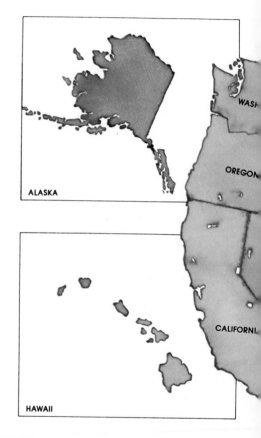

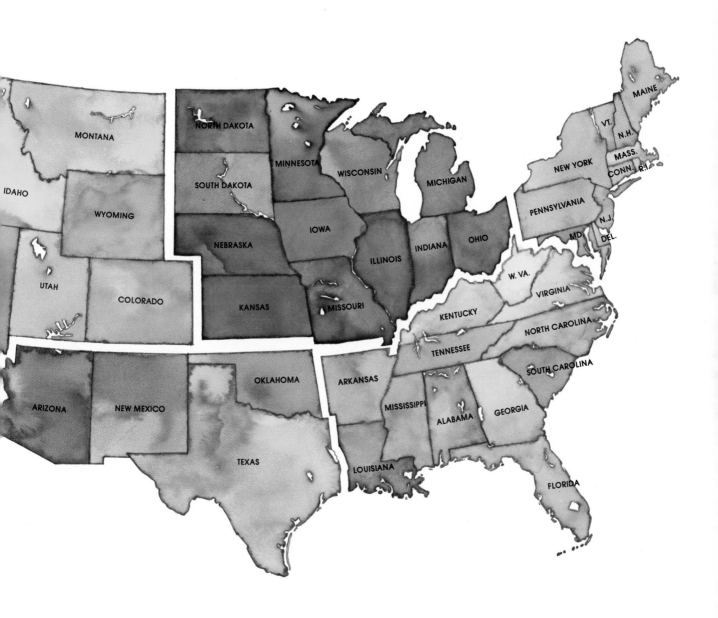

THE
EAST

The American culinary history has its richest heritage in the East where our country was first colonized. Foods from this region show the influences of immigrants who ventured to the United States from England, Germany, France, and the Netherlands. Food tastes range from plain hearty fare to more sophisticated cuisine.

The East is a prime source of fish and seafood because of its proximity to the Atlantic Ocean. Fresh crab, lobster, scrod, cod, scallops, oysters, and clams are a few of the bounties from the sea. Other examples of Eastern produce are maple syrup, cranberries, blueberries, tomatoes, pumpkin, and apples.

Typical Eastern recipes you'll find in this chapter are Boston Baked Beans, Manhattan- and New England-style clam chowders, Pennsylvania Dutch Shoofly Pie, Fish House Punch from Philadelphia, and Indian Pudding that's reminiscent of the early colonies.

Recipe pictured: *New England Boiled Dinner* (see recipe, page 10).

9

Philadelphia Pepper Pot

A main ingredient in this soup is tripe, which is the inner stomach lining of beef. Honeycomb tripe has a lacy appearance and is somewhat chewy. It is available at the butcher counter of most supermarkets.

This soup is seasoned with two kinds of pepper, which is reflected in its name.

2 pounds honeycomb tripe
1½ teaspoons salt
1 1½-pound veal knuckle
1 large onion, sliced (1 cup)
1 stalk celery, sliced (½ cup)
2 sprigs parsley
10 to 12 whole black peppercorns
1 teaspoon salt
1 teaspoon dried thyme, crushed
¼ teaspoon ground red pepper
2 bay leaves
2 medium potatoes, peeled and cut into ½-inch cubes (2 cups)

In a large saucepan or Dutch oven cover tripe with 6 cups *water*. Add 1½ teaspoons salt. Cover and simmer for 3 to 4 hours or till tripe has a clear, jellylike appearance. Drain. Cover and refrigerate.

Meanwhile, in a Dutch oven place the veal knuckle, onion, celery, parsley, peppercorns, salt, thyme, ground red pepper, and bay leaves. Add 6 cups *water*. Cover; simmer 2 hours or till meat is very tender. Remove knuckle. Cut any meat from bones; discard bones. Strain broth, discarding cooked vegetables. Cover and refrigerate broth and veal separately.

Cut tripe and veal into bite-sized pieces. Skim fat from broth. In saucepan heat *4 cups* of the broth. Add tripe, veal, and potatoes. Simmer 15 minutes or till potatoes are tender. Serves 6.

New England Boiled Dinner   *pictured on page 9*

1 3- to 4-pound corned beef brisket
10 small onions
4 medium potatoes, peeled and quartered
4 medium carrots, quartered
3 medium parsnips, peeled and sliced ½ inch thick
2 medium rutabagas, peeled and cut into 1-inch cubes
1 small head cabbage, cored and cut into wedges
Salt
Pepper
Prepared horseradish (optional)
Prepared mustard (optional)
Assorted pickles (optional)

Place corned beef brisket in a 6- or 8-quart Dutch oven; add enough water to cover. Bring to boiling; reduce heat. Cover and simmer about 2 hours or till meat is nearly tender. Add onions, potatoes, carrots, parsnips, and rutabagas. Cover and simmer 15 minutes. Add cabbage; cover and simmer for 15 to 20 minutes more or till cabbage is tender. Season to taste with salt and pepper.

Serve corned beef on a platter surrounded by the vegetables. Serve with horseradish, mustard, and pickles if desired. Pass some of the pan juices. Makes 8 to 10 servings.

Red Flannel Hash

For years cooks have used the leftover corned beef and vegetables from *New England Boiled Dinner* to make *Red Flannel Hash*. When beets are added and the entire mixture is finely chopped, the final result resembles red flannel fabric.

¼ pound salt pork, finely chopped
½ cup finely chopped onion
2 cups finely chopped cooked potatoes
1½ cups finely chopped cooked corned beef (8 ounces)
1 8¼-ounce can beets, drained and finely chopped
Pepper
¼ cup milk
Snipped parsley (optional)

In a 10-inch skillet cook salt pork and onion till pork is light brown and onion is tender. Drain off fat, reserving 2 tablespoons in skillet. In a mixing bowl combine pork, onion, potatoes, corned beef, and beets. Sprinkle with pepper. Toss lightly till well combined. Turn out onto cutting board and chop mixture finely.

Heat skillet; add meat mixture and milk, stirring till combined. Spread evenly in skillet. Cook over medium-low heat about 15 minutes or till bottom is brown. Transfer to a heated serving platter or serve from skillet. Sprinkle with snipped parsley if desired. Makes 4 servings.

Scrapple

The thrifty Pennsylvania Dutch created *Scrapple* as a way to use up scraps of pork left after hog butchering. It is traditionally served with maple syrup, but some people prefer it with catsup or fried apple slices.

1 pound boneless pork shoulder roast, cubed
1 cup cornmeal
¼ cup finely chopped onion
1¼ teaspoons salt
½ teaspoon dried sage, crushed
¼ teaspoon pepper
All-purpose flour
Shortening
Pure maple syrup *or* maple-flavored syrup

In a saucepan place pork and enough water to cover. Bring to boiling. Reduce heat; cover and simmer about 1 hour or till meat is tender. Drain, reserving broth. Add enough water to reserved broth to measure 3 cups. Return to saucepan.

Using 2 forks, pull meat apart into shreds. Stir shredded meat, cornmeal, onion, salt, sage, and pepper into broth in saucepan. Bring to boiling, stirring constantly. Cook and stir about 2 minutes or till very thick. Pour mixture into an 8x4x2-inch loaf pan. Cover and refrigerate several hours or overnight till firm.

Unmold; cut into ½-inch slices. Dip slices into flour. In a skillet cook slices, a few at a time, in a small amount of hot shortening over medium-high heat till golden brown. Drain on paper toweling. Serve with maple syrup or maple-flavored syrup. Makes 6 servings.

Schnitz un Knepp

Schnitz means "cut" and refers to the cut dried apples that team with *knepp* (dumplings) to accompany the pork in this dish.

Schnitz un Knepp (SHNITS uhn kuh-NEP) rivals *Scrapple* for popularity among the Pennsylvania Dutch.

1 3-pound smoked pork arm picnic
1 8-ounce package (2 cups) dried apples
¼ cup packed brown sugar
1½ cups all-purpose flour
2 teaspoons baking powder
¼ teaspoon salt
1 beaten egg
½ cup milk
2 tablespoons butter *or* margarine, melted

Remove skin and fat from outside of smoked pork. Place pork in a Dutch oven; add enough water to cover meat. Bring to boiling; reduce heat. Cover and simmer 30 minutes. Stir in dried apples and brown sugar. Cover and simmer 1 hour more.

Meanwhile, for dumplings, stir together flour, baking powder, and salt. Combine egg, milk, and melted butter or margarine. Add to flour mixture; stir just till mixture is moistened. Drop dough by rounded tablespoonfuls to make 10 mounds atop the simmering liquid. Cover and simmer 20 minutes (do not lift cover).

Serve pork on a serving platter with the dumplings and apples. Spoon a small amount of the remaining liquid over the meat. Serves 8 to 10.

Plymouth Succotash

This recipe differs from the more conventional corn and lima bean succotash in that it combines chicken, corned beef, pork, beans, and hominy in a hearty stew.

It traditionally is served in Plymouth, Massachusetts, on Forefathers' Day (December 21) to commemorate the Pilgrims' landing in America.

½ **pound dry navy beans**
2 **whole large chicken breasts**
1 **pound corned beef brisket**
2 **ounces salt pork, rinsed**
1½ **cups sliced potatoes**
½ **cup chopped turnip**
½ **cup chopped carrot**
1 **small onion, sliced**
1 **small bay leaf**
1 **14½-ounce can yellow hominy, drained**
 Salt
 Pepper

Rinse beans. In a Dutch oven or kettle combine beans and 2 cups cold *water*. Cover; soak overnight. (Or, bring to boiling; simmer 2 minutes. Remove from heat. Cover and soak 1 hour.) Drain and rinse beans.

Meanwhile, in a saucepan cook chicken in 2 cups *water*, covered, over low heat for 35 to 40 minutes or till tender. Drain chicken, reserving broth. Cool chicken; remove and discard skin and bones. Cut chicken into bite-sized pieces; chill.

Add enough water to reserved broth to make 3 cups liquid. Stir liquid, corned beef, and salt pork into beans. Cover; simmer 1 hour. Add potatoes, turnip, carrot, onion, and bay leaf. Cover; simmer 1 hour more.

Remove corned beef, salt pork, and bay leaf. Discard salt pork and bay leaf. Mash beans slightly. Dice corned beef; return to bean mixture. Add chicken and hominy. Season with salt and pepper. Simmer 15 minutes more. Serve in individual soup bowls. Makes 8 servings.

Chicken Stoltzfus

1 **2½- to 3-pound broiler-fryer chicken, cut up**
4 **cups water**
1 **cup sliced carrots**
½ **cup chopped onion**
½ **cup sliced celery**
1½ **teaspoons salt**
⅛ **teaspoon pepper**
¾ **cup all-purpose flour**
¼ **teaspoon salt**
3 **tablespoons shortening**
2 **tablespoons ice water**
¼ **cup butter *or* margarine**
⅓ **cup all-purpose flour**
⅛ **teaspoon crushed thread saffron**
½ **cup light cream *or* milk**
 Salt
 Pepper
 Parsley sprigs (optional)
 Whole spiced apples (optional)

In a large kettle or Dutch oven place chicken and the 4 cups water. Bring to boiling; skim off foam. Add carrot, onion, celery, the 1½ teaspoons salt, and the ⅛ teaspoon pepper. Cover and simmer about 45 minutes or till chicken is tender. Remove chicken from broth. Cool chicken till easy to handle. Skim fat from broth. Strain broth, reserving vegetables and 3 cups liquid. Remove and discard chicken skin and bones. Cut chicken into bite-sized pieces.

In a bowl combine the ¾ cup flour and the ¼ teaspoon salt. With a pastry blender cut in shortening till mixture resembles coarse crumbs. Sprinkle 2 tablespoons ice water over flour mixture; toss with fork. Press dough into a ball. On a lightly floured surface, roll dough to ⅛-inch thickness. Cut with a pastry wheel or sharp knife into 1½-inch squares or diamonds. Place on a baking sheet. Bake in a 450° oven for 12 to 15 minutes.

Meanwhile, melt the butter or margarine in the kettle or Dutch oven. Stir in the ⅓ cup flour and the saffron. Stir in reserved broth and light cream or milk. Cook and stir till mixture is thickened and bubbly. Cook and stir 1 minute more. Reduce heat; add reserved vegetables and chicken. Heat through. Season to taste with salt and pepper. Serve chicken mixture with pastry squares. Garnish with parsley sprigs and spiced apples if desired. Makes 6 servings.

Pictured:
Chicken Stoltzfus

Broiled Scrod with Lemon Butter *pictured on pages 4 and 5*

Scrod is young cod or haddock. It is extremely popular in New England, where cod and haddock are important to the economy as well as the cuisine.

2 **pounds fresh *or* frozen scrod fillets, cut 1 inch thick**
3 **tablespoons butter *or* margarine, melted**
1 **to 2 tablespoons lemon juice**
 Salt
 Pepper
 Snipped parsley
 Hot boiled potatoes

Thaw fish fillets, if frozen. Place in a single layer on greased rack of an unheated broiler pan. Tuck under any thin edges. Combine butter and lemon juice; brush fillets. Sprinkle with salt and pepper.

Broil fish 4 inches from heat for 10 to 12 minutes or till fish flakes easily when tested with a fork, brushing occasionally with lemon-butter mixture. Brush with lemon-butter mixture before serving. Garnish with snipped parsley. Serve with hot boiled potatoes. Makes 6 servings.

Poached Salmon with Egg Sauce

Salmon ran thick in New England coastal rivers in the early years of our nation. Abigail Adams, wife of our second president, began the custom of serving salmon on Independence Day. It was topped with a creamy sauce made with hard-cooked eggs and was served with new potatoes and fresh peas.

Atlantic salmon is now scarce, but it is still a Yankee favorite on the Fourth of July.

2 **pounds fresh *or* frozen salmon fillets**
2 **cups water**
2 **lemon slices**
1 **teaspoon salt**
1 **bay leaf**
2 **tablespoons butter *or* margarine**
2 **tablespoons all-purpose flour**
½ **teaspoon salt**
⅛ **teaspoon pepper**
1 **cup milk**
1 **tablespoon lemon juice**
2 **hard-cooked eggs, sliced**

Thaw fish, if frozen. Place salmon on large piece of cheesecloth; fold cloth over sides, leaving ends free to use as handles. Place in a large roasting pan or poaching pan (without rack). Add water, lemon, 1 teaspoon salt, and bay leaf. Cover and simmer about 18 minutes or till salmon flakes easily when tested with a fork. Lift from pan; drain. Remove cheesecloth; place salmon on a heated serving platter.

Meanwhile, for sauce, in a medium saucepan melt butter or margarine. Stir in flour, ½ teaspoon salt, and pepper. Add milk all at once. Cook and stir over medium heat till thickened and bubbly. Cook and stir 1 minute more. Stir in lemon juice. Fold in sliced eggs. Spoon some sauce over salmon; pass remaining sauce. Makes 6 servings.

Recipe note: If desired, use 6 fresh or thawed frozen salmon steaks. Poach the salmon as above for 8 to 10 minutes.

Codfish Balls

8 **ounces salt cod**
2 **cups chopped potatoes**
1 **egg**
2 **tablespoons butter *or* margarine**
½ **teaspoon Worcestershire sauce**
¼ **teaspoon pepper**
¼ **teaspoon dry mustard**
 Cooking oil for deep-fat frying

Soak salt cod in enough water to cover for several hours or overnight, changing water several times. Drain fish; cut into small pieces. In a saucepan cook cod and potatoes in boiling water about 10 minutes or till tender; drain well.

Place cod mixture in a mixer bowl; beat at medium speed with electric mixer till well combined. Add egg, butter or margarine, Worcestershire sauce, pepper, and dry mustard; beat till well combined.

In a saucepan or deep-fat fryer heat about 2 inches cooking oil to 375°. Carefully drop heaping tablespoons of cod mixture into hot fat. Fry 2 to 3 minutes or till golden, turning once. Drain on paper toweling. Keep warm in a 325° oven while frying the remaining mixture. Makes 4 servings.

Boiled Lobster

When preparing the *Boiled Lobster* for serving, don't discard the red roe (found in the female lobster) or the brownish-green liver. Both the roe and liver are edible and are considered delicacies. Serve them alongside the lobster with melted butter.

12 **cups water**
1 **tablespoon salt**
2 **1- to 1½-pound live lobsters**

In a large kettle combine water and salt. Bring to boiling. Choose active live lobsters. Holding one lobster just behind the eyes, rinse it in cold running water. Plunge it headfirst into the boiling salted water. Repeat with other lobster. Return to boiling; reduce heat and simmer over low heat for 20 minutes. Remove lobsters at once.

Place each lobster on its back. With a sharp knife, cut lobster in half lengthwise. With kitchen shears or knife, cut away membrane on tail. Remove and discard black vein and body organs except red roe and liver. Crack open large claws; break away from body.

Serve lobster in the shell with melted butter if desired, or use in recipes as cooked lobster. Use a seafood fork to remove meat from claws, tail, and body. Pull smaller claws away from body and gently suck out the meat. Makes 2 servings or about 2 cups meat.

Lobster Newburg

This elegant seafood dish was first served at Delmonico's in New York City in the 1890s. It was named after Ben Wenberg, a friend of restaurant manager Charles Delmonico. A disagreement between the men prompted Delmonico to transpose the letters in the first syllable.

1½ **cups whipping cream**
4 **beaten egg yolks**
1 **tablespoon butter *or* margarine**
¼ **teaspoon salt**
⅛ **teaspoon ground red pepper**
2 **5-ounce cans lobster, drained, broken into large pieces, and cartilage removed, *or* 10 ounces cooked lobster**
2 **tablespoons dry sherry**
Cooked wild rice, buttered toast, *or* patty shells

In a heavy saucepan combine whipping cream, beaten egg yolks, butter or margarine, salt, and ground red pepper. Cook and stir till mixture thickens and just comes to a gentle boil. Stir in lobster and dry sherry. Cook and stir just till heated through. Immediately serve atop wild rice, toast, or patty shells. Makes 4 servings.

Sautéed Bay Scallops

Bay scallops are smaller and more tender than common sea scallops. If you use larger scallops in this recipe, cook them 6 to 7 minutes or till tender.

¾ **pound fresh *or* frozen bay scallops**
2 **tablespoons butter *or* margarine**
1 **clove garlic, minced**
⅛ **teaspoon dried tarragon, crushed**

Thaw scallops, if frozen. In a skillet over medium heat melt butter or margarine. Add the minced garlic and dried tarragon; cook 1 minute. Remove from heat.

Add scallops. Sprinkle lightly with salt and pepper. Cook over medium heat about 4 minutes or just till tender, turning occasionally. Makes 3 or 4 servings.

Crab Cakes

Use canned snow crab to economize in this recipe. It is less expensive than other varieties of crab meat and has a finer texture that is suitable for these fried patties.

¼ **cup finely chopped onion**
2 **tablespoons butter** *or* **margarine**
4 **beaten eggs**
⅔ **cup fine dry bread crumbs**
2 **teaspoons Worcestershire sauce**
1 **teaspoon dry mustard**
½ **teaspoon salt**
2 **6-ounce cans crab meat, drained, flaked, and cartilage removed**
¼ **cup fine dry bread crumbs**
2 **tablespoons shortening** *or* **cooking oil**
Lemon wedges

In a saucepan cook onion in the butter or margarine till tender. In a bowl stir together the eggs, ⅔ cup bread crumbs, Worcestershire sauce, dry mustard, and salt. Stir in onion and crab meat.

Using about ¼ *cup* crab mixture for each, shape into ten ½-inch-thick patties. Coat with the ¼ cup fine dry bread crumbs. Cover and refrigerate for 30 minutes.

In a skillet heat shortening or cooking oil. Add *half* the patties; cook over medium heat about 3 minutes on each side or till golden brown, turning once. Drain on paper toweling; keep warm while frying remaining patties. Add more shortening or oil to skillet if necessary. Serve warm with lemon wedges. Makes 5 servings.

Steamed Clams

48 **soft-shell clams in shells**
3 **gallons cold water**
1 **cup salt**
1 **cup hot water**
Butter, melted

Thoroughly wash clams. In a large kettle combine *1 gallon* of the cold water and ⅓ *cup* of the salt. Add clams. Let stand 15 minutes; drain and rinse well. Repeat soaking and rinsing twice more.

Place clams on a rack in a kettle with the hot water. Cover tightly and steam for 5 to 10 minutes or just till shells open. Discard any clams that do not open. Loosen clams from shells. Serve with melted butter. Makes 4 servings.

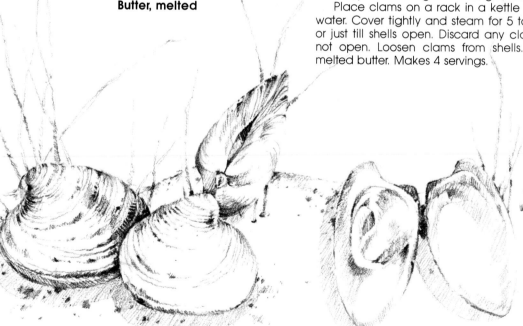

New England Clam Chowder

The earliest version of clam chowder was *New England Clam Chowder*. It combined salt pork, potatoes, and clams in a smooth cream mixture.

Later, tomatoes and clams were combined and *Manhattan Clam Chowder* was created. There has been a battle raging ever since over the virtue of this combination.

Rhode Island and Connecticut stand up for the Manhattan chowder, while the rest of New England is devoted to the creamy version.

1 **pint shucked clams** *or two* **6½-ounce cans minced clams**
¼ **pound salt pork, diced,** *or 3* **slices bacon, cut up**
3 **cups diced potatoes**
1 **large onion, chopped (1 cup)**
2 **cups milk**
1 **cup light cream**
3 **tablespoons all-purpose flour**
½ **teaspoon salt**
½ **teaspoon dried thyme, crushed**
   Dash pepper

Drain the clams, reserving clam liquid. Chop shucked clams. Add enough water to reserved liquid to measure 2 cups. In a large saucepan cook salt pork or bacon till crisp; remove pork or bacon and set aside. Add clam liquid, potatoes, and onion to drippings. Cover; cook about 15 minutes or till potatoes are tender.

Stir in clams, 1½ cups of the milk, and the cream. Combine remaining ½ cup milk and the flour; stir into chowder. Cook and stir till thickened and bubbly. Cook and stir 1 minute more. Stir in salt, thyme, and pepper. Sprinkle cooked salt pork or bacon atop. Makes 6 main-dish servings or 8 to 10 side-dish servings.

Manhattan Clam Chowder

1 **pint shucked clams** *or two* **6½-ounce cans minced clams**
3 **slices bacon, cut up**
1 **cup finely chopped celery**
1 **large onion, chopped (1 cup)**
1 **16-ounce can tomatoes, cut up**
2 **medium potatoes, peeled and chopped**
½ **cup finely chopped carrots**
½ **teaspoon dried thyme, crushed**

Drain the clams, reserving clam liquid. Chop shucked clams. Add enough water to reserved liquid to measure 3 cups. In a large saucepan partially cook bacon; add celery and onion. Cook and stir till vegetables are tender. Stir in reserved clam liquid, *undrained* tomatoes, potatoes, carrots, thyme, 1 teaspoon *salt*, and ⅛ teaspoon *pepper*. Cover and simmer for 30 to 35 minutes. Mash vegetables slightly to thicken. Stir in clams; heat through. Makes 6 main-dish servings or 8 to 10 side-dish servings.

Snapper Soup

Turtle meat is a relatively rare delicacy with a flavor similar to veal. The fresh meat is available in Eastern states, although some fish markets in other regions also carry it.

If you wish, substitute a 2½- to 3-pound broiler-fryer chicken for the turtle meat.

1 **1½-pound veal knuckle**
¼ **cup butter** *or* **margarine**
¼ **cup all-purpose flour**
1 **large onion, chopped (1 cup)**
½ **cup chopped celery**
½ **cup chopped carrot**
½ **teaspoon dried marjoram, crushed**
¼ **teaspoon dried thyme, crushed**
¼ **teaspoon pepper**
1 **small bay leaf**
1 **whole clove**
2 **10½-ounce cans condensed beef broth**
1 **7½-ounce can tomatoes, cut up**
2½ **to 3 pounds turtle meat, cut up**
½ **cup dry sherry**
1 **lemon slice**
   Dash bottled hot pepper sauce
2 **hard-cooked eggs, chopped**

Place veal knuckle in a shallow roasting pan. Bake in a 450° oven 30 minutes. Meanwhile, in a Dutch oven combine butter and flour. Cook and stir over medium heat 15 to 20 minutes or till golden brown.

Add onion, celery, carrot, marjoram, thyme, pepper, bay leaf, and clove. Stir in beef broth and *undrained* tomatoes. Add browned knuckle. Bring to boiling; reduce heat. Cover and simmer 1½ hours. Remove knuckle. Cut any meat from bones; discard bones. Strain broth, discarding vegetables. Cover; chill broth and veal separately.

Meanwhile, in a large kettle combine turtle meat and 6 cups *water*. Cover; cook 1 hour or till tender. Drain, reserving 2 cups liquid. Cut meat from bones; discard bones.

Dice veal and turtle meat. Skim fat from veal broth. In Dutch oven combine veal, veal broth, turtle meat, reserved cooking liquid, sherry, lemon, and hot pepper sauce. Bring to boiling; reduce heat. Cover; simmer 10 minutes. Remove lemon slice; stir in chopped eggs. Season. Serves 6.

Boston Baked Beans

Boston Baked Beans has changed little through the years. However, local cooks have introduced their own favorite flavorings to the dish. In Connecticut they bury an onion in the beans to impart flavor. Some even stud the onion with whole cloves. Maple syrup sweetens the pot in Vermont. Cape Cod cooks are known to pour cream over the beans the last hour of baking.

1 pound dry navy beans
8 cups cold water
6 cups cold water
½ teaspoon salt
⅓ cup molasses
¼ cup packed brown sugar
1 teaspoon dry mustard
½ teaspoon salt
⅛ teaspoon pepper
1 small onion
¼ pound salt pork

Rinse beans. In a heavy 3-quart saucepan combine beans and the 8 cups cold water. Cover; soak overnight. (Or, bring to boiling; simmer 2 minutes. Remove from heat. Cover and soak 1 hour.) Drain beans; rinse and cover with 6 cups cold water. Stir in ½ teaspoon salt. Bring to boiling. Cover; reduce heat. Simmer 1¼ to 1½ hours or till tender.

Drain beans, reserving liquid. In a 2½-quart bean pot or casserole combine the drained beans, molasses, brown sugar, dry mustard, ½ teaspoon salt, and the pepper. Stir in 1 cup of the reserved bean liquid.

Place the whole onion in the beans so it is covered. Score the salt pork at 1-inch intervals. Place pork in the beans, covering all but the rind. Cover bean pot or casserole and bake in a 300° oven about 3 hours, adding additional reserved bean liquid if necessary. If using bean pot, uncover the last half hour or till pork rind is crisp. Makes 6 to 8 servings.

Harvard Beets

Harvard's school color of crimson is said to have inspired the name for these sweet and sour beets.

To make Yale beets, substitute orange juice for the vinegar.

4 fresh medium beets or
   one 16-ounce can sliced or
   diced beets
2 tablespoons sugar
2 teaspoons cornstarch
⅛ teaspoon salt
3 tablespoons vinegar
1 tablespoon butter or
   margarine

Peel fresh beets; slice or cut into ½-inch cubes. Cover and cook in a small amount of boiling salted water about 20 minutes or till tender. Drain, reserving ⅓ cup liquid. (Or, drain canned beets, reserving ⅓ cup liquid.)

Combine sugar, cornstarch, and salt. Stir in reserved beet liquid, vinegar, and butter or margarine. Cook and stir till thickened and bubbly. Cook and stir 2 minutes more. Stir in cooked or canned beets. Cook and stir about 5 minutes more or till heated through. Makes 4 servings.

Maple Syrup Acorn Squash

2 acorn squash
4 teaspoons butter or
   margarine
¼ cup pure maple syrup or
   maple-flavored syrup
¼ teaspoon salt
¼ teaspoon ground cinnamon
⅛ teaspoon ground allspice
¼ cup coarsely chopped walnuts

Halve squash lengthwise; remove seeds. Place halves, cut side down, in a 13x9x2-inch baking pan. Cover with foil. Bake in a 350° oven 40 minutes.

Turn squash cut side up; halve pieces. Add ½ teaspoon of the butter or margarine and 1½ teaspoons of the maple syrup to each squash portion. Sprinkle each with salt, cinnamon, and allspice. Sprinkle with walnuts. Bake, uncovered, about 20 minutes more or till squash is tender. Serves 4.

Pictured:
Maple Syrup Acorn Squash, Boston Baked Beans, and Pumpkin Bread (see recipe, page 23).

Corn Oysters

Also known as "mock oysters," these corn fritters are considered by some to taste like deep-fried oysters.

- **2 fresh ears of corn** *or* **one 8¾-ounce can whole kernel corn, drained**
- **1 beaten egg**
- **¼ cup all-purpose flour**
- **3 tablespoons light cream** *or* **milk**
- **1 tablespoon butter, melted Cooking oil for shallow-fat frying**

Remove husks and silk from fresh ears of corn. With a sharp knife cut down through the center of kernels on each row of corn. Cut corn from cob; scrape cob. (Or, coarsely chop canned whole kernel corn.) In a bowl combine the corn, egg, flour, light cream or milk, butter, ¼ teaspoon *salt*, and ⅛ teaspoon *pepper*.

In a heavy skillet heat about ½ inch cooking oil to 365°. Carefully drop corn mixture by tablespoons into hot fat. Fry 2 minutes or till golden, turning once. Makes about 12.

Scootin' 'Long the Shore

Cape Cod fishermen for years have prepared this simple potato dish while at work and enjoy it while "scootin' 'long the shore."

- **4 cups sliced, peeled potatoes**
- **1 large onion, sliced (1 cup)**
- **3 tablespoons bacon drippings**
- **3 slices bacon, crisp-cooked, drained, and crumbled (optional)**

Combine potatoes and onion; season with salt and pepper. In skillet cook potato mixture, covered, in drippings over medium-low heat about 15 minutes or just till tender. Uncover; turn and cook 5 to 10 minutes more or till done, loosening occasionally. Garnish with bacon if desired. Serves 6.

Dutch Fried Green Tomatoes

Although this Pennsylvania Dutch recipe is traditionally made with green tomatoes, firm ripe tomatoes may be used. Prepare as directed for green tomatoes, except fry the ripe tomato slices for 3 to 4 minutes on each side or till light brown.

- **2 green medium tomatoes, cut into ½-inch-thick slices**
- **1 teaspoon sugar**
- **⅓ cup all-purpose flour**
- **½ teaspoon salt**
- **¼ teaspoon pepper**
- **1 beaten egg**
- **¼ cup butter** *or* **margarine**
- **1 cup milk**

Sprinkle tomato slices with sugar. In a bowl stir together flour, salt, and pepper. Dip tomato slices into beaten egg, then into flour mixture. (Reserve remaining flour mixture.) In a 10-inch skillet melt the butter or margarine. Fry the tomato slices over medium-low heat about 8 minutes on each side or till brown. Place on heated serving plate.

For sauce, stir remaining flour mixture into pan drippings; add milk. Cook and stir till thickened and bubbly; cook and stir 1 minute more. If necessary add a little more milk till desired consistency. Serve over tomato slices. Makes 4 to 6 servings.

Pumpkin Soup

- **2 tablespoons butter**
- **1 16-ounce can pumpkin** *or* **2 cups mashed cooked pumpkin**
- **3 cups milk**
- **2 teaspoons instant chicken bouillon granules**
- **⅛ teaspoon ground allspice Croutons**

In a saucepan melt butter or margarine; stir in pumpkin. Stir in milk, chicken bouillon granules, allspice, and ¼ teaspoon *pepper*. Bring mixture to boiling, stirring constantly. Pour soup into individual soup bowls. Top each serving with the croutons. Makes 4 servings.

Shaker Spinach with Rosemary

Shaker cooking stressed simple, wholesome food, the importance of vegetables, and the use of herbs. This recipe is a perfect example of that philosophy.

1 **pound spinach (12 cups)**
2 **tablespoons butter** *or* **margarine**
1 **green onion, chopped**
1 **teaspoon snipped parsley**
¼ **teaspoon dried rosemary, crushed**

Trim stems from spinach. Tear leaves into bite-sized pieces. In a large saucepan simmer spinach, covered, in a small amount of water 3 minutes; drain well.

In a saucepan melt butter or margarine. Add spinach, green onion, parsley, and rosemary. Cook and toss for 2 to 3 minutes or till spinach is well coated and heated through. Makes 4 servings.

Waldorf Salad

The maître d' of New York's Waldorf-Astoria created *Waldorf Salad* in the late 1800s. Although walnuts were not in the first salad, they are now a characteristic ingredient.

2 **medium apples**
1 **tablespoon lemon juice**
1½ **cups chopped celery**
¾ **cups coarsely chopped walnuts**
½ **cup mayonnaise** *or* **salad dressing**
Lettuce leaves

Core and dice apples. In a large bowl sprinkle diced apples with lemon juice. Add celery, walnuts, and mayonnaise or salad dressing; toss to coat. Serve on individual lettuce-lined plates. Makes 8 servings.

Recipe note: If desired stir in 1 cup grapes, halved and seeded, and additional mayonnaise.

Cucumber Salad

½ **cup dairy sour cream**
2 **tablespoons sugar**
2 **tablespoons white vinegar**
½ **teaspoon salt**
¼ **teaspoon pepper**
2 **cups thinly sliced unpeeled cucumbers**
1 **small onion, thinly sliced and separated into rings**

In a bowl stir together sour cream, sugar, vinegar, salt, and pepper. Place cucumber and onion slices in a serving bowl. Pour sour cream mixture atop. Toss to coat. If desired, cover and refrigerate to chill. Makes 6 servings.

Parker House Rolls

Parker House Rolls, named for the famed Parker House Hotel and restaurant in Boston, are also called pocketbook rolls because they resemble small purses. These rich rolls are an ideal accompaniment for everything from plain pot roast to the most elegant beef tournedos.

3 to 3½ cups all-purpose flour
1 package active dry yeast
¾ cup milk
⅓ cup butter *or* margarine
¼ cup sugar
½ teaspoon salt
2 eggs
Butter *or* margarine, melted

In a large mixer bowl combine *1½ cups* of the flour and the yeast. In a saucepan heat milk, the ⅓ cup butter or margarine, the sugar, and salt just till warm (115° to 120°) and butter is almost melted; stir constantly. Add to flour mixture; add eggs. Beat at low speed with electric mixer for 30 seconds, scraping sides of bowl constantly. Beat 3 minutes at high speed.

Stir in as much of the remaining flour as you can with a spoon. Turn out onto a lightly floured surface. Knead in enough of the remaining flour to make a moderately stiff dough that is smooth and elastic (6 to 8 minutes total). Shape into a ball. Place in a lightly greased bowl; turn once to grease surface. Cover; let rise in warm place till double (about 1 hour). Punch down; divide dough in half. Cover; let rest 10 minutes.

On a lightly floured surface, roll each half of the dough to ¼-inch thickness. Cut with a floured 2½-inch round cutter. Brush with melted butter or margarine. Make an off-center crease in each round. Fold so large portion overlaps small portion slightly. Place rolls, with large portions up, side by side in a greased 13x9x2-inch baking pan. Cover; let rise till nearly double (about 30 minutes). Bake in a 375° oven for 15 to 18 minutes or till done. Makes about 24 rolls.

Anadama Bread

Anadama Bread, so the story goes, was invented by a New England fisherman with a lazy wife. Out of desperation, he baked his own bread and sat down to eat it mumbling, "Anna, damn her."

4½ to 4¾ cups all-purpose flour
2 packages active dry yeast
2 cups cold water
1 cup cornmeal
½ cup molasses
⅓ cup lard *or* shortening
1 tablespoon salt
2 eggs
2 tablespoons butter *or* margarine, melted

In a large mixer bowl combine *1 cup* of the flour and the yeast. In a saucepan combine water and cornmeal. Cook and stir till thickened and bubbly. Remove from heat; stir in molasses, lard or shortening, and salt. Cool just till warm (115° to 120°). Add to flour mixture; add eggs. Beat at low speed with electric mixer for 30 seconds, scraping sides of bowl. Beat 3 minutes at high speed.

Stir in as much of the remaining flour as you can with a spoon. Turn out onto a lightly floured surface. Knead in enough of the remaining flour to make a moderately stiff dough that is smooth and elastic (8 to 10 minutes). Place in a greased bowl; turn once. Cover and let rise in warm place till double (about 1 hour). Punch down; divide dough in half. Cover and let rest 10 minutes.

Shape into two loaves and place in two greased 8x4x2-inch loaf pans. Cover; let rise till nearly double (about 45 minutes). Brush with melted butter or margarine. Bake in a 375° oven for 20 minutes. Cover with foil. Bake 20 minutes more. Remove from pans; cool on wire rack. Makes 2 loaves.

Pumpkin Bread *pictured on page 19*

pictured on page 19

Pumpkin was so important to the colonists' survival that it was described as "fruit which the Lord fed his people with till corn and cattle increased."

Now a people with an ample food supply, Americans still appreciate pumpkin, especially in baked goods such as this moist *Pumpkin Bread.*

 2 **cups all-purpose flour**
 2 **teaspoons baking powder**
 ½ **teaspoon salt**
 ½ **teaspoon ground cinnamon**
 ½ **teaspoon ground nutmeg**
 ¼ **teaspoon baking soda**
 ⅓ **cup shortening**
 ½ **cup sugar**
 ½ **cup packed brown sugar**
 2 **eggs**
 1 **cup canned pumpkin** *or*
   mashed cooked pumpkin
 ½ **cup milk**
 ½ **cup coarsely chopped walnuts**
 ½ **cup raisins**

Stir together flour, baking powder, salt, cinnamon, nutmeg, and baking soda. In a large mixer bowl beat shortening at medium speed with electric mixer for 30 seconds. Add sugar and brown sugar; beat till well combined. Add eggs, one at a time, beating 1 minute after each addition.

Stir together pumpkin and milk. Add flour mixture and pumpkin mixture alternately to beaten mixture, beating at low speed after each addition just till combined. Stir in nuts and raisins.

Turn batter into a greased 9x5x3-inch loaf pan. Bake in a 350° oven for 50 to 55 minutes or till wooden pick inserted near center comes out clean. Cool 10 minutes on wire rack. Remove from pan; cool thoroughly. Wrap in foil and store overnight before slicing. Makes 1 loaf.

Boston Brown Bread

Early New England Puritans steamed *Boston Brown Bread* on Saturday afternoons in accordance with their Sabbath cooking ban. Because tradition dies hard in New England, the custom of serving this bread at Saturday night supper is still followed in some households today.

 ½ **cup whole wheat flour**
 ¼ **cup all-purpose flour**
 ¼ **cup yellow cornmeal**
 ½ **teaspoon baking powder**
 ¼ **teaspoon baking soda**
 ¼ **teaspoon salt**
 1 **beaten egg**
 ¼ **cup molasses**
 2 **tablespoons sugar**
 2 **teaspoons cooking oil**
 ¾ **cup buttermilk** *or* **sour milk**
 ¼ **cup raisins**

Stir together whole wheat and all-purpose flours, cornmeal, baking powder, baking soda, and salt. In a mixing bowl combine egg, molasses, sugar, and oil. Add flour mixture and buttermilk alternately to molasses mixture, beating well. Stir in raisins. Turn batter into two well-greased 16-ounce vegetable cans. Cover cans tightly with foil.

Place a rack in a large Dutch oven. Pour in hot water to depth of 1 inch (water should not cover rack). Place cans on rack. Bring water to boiling; reduce heat. Cover and simmer 2½ to 3 hours or till done. Add boiling water as needed. Remove cans; let stand 10 minutes. Remove bread from cans. Serve warm. Makes 2 loaves.

Funnel Cakes

Funnel Cakes are a Pennsylvania Dutch original often served with sausage and syrup for breakfast.

Try creating interesting shapes with the batter, or make the traditional spiral pattern.

 2 **beaten eggs**
 1½ **cups milk**
 2 **cups all-purpose flour**
 1 **teaspoon baking powder**
 ½ **teaspoon salt**
 2 **cups cooking oil**
   Powdered sugar
   Pure maple syrup *or*
   maple-flavored syrup
   (optional)

For batter, in a mixing bowl combine eggs and milk. Stir together flour, baking powder, and salt. Add to egg mixture; beat with rotary beater till smooth.

In an 8-inch skillet heat oil to 360°. Using a finger to cover the bottom opening of a funnel with a ½-inch spout (inside diameter), pour a generous ½ cup batter into funnel. To release batter into the hot oil, remove finger and move funnel in a circular motion. Fry about 2½ minutes or till golden brown. Using 2 wide metal spatulasn turn cake carefully. Cook about 1 minute more.

Drain on paper toweling; sprinkle with powdered sugar. Repeat with remaining batter. Serve warm with syrup if desired. Makes 4 or 5 cakes.

Joe Froggers

Uncle Joe was an old man who made the best molasses cookies in Marblehead, Massachusetts. They were called *Joe Froggers* because they were as big and dark as the frogs in Joe's pond. Fishermen found they kept well at sea and traded them for rum, one of Joe's secret ingredients.

4 cups all-purpose flour
1½ teaspoons ground ginger
1 teaspoon baking soda
½ teaspoon ground cloves
½ teaspoon ground nutmeg
⅛ teaspoon ground allspice
¾ cup butter *or* margarine
1 cup sugar
1 cup dark molasses
2 tablespoons water
2 tablespoons rum *or* milk

Stir together flour, ginger, baking soda, cloves, nutmeg, and allspice. In a mixer bowl beat butter with electric mixer for 30 seconds. Add sugar and beat till fluffy. Combine molasses, water, and rum or milk. Add flour mixture and molasses mixture alternately to beaten mixture; beat till well blended. Cover; chill several hours or overnight.

On a well-floured surface roll dough to ¼-inch thickness. Cut with a floured 4-inch round cutter. Place on greased cookie sheet. Bake in a 375° oven for 10 to 12 minutes or till done. Cool about 1 minute before removing to wire rack. Cool. Makes 18 to 22 cookies.

Lord Baltimore Cake

Lord Baltimore Cake is thought to have been named after the founder of the colony of Maryland.

Unlike the white Lady Baltimore cake, this stately cake is made with egg yolks and flavored with rum. Other points of difference are the use of brown sugar in the fluffy frosting and crushed macaroons in the filling.

2¼ cups all-purpose flour
1 tablespoon baking powder
1 teaspoon salt
¾ cup butter *or* margarine
1¼ cups sugar
8 egg yolks
1 tablespoon rum
½ teaspoon lemon extract
¾ cup milk
Lord Baltimore Frosting
Lord Baltimore Filling

Grease and lightly flour two 9x1½-inch round baking pans; set aside. Stir together flour, baking powder, and salt. In a mixer bowl beat butter or margarine at medium speed with electric mixer for 30 seconds. Add sugar and beat till fluffy. Add egg yolks, two at a time, beating 1 minute after each addition. Beat in rum and lemon extract.

Add flour mixture and milk alternately to beaten mixture, beating on low speed after each addition just till combined. Turn batter into prepared pans. Bake in a 350° oven for 25 to 30 minutes or till a wooden pick inserted in center comes out clean. Cool 10 minutes on wire racks. Remove from pans. Cool thoroughly.

Meanwhile, prepare Lord Baltimore Frosting and Filling. Spread filling between cake layers. Frost sides and top with frosting. Serves 12.

Lord Baltimore Frosting: In top of double boiler combine 1½ cups packed *brown sugar,* ⅓ cup cold *water,* 2 *egg whites,* 2 teaspoons *light corn syrup,* and a dash *salt.* Beat at low speed with electric mixer for 30 seconds to blend. Place over boiling water (upper pan should not touch water). While beating constantly at high speed with electric mixer, cook about 7 minutes or till frosting forms stiff peaks. Remove from heat; add 1 teaspoon *vanilla.* Beat 2 to 3 minutes more or till of spreading consistency.

Lord Baltimore Filling: Combine *1 cup* of the *Lord Baltimore Frosting,* ½ cup crumbled *soft macaroons,* ½ cup chopped *pecans,* and 12 *candied cherries,* chopped (about ¼ cup).

Pictured:
Lord Baltimore Cake and Joe Froggers.

Hartford Election Cake

When the first town meetings were held in New England, village stores sold yeast cakes to hungry colonists. Later, politicians in Hartford, Connecticut used such cakes to repay straight-ticket voters. *Hartford Election Cake* is served today as a traditional refreshment at election-day celebrations.

½ cup dry sherry
1½ cups raisins
1½ cups milk
5 cups all-purpose flour
⅔ cup sugar
1 package active dry yeast
½ teaspoon salt
¾ cup butter *or* margarine
½ cup packed brown sugar
2 eggs
1 teaspoon ground cinnamon
½ teaspoon ground nutmeg
¼ teaspoon ground cloves
1 cup chopped pecans
½ cup diced candied citron
  Sherry Icing
  Pecan halves
  Candied citron, cut into thin strips, *or* candied fruit (optional)

Grease and lightly flour a 10-inch fluted tube pan. In a small saucepan heat sherry till warm; add raisins. Remove from heat. Let stand several hours or overnight. In a saucepan heat milk till lukewarm (110° to 115°); remove from heat. Combine *1½ cups* of the flour, ⅓ *cup* of the sugar, yeast, and salt. Add milk; stir till combined. Cover; let stand in warm place till double (45 to 60 minutes).

Stir dough down. In a mixer bowl beat butter, brown sugar, and remaining ⅓ cup sugar. Add eggs, one at time, beating 1 minute after each. Combine remaining 3½ cups flour, the cinnamon, nutmeg, and cloves. Stir in the 1 cup chopped pecans and ½ cup diced citron.

Stir yeast mixture and raisin-sherry mixture into egg mixture. Stir in dry ingredients. Turn dough into prepared pan. Cover; let rise till double (about 1½ hours).

Bake in a 350° oven 1 hour or till done, covering with foil the last 15 minutes if necessary, to prevent overbrowning. Invert onto wire rack to cool. Frost with Sherry Icing. Top with pecan halves. Garnish with strips of citron rolled into flower shapes or candied fruit if desired. Serves 12.

Sherry Icing: Combine 2 cups sifted *powdered sugar,* 1 teaspoon *vanilla,* and enough *dry sherry* (about 2 tablespoons) till the icing is of drizzling consistency.

Mother Ann's Birthday Cake *pictured on the cover*

Mother Ann's Birthday Cake is the traditional birthday cake of Ann Lee, founder of the Shakers, one of the earliest religious societies in America.

In the original recipe for this light layer cake, a twig from a peach tree was used to beat the batter, giving it a delicate peach flavor.

2½ cups all-purpose flour
¼ cup cornstarch
4 teaspoons baking powder
1 teaspoon salt
1 cup butter *or* margarine
2¼ cups sugar
1 tablespoon vanilla
1½ cups milk
7 egg whites
½ teaspoon cream of tartar
  Butter Frosting
1 cup peach preserves

Grease and lightly flour three 9x1½-inch round baking pans. Combine flour, cornstarch, baking powder, and salt. In mixer bowl beat butter with electric mixer for 30 seconds. Add sugar and vanilla; beat till well combined. Add flour mixture and milk alternately to beaten mixture, beating after each addition till combined.

In large mixing bowl beat egg whites and cream of tartar with rotary beater till stiff peaks form. Fold into beaten mixture. Turn into pans. Bake in a 350° oven about 25 minutes or till done. Cool 10 minutes on wire racks. Remove from pans; cool.

Meanwhile, prepare Butter Frosting. To assemble, spread one cake layer with ½ cup peach preserves. Top with another cake layer; spread with remaining ½ cup preserves. Top with remaining cake layer. Frost sides and top with frosting. Serves 12 to 16.

Butter Frosting: In small mixer bowl beat ½ cup *butter or margarine* till fluffy. Add 2½ cups sifted *powdered sugar;* beat well. Beat in ¼ cup *milk* and 1½ teaspoons *vanilla.* Gradually beat in 2¼ cups sifted *powdered sugar.* Beat in additional milk, if necessary, till of spreading consistency.

Shoofly Pie

All recipes for Pennsylvania Dutch *Shoofly Pie* must contain molasses to be authentic. Flies are attracted to molasses, and it is a popular notion that the nuisance they cause when the pie is made is responsible for the recipe's name.

Pastry for Single-Crust Pie (see recipe, page 141)
1½ **cups all-purpose flour**
½ **cup packed brown sugar**
6 **tablespoons butter *or* margarine**
½ **cup molasses**
½ **cup hot water**
½ **teaspoon baking soda**

Prepare and roll out pastry. Line a 9-inch pie plate. Trim pastry to ½ inch beyond edge of plate. Flute edge; *do not prick pastry.* Bake in a 450° oven for 5 minutes. Cool on wire rack.

For the filling, combine flour and brown sugar. Cut in butter till mixture resembles coarse crumbs. Combine molasses, hot water, and baking soda. Pour *one-third* of the molasses mixture into pastry shell. Sprinkle *one-third* of the flour mixture atop. Repeat layers, ending with flour mixture. To prevent overbrowning, cover edge of pie with foil. Bake in a 375° oven for 15 minutes. Remove foil; bake 15 to 20 minutes more or till set. Cool on wire rack before serving. Cover; refrigerate to store. Makes 8 servings.

Maple Custard Pie

Pastry for Single-Crust Pie (see recipe, page 141)
4 **eggs**
½ **cup pure maple syrup *or* maple-flavored syrup**
1 **teaspoon vanilla**
¼ **teaspoon salt**
1½ **cups light cream**
¾ **cup milk**
Unsweetened whipped cream (optional)

Prepare and roll out pastry. Line a 9-inch pie plate. Trim pastry to ½ inch beyond edge of plate. Flute edge high; *do not prick pastry.* Bake in a 450° oven for 5 minutes. Cool on wire rack.

For the filling, in a mixing bowl beat eggs slightly with rotary beater or fork. Stir in maple syrup, vanilla, and salt. Gradually stir in light cream and milk; mix well. Place partially baked pie shell on oven rack; pour filling into pie shell. Bake in a 350° oven about 40 minutes or till a knife inserted near center comes out clean. Cool on wire rack. To serve, top with whipped cream if desired. Cover; refrigerate to store. Makes 8 servings.

Apple Pandowdy

Apple Pandowdy is a molasses-flavored deep-dish apple dessert. To keep with tradition, "dowdy" it by breaking up the flaky crust. As you serve it, stir the crust into the apple filling.

Pastry for Single-Crust Pie
(see recipe, page 141)
2 tablespoons butter *or* margarine, melted
¼ cup sugar
¼ teaspoon ground cinnamon
⅛ teaspoon ground nutmeg
Dash salt
5 cups thinly sliced, peeled apples
¼ cup molasses
2 tablespoons water
2 tablespoons butter *or* margarine, melted

Prepare and roll out pastry into a 10-inch square; brush with some of 2 tablespoons melted butter or margarine. Fold in half. Brush with more butter or margarine; fold again and seal edges. Roll again into a 10-inch square and repeat brushing with butter or margarine and folding. Refrigerate.

Stir together sugar, cinnamon, nutmeg, and salt; toss with apple slices. Turn apple mixture into an 8x8x2-inch baking dish. Combine the molasses, water, and 2 tablespoons melted butter or margarine; pour over apple mixture in baking dish.

Roll pastry into a 10-inch square. Place over apples; turn under and flute pastry to sides but not over edge of dish. Bake in a 400° oven 10 minutes. Reduce heat to 325°; bake 30 minutes more. Remove from oven. Using a sharp knife, "dowdy" the crust by making several gashes through crust and apples about 1 inch apart in each direction. Return to oven; bake 10 minutes more. Serve warm. Serves 6 to 8.

Blueberry Grunt

Known on Cape Cod as *Blueberry Grunt* and elsewhere in the East as Blueberry Slump, this is a dessert of light, airy dumplings baked on top of a bubbling blueberry mixture. Its peculiar names add to its home-style appeal.

2 cups fresh *or* frozen blueberries
½ cup sugar
1 tablespoon lemon juice
½ teaspoon ground cinnamon
¼ teaspoon ground nutmeg
¾ cup all-purpose flour
2 tablespoons sugar
1 teaspoon baking powder
¼ cup butter *or* margarine
3 tablespoons milk
Light cream *or* milk

In 3-quart saucepan combine blueberries, ½ cup sugar, lemon juice, cinnamon, nutmeg, and 1 cup *water*. Bring to boiling; reduce heat. Cover and simmer 5 minutes.

For dumplings, combine flour, 2 tablespoons sugar, and baking powder. Cut in butter till mixture resembles coarse crumbs. Stir in 3 tablespoons milk just till moistened. Drop by tablespoons to make 6 mounds atop bubbling blueberry mixture. Cover and simmer 15 minutes (do not lift cover). To serve, spoon dumplings into serving bowls; spoon blueberry mixture atop. Serve with light cream or milk. Makes 6 servings.

Indian Pudding

This cornmeal-molasses dessert did not originate with the Indians, as the name suggests. It is called *Indian Pudding* because colonists referred to corn as "Indian corn" to distinguish it from wheat, which they had always called corn.

1 cup milk
⅓ cup yellow cornmeal
2 tablespoons butter *or* margarine
⅓ cup molasses
¼ cup sugar
½ teaspoon ground ginger
½ teaspoon ground cinnamon
2 beaten eggs
1½ cups milk
Whipped cream *or* vanilla ice cream

In a saucepan combine milk, cornmeal, and butter or margarine. Bring to boiling, stirring constantly. Reduce heat; cover and cook over low heat for 10 minutes. Stir in molasses, sugar, ginger, cinnamon, and ¼ teaspoon *salt*; mix well. Combine the eggs and milk; stir into the cornmeal mixture. Turn into a 1-quart casserole.

Bake, uncovered, in a 325° oven about 1 hour or till a knife inserted near center comes out clean. Serve warm or chilled. Top with whipped cream or vanilla ice cream. Makes 6 servings.

Philadelphia Ice Cream

Philadelphia became known for its commercially produced ice cream as far back as the late 1700s.

Creamy *Philadelphia Ice Cream* is different because it is made without eggs or other thickeners. The tiny black specks in this white ice cream are the flavorful seeds from the vanilla bean.

2 **cups light cream**
1 **vanilla bean, split in half**
   lengthwise
2 **cups sugar**
¼ **teaspoon salt**
4 **cups light cream**
2 **cups whipping cream**

In a saucepan heat the 2 cups light cream and the split vanilla bean over low heat for 10 minutes, stirring occasionally; *do not boil.* Remove from heat; remove vanilla bean and set aside. Stir sugar and salt into cream in saucepan.

When vanilla bean is cool enough to handle, scrape out seeds and soft part from inside bean; stir into cooked mixture. Discard bean. Cover and refrigerate about 2 hours or till well chilled.

Combine the 4 cups light cream, the whipping cream, and chilled mixture. Pour into ice cream freezer. Freeze according to manufacturer's directions. After freezing let ripen 4 hours. Makes about 2½ quarts.

Recipe note: Vanilla extract can be substituted for the vanilla bean. Heat the 2 cups light cream just till heated through; remove from heat. Stir in sugar and salt. Cool as above. Stir 4 teaspoons *vanilla* into mixture along with the 4 cups light cream and whipping cream.

Yard of Flannel

A Yard of Flannel is a hot rum and beer drink that was popular in the 1800s. It was originally made by plunging a hot poker into the brew, giving it a burned flavor and a fleecy look.

3 **12-ounce cans beer**
4 **eggs (at room temperature)**
⅓ **cup sugar**
⅔ **cup dark rum**
1 **teaspoon grated gingerroot** *or*
   grated nutmeg

In a saucepan heat beer. In a mixing bowl beat together the eggs and sugar till smooth. Stir in rum and gingerroot or nutmeg. When the beer is almost boiling, combine with the egg mixture by gradually stirring about *1 cup* of the hot beer into the egg mixture. Then stir about *1 cup* of the egg mixture into remaining beer mixture. Continue pouring back and forth till smooth. Serve in mugs. Makes 8 (6-ounce) servings.

Fish House Punch

This strong lemony concoction was served at an elegant Philadelphia eating club known as the Fish House. The officers of George Washington's army declared it their favorite drink.

2 **cups water**
½ **cup sugar**
2 **cups rum**
1 **cup brandy**
¾ **cup lemon juice**
2 **tablespoons peach brandy**
1 **cup ice cubes (10 ice cubes)**
   Ice ring *or* **ice cubes**

In a bowl or pitcher combine water and sugar; stir till sugar is dissolved. Stir in the rum, brandy, lemon juice, and peach brandy. Add the 1 cup ice cubes. Cover; refrigerate several hours. Remove ice. Serve in a punch bowl with ice ring or in glasses over ice cubes. Makes 12 (4-ounce) servings.

THE SOUTH

The South covers a large tract of land that varies widely in climate and geography. It's a land with orange groves, the Appalachian Mountains, the Atlantic and Gulf waters, plantations, and small farms.

The people are descendants of different nationalities: German, Swiss, Scottish, Irish, English, French, African, and Spanish.

In the past, legendary Southern hospitality included lavish spreads served by merchants and plantation owners. Sharecroppers and slaves created simpler recipes.

The Cajuns and Creoles contributed to Southern Louisiana cookery. Cajuns, also known as Acadians, were French-Canadians who left Canada in 1755 to settle in Louisiana swamps and bayous. These country people prepared distinctively spicy recipes.

New Orleans inherited a more sophisticated fare from the Creoles, the aristocratic French who settled there before the Louisiana Purchase of 1803. Delicate seasonings and the use of separate sauces flavor their recipes.

Recipes pictured: *Shrimp Creole* (see recipe, page 38) and *Lane Cake* (see recipe, page 45).

Grillades and Grits

Traditionally, *Grillades* (gree-ODD) *and Grits* is a hearty breakfast dish, but it's good for other meals too.

The rich, thick meat-vegetable mixture is served over hot cooked grits. Beef round steak can be substituted for the veal.

1½ **pounds veal leg round steak, cut ¾ inch thick**
¼ **cup all-purpose flour**
2 **tablespoons lard *or* shortening**
2 **medium onions, chopped**
1 **16-ounce can tomatoes, cut up**
½ **teaspoon instant chicken bouillon granules**
1 **clove garlic, minced**
⅛ **teaspoon ground red pepper**
Hot cooked grits

Trim excess fat from meat. Remove bones. Cut meat into 3-inch pieces. Using meat mallet, pound meat to ¼-inch-thick pieces. Coat meat with flour.

In skillet brown meat, half at a time, on both sides in hot lard or shortening. Remove from skillet; set aside. In the skillet stir together onions, *undrained* tomatoes, bouillon granules, garlic, red pepper, and ½ cup *water*. Return meat to skillet.

Bring mixture to boiling. Reduce heat. Cover and simmer over low heat about 20 minutes. Uncover and simmer 10 minutes more. Serve meat atop hot cooked grits. Spoon gravy in pan over meat. Serves 6.

Red Beans and Rice

Creole *Red Beans and Rice* usually was prepared on Mondays in New Orleans because Monday was wash day. The beans cooked while the clothes dried, which took all day in humid New Orleans.

1 **pound dry red beans *or* dry red kidney beans**
6 **cups cold water**
6 **cups hot water**
1 **pound meaty ham bone *or* smoked pork hocks**
1 **large onion, chopped (1 cup)**
2 **cloves garlic, minced**
1 **bay leaf**
¼ **to ½ teaspoon ground red pepper**
1 **pound smoked sausage, cut into bite-sized pieces**
Hot cooked rice

Rinse beans. In Dutch oven cover beans with 6 cups cold water. Bring to boiling. Reduce heat; simmer 2 minutes. Remove from heat. Cover; let stand 1 hour. (Or, soak beans in water overnight in covered pan.) Drain and rinse.

In the same Dutch oven combine rinsed beans, 6 cups hot water, the ham bone or smoked pork hocks, onion, garlic, bay leaf, and red pepper. Bring to boiling; reduce heat. Cover and simmer about 2½ hours or till beans are tender, adding more water if necessary and stirring occasionally. Remove ham bone or hocks; cut meat from bone and add to bean mixture. Add sausage to bean mixture. Boil gently, uncovered, 15 to 20 minutes more or till a thick gravy forms, stirring occasionally. Serve over rice. Serves 8.

Recipe note: Freeze any leftover bean mixture. To serve, just thaw and reheat in a saucepan, adding additional water as necessary.

Kentucky Burgoo

There are different forms of burgoo, but they're all basically a variety of meats and vegetables in a thick and savory soup or stew. The burgoo originally was served at outdoor feasts in many parts of the South.

1   4- to 4½-pound stewing chicken cut up
2   to 2½ pounds beef shank crosscuts
5   cups water
1   16-ounce can tomatoes, cut up
1½ teaspoons salt
2   medium onions, chopped
1   10-ounce package frozen lima beans
1   10-ounce package frozen whole kernel corn
1   10-ounce package frozen cut okra
1   cup chopped celery
1   medium green pepper, chopped
1   tablespoon sugar
1   tablespoon Worcestershire sauce
1   teaspoon salt
1   teaspoon dried thyme, crushed
¼   teaspoon bottled hot pepper sauce
1   bay leaf
½   cup cold water
2   tablespoons all-purpose flour
¼   cup snipped parsley

In large kettle or Dutch oven combine chicken, beef shanks, the 5 cups water, the *undrained* tomatoes, and the 1½ teaspoons salt. Bring to boiling. Reduce heat; cover and simmer for 1¼ to 1¾ hours or till meats are tender. Remove chicken and beef; let stand till cool enough to handle. Remove meat from bones; discard skin and bones. Dice meat; return to broth mixture. Add onions, lima beans, corn, okra, celery, green pepper, sugar, Worcestershire sauce, the 1 teaspoon salt, the thyme, hot pepper sauce, and bay leaf. Cover and simmer the mixture about 30 minutes or till the vegetables are tender.

In screw-top jar shake together the ½ cup cold water and the flour; stir into stew. Cook and stir till mixture thickens slightly and boils. Cook and stir 1 minute more. Remove bay leaf. Stir in parsley. Makes 12 to 15 servings.

New Orleans Muffuletta *pictured on pages 4 and 5*

The *Muffuletta* is an Italian-style sandwich said to have been created in New Orleans in the early 1900s.

This jumbo-sized sandwich is built on a 1½-pound loaf of round Italian bread. It is filled with salami, cheese, and capacola or ham. A juicy pickled vegetable mixture gives this sandwich its distinctive flavor.

Order the unsliced bread from a bakery, or use two smaller loaves of unsliced bread (about 12 ounces each) instead of the round loaf.

½   cup chopped pimiento-stuffed olives
½   cup chopped ripe olives
½   cup chopped celery
½   cup chopped mixed pickled vegetables
⅓   cup olive oil *or* salad oil
¼   cup snipped parsley
3   tablespoons lemon juice
1   clove garlic, minced
1   teaspoon dried oregano, crushed
    Several dashes freshly ground pepper
1   1½-pound loaf unsliced round Italian bread
4   ounces thinly sliced Genoa salami
4   ounces sliced provolone cheese
4   ounces sliced capacola *or* fully-cooked ham
    Lettuce leaves (optional)

In a bowl combine the pimiento-stuffed olives, ripe olives, celery, pickled vegetables, olive oil or cooking oil, parsley, lemon juice, garlic, oregano, and pepper. Cover and refrigerate for 8 hours or overnight, tossing once or twice.

To assemble sandwich, cut the loaf of bread in half horizontally; cut a ½-inch slice from the cut side of one of the bread halves. (Use slice another time.) Drain olive mixture, reserving the liquid. Brush cut sides of bread with some of the reserved liquid. Layer bottom of loaf with the sliced salami, *half* of the olive mixture, the provolone cheese, the remaining olive mixture, and the capacola or ham. Top with lettuce leaves if desired. Cover with bread top. Cut sandwich into sections to serve. Makes 6 servings.

Ham with Red-Eye Gravy

A Southern breakfast favorite is *Ham with Red-Eye Gravy.* It is traditionally served over hot cooked grits, hot biscuits, or with both.

The red-eye gravy can be made from ham juices and water cooked down, or with coffee added, as in this recipe.

3 **country-style ham slices** *or* **fully-cooked ham slices, cut ½-inch thick**
1 **teaspoon instant coffee crystals**
   Few drops liquid smoke (optional)
   Hot cooked grits
   Hot biscuits

Cut ham slices in half crosswise. Trim excess fat from the ham slices. In skillet cook fat trimmings till crisp; discard trimmings. Cook ham slices in hot fat for 5 to 6 minutes on each side or till brown. Remove ham to warm platter. Stir in the instant coffee crystals and ⁓⅔ cup *boiling water.* If ham is mild-cured, add the liquid smoke. Cook for 2 to 3 minutes, scraping pan to loosen crusty bits. Serve warm gravy over ham with grits and biscuits. Makes 6 servings.

Chicken Andouille Gumbo

Gumbos are a source of controversy in the South. The debate centers on whether to thicken them with okra or with filé (FEE-lay) powder. *Chicken Andouille* (on-DOV-ee) *Gumbo* is thickened with filé, and *Seafood Gumbo* (see recipe, page 37) is thickened with okra.

There are many kinds of gumbos. Ingredients can include a variety of meats, shellfish, poultry, herbs, or andouille, a smoked sausage.

1 **4- to 6-pound stewing chicken, cut up**
⅛ **teaspoon ground red pepper**
½ **cup cooking oil**
½ **cup all-purpose flour**
1 **large onion, chopped (1 cup)**
1 **large green pepper, chopped**
1 **bunch green onions, chopped**
1 **cup chopped celery**
1 **clove garlic, minced**
3 **quarts hot water**
1 **pound andouille** *or* **smoked sausage, cut into ½-inch slices**
2 **to 3 tablespoons filé powder**
   Hot cooked rice

Sprinkle chicken with red pepper, 1 teaspoon *salt,* and ¼ teaspoon *pepper.* In Dutch oven brown chicken in hot oil. Remove chicken and set aside. Add flour to pan drippings, scraping bottom of pan to loosen drippings. Cook over medium heat, *stirring constantly,* for 30 to 45 minutes or till a dark reddish brown roux is formed. Add onion, green pepper, green onion, celery, and garlic; cook and stir over medium heat for 5 to 10 minutes or till vegetables are tender.

Gradually stir in hot water. Add chicken; bring to boiling. Reduce heat; cover and simmer for 2 to 2½ hours or till chicken is very tender, adding more water if necessary. Add andouille or smoked sausage and 1 teaspoon *salt;* simmer 20 to 30 minutes more. Remove from heat; skim off fat. Stir in filé powder; let stand 5 minutes. Serve with hot cooked rice. Makes 8 servings.

Southern Fried Chicken with Cream Gravy

1 **beaten egg**
¼ **cup milk**
¾ **cup finely crushed saltine crackers (21 crackers)**
½ **teaspoon salt**
   Dash pepper
1 **2½- to 3-pound broiler-fryer chicken, cut up**
3 **tablespoons shortening** *or* **cooking oil**
1 **cup milk**
3 **tablespoons all-purpose flour**
¼ **teaspoon salt**
   Dash pepper
1 **cup milk**

Combine the egg and ¼ cup milk. Combine the crackers, ½ teaspoon salt, and dash pepper. Dip chicken in egg mixture; roll in cracker mixture.

In skillet slowly brown chicken pieces in hot shortening, turning occasionally. Add 1 cup milk. Reduce heat; cover and simmer 35 minutes. Uncover and cook about 10 minutes more or till chicken is tender. Remove chicken to serving platter; keep warm. Reserve pan drippings.

In a screw-top jar combine the flour, ¼ teaspoon salt, and dash pepper. Add 1 cup milk; cover and shake well. Stir into reserved drippings. Cook and stir till thickened and bubbly. Cook and stir 1 minute more. If necessary, add additional milk. Serve with fried chicken. Makes 6 servings.

Pictured:
Chicken Andouille Gumbo.

Courtbouillon

Courtbouillon (pronounced KOO-bee-yon in the South) is a spicy fish stew with a tomato base. The tomato mixture is simmered 30 minutes to mellow the flavors. Then the fish is added and cooked just until it flakes with a fork. For a spicy hotness, add the higher level of ground red pepper.

2 pounds fresh *or* frozen redfish, red snapper, *or* halibut fillets
¼ cup cooking oil
¼ cup all-purpose flour
2 medium onions, chopped
½ cup chopped green pepper
⅓ cup chopped celery
2 cloves garlic, minced
1 16-ounce can tomatoes, cut up
½ of 6-ounce can tomato paste
1 bay leaf
⅛ to ¼ teaspoon ground red pepper
½ cup dry red wine
1 small lemon, thinly sliced
2 tablespoons snipped parsley
Hot cooked rice

Thaw fish, if frozen. Skin fish if necessary and cut into 2-inch pieces. In heavy Dutch oven combine cooking oil and flour; cook and stir over medium heat *stirring constantly,* about 15 minutes or till a medium brown roux is formed. Add chopped onion, chopped green pepper, celery, and garlic. Cook and stir for 5 minutes.

Stir in *undrained* tomatoes, tomato paste, bay leaf, ground red pepper, 2 cups *water,* and 1 teaspoon *salt.* Bring mixture to boiling. Reduce heat and simmer, uncovered, for 30 minutes. Add fish pieces; cook 5 minutes more. Stir in wine, lemon slices, and parsley. Cook about 5 minutes more or till fish flakes easily when tested with fork. Remove bay leaf. Serve with hot cooked rice. Makes 6 to 8 servings.

Pompano en Papillote

This "pompano-in-a-bag" is said to resemble a balloon and was made in honor of French balloonist, Alberto Santos-Dumont, a visitor to Antoine's restaurant in New Orleans in 1901.

Florida pompano is found from the Gulf of Mexico to the Carolinas. It is a firm but delicate white fish that is delightful when combined with the rich sauce and baked in a paper bag. Other fish fillets can be used instead of pompano.

4 fresh *or* frozen pompano fillets *or* other fish fillets (about ¾ pound)
2 cups water
½ teaspoon salt
2 lemon slices
1 bay leaf
¼ cup chopped green onion
2 tablespoons snipped parsley
2 tablespoons butter *or* margarine
2 tablespoons all-purpose flour
⅛ teaspoon ground red pepper
¼ cup milk
2 slightly beaten egg yolks
3 tablespoons dry white wine
6 ounces fresh *or* frozen crab meat, thawed, flaked, and cartilage removed, *or* one 6-ounce can crab meat, drained, flaked, and cartilage removed
12 ounces fresh *or* frozen tiny shrimp, cooked, peeled, and deveined

Thaw fish, if frozen. In saucepan combine water, salt, lemon slices, and bay leaf. Bring to boiling. Add fish fillets. Cover and simmer about 15 minutes or till fish flakes easily when tested with a fork.

Remove fish, reserving broth. Cut 4 pieces of parchment or brown paper into heart shapes, about 12x9 inches each. Place one fillet on *half* of each parchment heart.

Strain broth, reserving ¾ cup. In saucepan cook green onion and parsley in butter or margarine till onion is tender. Stir in the flour and ground red pepper. Stir in the reserved broth and the milk. Cook and stir till thickened and bubbly. Cook and stir 1 minute more.

Gradually stir a small amount of the hot mixture into beaten egg yolks; return all to saucepan. Add wine. Cook and stir over low heat just till mixture is bubbly. Stir in crab meat and shrimp; heat through.

Spoon about ½ *cup* sauce over each fillet. Fold other half of paper heart over fillet to form individual packets. Seal, starting at top of heart, by turning edges up and folding, twisting tip of heart to hold packet closed. Place filled packets in a shallow baking pan. Bake in a 400° oven for 10 to 15 minutes. To serve, cut a large X on the top of each packet, folding back each segment. Transfer paper packets to dinner plates. Serves 4.

Shrimp Jambalaya

The Creole name, jambalaya, is derived from jambon, the French word for ham. Ham is just one of the ingredients that can go into this rice dish. Seafood, meats, chicken, and vegetables are also acceptable.

Jambalaya is said to have evolved from the Spanish dish paella. This culinary influence occurred when New Orleans was under Spanish rule from 1792 to 1803.

½ cup celery leaves
2 tablespoons vinegar
1 slice onion
2 teaspoons salt
1 teaspoon seafood seasoning
4 cups water
1½ pounds fresh *or* frozen shrimp in shells *or* 1 pound frozen shelled and cooked shrimp, thawed
1 medium onion, chopped (½ cup)
½ cup chopped celery
1 clove garlic, minced
¼ cup butter *or* margarine
1 16-ounce can tomatoes, cut up
1½ cups water
1 6-ounce can tomato paste
1 teaspoon sugar
1 teaspoon Worcestershire sauce
½ teaspoon salt
½ teaspoon seafood seasoning
Several dashes bottled hot pepper sauce
1 cup sliced fresh mushrooms
1 teaspoon filé powder
Hot cooked rice

When using fresh or frozen shrimp in shells, in a large saucepan combine celery leaves, vinegar, the onion slice, the 2 teaspoons salt, and the 1 teaspoon seafood seasoning. Stir in the 4 cups water; bring to boiling. Add fresh or frozen shrimp in shells; return to boiling. Simmer about 3 minutes or till shrimp turn pink. Drain. Peel shrimp under running water; remove vein that runs down the back. (Omit cooking and cleaning shrimp when using thawed frozen shelled and cooked shrimp.)

Cook the chopped onion, celery, and garlic in butter or margarine till tender. Add *undrained* tomatoes, the 1½ cups water, the tomato paste, sugar, Worcestershire sauce, the ½ teaspoon salt, the ½ teaspoon seafood seasoning, and hot pepper sauce. Cover and simmer 30 minutes. Add shrimp and mushrooms; simmer, uncovered, till shrimp are heated through and mushrooms are tender. Stir in filé powder; serve with hot cooked rice. Makes 6 servings.

Seafood Gumbo

The roux (ROO) is the base for all gumbos and some other Creole soups and stews. It is a thickener made from equal parts of oil or butter and flour. It is cooked slowly and stirred constantly to avoid burning or scorching. If the roux is burned, it won't thicken the mixture.

To judge doneness, cook and stir until the roux is the rich brown color of a tarnished copper penny.

1 pound fresh *or* frozen shelled shrimp
1 6-ounce package frozen crab meat
½ cup all-purpose flour
½ cup cooking oil
2 cups chopped onion
1 cup chopped green pepper
5 or 6 cloves garlic, minced
6 cups hot water
2 cups sliced okra *or* 1 10-ounce package frozen cut okra, thawed
2 teaspoons salt
¼ teaspoon pepper
¼ to ½ teaspoon ground red pepper
1 bay leaf
Hot cooked rice

Thaw shrimp, if frozen, and crab meat. In a heavy 4-quart Dutch oven, stir together flour and oil till smooth. Cook over medium heat, *stirring constantly*, about 35 minutes or till a dark reddish brown roux is formed. Add the onion, green pepper, and garlic; cook and stir over medium heat for 10 to 15 minutes or till vegetables are very tender. Gradually stir in hot water. Stir in okra, salt, pepper, red pepper, and bay leaf. Bring to boiling. Reduce heat; cover and simmer about 1 hour. Add shrimp and crab meat; simmer about 5 minutes or till shrimp turn pink. Remove bay leaf. Season to taste. Serve over hot cooked rice. Makes 6 servings.

Crawfish Étouffée

An étouffée (A-too-FAY) is a Cajun dish usually made with shrimp or crawfish. The shellfish is cooked smothered in the chopped vegetables, resulting in a rich savory sauce that is served with rice.

Crawfish are freshwater crustaceans that look like miniature lobsters. They also are known as crayfish, crawdads, creekcrabs, and yabbies. You'll find crawfish available fresh or frozen.

One pound fresh or frozen peeled shrimp can be substituted for the crawfish in *Crawfish Étouffée.*

1 **pound fresh** *or* **frozen peeled crawfish tails**
¼ **cup butter** *or* **margarine**
¼ **cup all-purpose flour**
¼ **cup butter** *or* **margarine**
1 **medium onion, chopped (½ cup)**
½ **cup chopped green pepper**
½ **cup chopped celery**
1 **clove garlic, minced**
2 **tablespoons snipped parsley**
⅛ **to ¼ teaspoon ground red pepper**
Hot cooked rice

Thaw crawfish, if frozen. In heavy saucepan melt ¼ cup butter or margarine. Stir in the flour. Cook over medium-low heat, *stirring constantly,* about 20 minutes or till a dark reddish brown roux is formed. Add ¼ cup butter or margarine, stirring till melted. Add onion, green pepper, celery, and garlic; cook and stir 15 minutes or till vegetables are very tender.

Add the crawfish, snipped parsley, ground red pepper, ½ teaspoon *salt,* and ¼ teaspoon *pepper.* Stir in ½ cup *water.* Bring to boiling. Reduce heat; simmer, uncovered, for 5 to 10 minutes or till crawfish are tender. Serve with hot cooked rice. Makes 4 servings.

Shrimp Creole   *pictured on page 30*

1 **pound fresh** *or* **frozen shelled shrimp**
1 **medium onion, chopped (½ cup)**
½ **cup chopped green pepper**
½ **cup chopped celery**
2 **cloves garlic, minced**
¼ **cup butter** *or* **margarine**
1 **16-ounce can tomatoes, cut up**
2 **tablespoons snipped parsley**
⅛ **to ¼ teaspoon ground red pepper**
1 **bay leaf**
4 **teaspoons cornstarch**
Hot cooked rice

Thaw shrimp, if frozen. In a 10-inch skillet cook onion, green pepper, celery, and garlic in butter or margarine till tender but not brown. Add *undrained* tomatoes, parsley, ground red pepper, the bay leaf, and ½ teaspoon *salt.* Cover and simmer 15 minutes. Combine cornstarch and 2 tablespoons cold *water;* stir into tomato mixture. Cook and stir till thickened and bubbly. Cook and stir 2 minutes more. Stir in shrimp; return to boiling. Reduce heat; cover and simmer for 5 to 10 minutes or till shrimp are tender. Remove bay leaf. Serve atop hot cooked rice. Garnish with parsley if desired. Makes 4 servings.

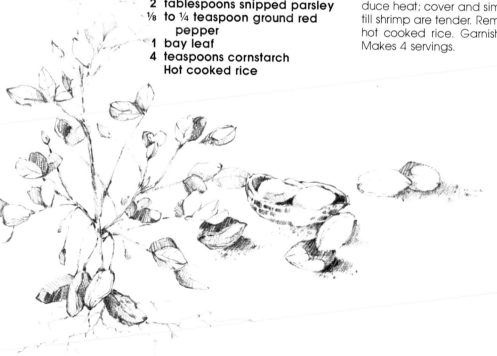

Fried Frog Legs

Fried Frog Legs are a delicacy that can prove to be tricky to eat. Pick up small pieces with your fingers, gripping one end. Put the other end in your mouth and suck the meat off. For larger legs, use a knife and fork.

 2 pounds fresh *or* frozen frog legs
⅓ cup all-purpose flour
1¼ teaspoons salt
 ¼ teaspoon ground red pepper
Cooking oil for deep-fat frying

Thaw frog legs, if frozen. Separate into individual legs. In shallow dish combine flour, salt, and ground red pepper. Dip frog legs into flour mixture a few at a time to coat thoroughly.

In a saucepan or deep-fat fryer heat about 2 inches of cooking oil to 375°. Fry coated frog legs a few at a time in deep hot fat about 2 minutes or till done. Keep warm in a 325° oven while frying the remainder. Makes 6 servings.

Peanut Soup

Peanuts are essential to Afro-American cuisine. Botanically, peanuts are peas that are called nuts because of their flavor and oil. Other names for peanuts are groundnuts, goober peas, and goobers.

⅓ cup thinly sliced celery
 ¼ cup chopped onion
 1 tablespoon butter *or* margarine
 2 tablespoons all-purpose flour
 1 13¾-ounce can chicken broth
1½ cups milk
 ½ cup peanut butter
Coarsely chopped peanuts
Snipped parsley

In large saucepan cook celery and onion in butter or margarine till vegetables are tender. Stir in flour. Add the chicken broth and milk. Cook and stir till mixture is slightly thickened and bubbly. Cook and stir 1 minute more.

Add the peanut butter; cook and stir till smooth and heated through. To serve, ladle into individual soup bowls. Sprinkle with chopped peanuts and snipped parsley. Makes 6 servings.

Black Bean Soup

 8 ounces dry black beans (1 cup)
 2 cups water
 ½ pound smoked pork hock, cut into 2-inch pieces
2½ cups chicken broth
1½ cups water
 1 medium onion, chopped (½ cup)
 ¼ cup chopped celery
 ¼ cup chopped carrot
 1 clove garlic, minced
 1 bay leaf
 1 tablespoon lemon juice
 ¼ cup madeira wine
Salt
Pepper
 1 hard-cooked egg, finely chopped
 1 small lemon, thinly sliced

Rinse beans. In a Dutch oven or kettle cover beans with the 2 cups water. Bring to boiling. Reduce heat and simmer, uncovered, for 2 minutes. Remove from heat; cover and let stand 1 hour. (Or, soak beans in water overnight in a covered pan.) Drain beans and rinse.

In the same Dutch oven or kettle combine the beans, pork hock, chicken broth, 1½ cups water, onion, celery, carrot, garlic, and bay leaf. Bring mixture to boiling. Reduce heat; cover and simmer about 1½ hours or till beans are soft. Remove from heat. Remove the bay leaf and pork hock; reserve pork hock if desired. Place bean mixture, *half* at a time, in a blender container; cover and blend till smooth. Return mixture to saucepan. (Or, rub beans with liquid through a sieve.)

Stir lemon juice into bean mixture. (If desired, cut meat from pork hock; coarsely chop meat and discard bones. Add meat to bean mixture.) Bring mixture to boiling. Remove from heat; stir in the madeira wine. Season to taste with salt and pepper. Ladle into individual serving bowls. Garnish with chopped egg and lemon slices. Serves 6.

Dirty Rice

Dirty Rice is a Cajun dish that is served as an accompaniment to poultry and meat. Its "dirty" appearance comes from the pieces of chicken livers and gizzards that are cooked with the rice. Don't let the name discourage you from preparing this savory Southern dish.

2 cups water
1 cup long grain rice
3 tablespoons all-purpose flour
3 tablespoons butter *or* margarine
1 large onion, finely chopped (1 cup)
½ cup finely chopped celery
½ cup finely chopped green pepper
1 clove garlic, minced
½ teaspoon salt
½ teaspoon pepper
⅛ teaspoon ground red pepper
8 ounces chicken livers
8 ounces chicken gizzards
¼ cup snipped parsley

In a saucepan bring water to boiling. Add rice; return to boiling. Reduce heat. Cover and simmer 20 minutes or till rice is done. Meanwhile, in another saucepan combine flour and butter or margarine. Cook over medium-low heat, *stirring constantly,* for 10 to 25 minutes or till a dark reddish brown roux is formed. Stir in onion, celery, green pepper, garlic, salt, pepper, and ground red pepper. Cook till onion is tender but not brown.

Coarsely cut chicken livers and gizzards into pieces. Use coarse blade of food grinder to grind meat. Stir into onion mixture. Cover and cook over low heat for 8 to 10 minutes or till ground gizzards are tender, stirring often. Toss together the gizzard mixture, cooked rice, and parsley. Heat through. Makes 10 servings.

Glazed Sweet Potatoes

Sweet potatoes frequently are featured fresh in *Glazed Sweet Potatoes.* They also are used in a host of other Southern dishes such as soufflés, biscuits, and pies.

1 cup packed brown sugar
¼ cup unsweetened pineapple juice
2 tablespoons lemon juice
½ teaspoon ground cinnamon
¼ teaspoon ground mace
6 medium sweet potatoes, cooked, peeled, and sliced ¾ inch thick (2¼ pounds)
½ cup broken pecans
2 tablespoons butter *or* margarine

In a bowl combine sugar, pineapple juice, lemon juice, cinnamon, and mace. Gently toss with potatoes and pecans. Turn into a 1½-quart casserole. Dot with butter or margarine. Bake, uncovered, in a 350° oven for 40 to 45 minutes or till heated through and glazed, spooning glaze over potatoes occasionally. Makes 6 to 8 servings.

Okra Pickles

When choosing fresh okra, select fresh tender pods and avoid those that look dull, dry, or shriveled. The peak quantities of okra come to market from June to September.

2 pounds okra
3 cups water
1 cup white vinegar
¼ cup pickling salt
2 teaspoons dillseed
½ teaspoon crushed red pepper

Thoroughly wash okra; drain. Pack into hot, clean pint jars, leaving ½ inch of headspace. In saucepan combine water, vinegar, pickling salt, dillseed, and red pepper; bring to boiling. Pour hot liquid over okra in jars, leaving ½ inch of headspace. Wipe rims; adjust lids. Process in boiling water bath for 10 minutes (start timing when water starts to boil). Makes 4 pints.

Pictured clockwise: *Glazed Sweet Potatoes, Okra Pickles, Corn Sticks (see recipe, page 43), and Southern Corn Bread (see recipe, page 43).*

41

Eggplant Soufflé

1 medium eggplant, peeled and cubed
¼ cup butter *or* margarine
¼ cup all-purpose flour
½ teaspoon dried chervil, crushed
¼ teaspoon salt
    Several dashes ground red pepper
1 cup milk
4 eggs

Cook cubed eggplant in a small amount of boiling salted water till tender; mash to make about 1 cup. Set aside.

In a saucepan melt butter or margarine; stir in flour, chervil, salt, and ground red pepper. Add milk all at once. Cook and stir till thickened and bubbly. Cook and stir 1 minute more. Remove from heat. Stir in mashed eggplant.

Separate eggs. Beat yolks till thick and lemon colored; slowly stir in hot mixture. Wash beaters thoroughly. Beat egg whites till stiff peaks form; fold into vegetable mixture. Turn into an ungreased 2-quart soufflé dish. Bake in a 350° oven for 35 to 40 minutes or till knife inserted near center comes out clean. Serve at once. Makes 6 servings.

Spoon Bread

Spoon Bread is similar to a heavy soufflé. It's a quick bread that is soft enough to dish out with a spoon.

Serve it at a meal as a side-dish substitute for potatoes or rice. It's delicious topped with butter or margarine.

2 cups milk
1 cup yellow cornmeal
1 cup milk
2 tablespoons butter *or* margarine
1 teaspoon salt
1 teaspoon baking powder
3 beaten egg yolks
3 stiff-beaten egg whites
    Butter *or* margarine

In saucepan stir the 2 cups milk into the cornmeal. Cook, stirring constantly, till mixture is very thick and pulls away from the sides of the pan. Remove from heat. Stir in the 1 cup milk, 2 tablespoons butter or margarine, salt, and baking powder. Stir about 1 cup of the hot mixture into egg yolks; return to saucepan. Gently fold in egg whites. Turn mixture into a greased 2-quart casserole. Bake in a 325° oven about 50 minutes or till knife inserted near center comes out clean. Serve immediately with butter or margarine. Makes 6 servings.

Pain Perdu

Pain Perdu (PAN per-DOO), which literally translated means "lost bread," is an elaborate version of French toast. It is typically made with day-old French bread, dusted with powdered sugar, and drizzled with Southern cane syrup.

It is said that orange flower water was in the original recipe, but it can be omitted if desired.

⅔ cup milk
2 beaten eggs
3 tablespoons sugar
    Few drops orange flower water *or* orange extract (optional)
1 teaspoon finely shredded lemon peel
8 slices day-old French bread, cut 1 inch thick
    Butter *or* margarine
    Powdered sugar
    Cane syrup, honey, *or* maple-flavored syrup

Stir together milk, eggs, sugar, orange flower water or orange extract if desired, and the shredded lemon peel; beat well. Dip both sides of the French bread slices in beaten mixture; let stand till well saturated.

In a skillet cook the bread on both sides in a small amount of hot butter or margarine over medium-high heat till golden brown; add more butter as needed. Sprinkle with powdered sugar. Serve with cane syrup, honey, or maple-flavored syrup. Makes 4 servings.

Southern Corn Bread *recipe and variation pictured on page 40*

The obvious difference between *Southern Corn Bread* and corn breads from other parts of the United States is that the Southern version is served in a skillet.

Typically, the corn bread batter is added to bacon drippings in a hot skillet. Then, it is baked in the skillet to a golden brown.

1½ **cups yellow** *or* **white cornmeal**
½ **cup all-purpose flour**
4 **teaspoons baking powder**
½ **teaspoon salt**
2 **eggs**
1¼ **cups milk**
⅓ **cup bacon drippings** *or* **shortening**

Stir together the cornmeal, flour, baking powder, and salt. Beat together eggs and milk. In 10-inch oven-going skillet melt the bacon drippings or shortening; pour fat into egg-milk mixture, leaving about 1 tablespoon fat in the hot skillet. Add egg mixture to dry ingredients; beat just till smooth (do not overbeat). Pour batter into the hot skillet; bake in a 425° oven for 18 to 20 minutes or till done. Cut into wedges to serve. Makes 8 or 9 servings.

• **Corn Sticks:** Prepare Southern Corn Bread batter as directed, melting fat in a small skillet or saucepan and brushing corn stick pans with the remaining 1 tablespoon melted bacon drippings or shortening. Heat the pans in a 425° oven for 5 minutes. Spoon batter into heated corn stick pans, filling ⅔ full. Bake in a 425° oven about 12 minutes or till done. Makes about 20.

Beaten Biscuits

Beaten Biscuits were a breakfast specialty in the Deep South before the Civil War. Unlike other kinds of biscuits, beaten biscuits are kneaded by repeatedly pounding the dough with the flat side of a wooden spoon or a metal mallet.

The biscuits are shaped with a cutter or by hand, pricked with a fork, and baked until they're crisp on the outside and soft on the inside. They're best when served warm with butter or margarine.

2 **cups all-purpose flour**
1 **teaspoon sugar**
½ **teaspoon salt**
⅛ **teaspoon baking powder**
¼ **cup lard** *or* **shortening**
⅓ **cup cold milk**
⅓ **cup cold water**
    Butter *or* **margarine**

In mixing bowl stir together flour, sugar, salt, and baking powder. Cut in lard or shortening till mixture resembles coarse crumbs. Make a well in the center. Add the milk and water all at once; stir well. Stir in additional water if necessary to make dough stick together. (Dough should be stiff.)

Turn dough out onto lightly floured surface. Beat vigorously with the flat side of a wooden spoon or a metal mallet for 15 minutes, turning and folding dough frequently. Dip spoon or mallet in flour as necessary to prevent sticking. Roll or pat the dough to ⅜-inch thickness. Cut dough with floured 2-inch biscuit cutter. Dip the cutter in flour between cuts to prevent sticking. (Or, for each biscuit pinch off about 2 tablespoons of dough; shape into 1½-inch ball. Flatten to about ⅜-inch thickness.)

Place the biscuits on an ungreased baking sheet. Prick the tops of each biscuit 3 times with the tines of a fork. Bake in a 450° oven about 20 minutes or till crisp and light brown. Serve biscuits warm with butter or margarine. Makes 16 to 18.

Beignets

Beignets (BEN-yaze) is the French word for fritters. These tasty rectangular doughnuts are a trademark of the coffeehouses of the French Market in New Orleans. The traditional accompaniment is *New Orleans Café au Lait* (see recipe, page 51) made from strong coffee with chicory.

2¾ to 3¼ cups all-purpose flour
1 package active dry yeast
½ teaspoon ground nutmeg (optional)
1 cup milk
¼ cup sugar
2 tablespoons shortening
½ teaspoon salt
1 egg
Shortening *or* cooking oil for deep-fat frying
Powdered sugar

In a mixer bowl stir together 1½ cups of the flour, the yeast, and nutmeg if desired. In a saucepan heat the milk, sugar, shortening, and salt just till warm (115° to 120°) and the shortening is almost melted; stir constantly. Add heated mixture to flour mixture. Add the egg. Beat at low speed of electric mixer ½ minute, scraping bowl. Beat 3 minutes at high speed. Stir in enough of the remaining flour to make a soft dough. Place in a greased bowl; turn once. Cover; refrigerate till well chilled.

Turn dough out onto a lightly floured surface. Cover; let rest 10 minutes. Roll into an 18x12-inch rectangle; cut into 3x2-inch rectangles. Cover; let rest for 30 minutes (dough will not be doubled).

In a saucepan or deep-fat fryer heat the shortening or cooking oil to 375°. Carefully add 2 or 3 of the dough rectangles; fry about 1 minute or till golden, turning once. Drain on paper toweling. Repeat with the remaining dough. Sprinkle with powdered sugar. Makes 36.

Moravian Sugar Cake

The Moravians were members of the Church of the Brethren, which started in Bohemia, Moravia, and Poland. They came to evangelize in Pennsylvania in 1734 and a year later established a mission in Savannah, Georgia. Eventually, another mission was established at Salem, which is now part of Winston-Salem, North Carolina.

In addition to the heritage of religious beliefs the Moravians left behind, they also left us *Moravian Sugar Cake.*

For best results, let the butter and eggs come to room temperature before preparing this yeast-leavened batter cake.

1 small potato, peeled and cubed
1 cup water
2 packages active dry yeast
½ cup sugar
¼ cup shortening
¼ cup butter *or* margarine, softened
½ teaspoon salt
2¾ cups all-purpose flour
2 beaten eggs
¼ cup butter *or* margarine, melted
½ cup packed brown sugar
1 teaspoon ground cinnamon

In a saucepan cook the potato in the water till tender. Cool mixture to 110° to 115°. Set aside ½ cup of the cooking liquid. Soften the yeast in the reserved ½ cup cooking liquid. Mash the potato in the remaining liquid, adding water if necessary, to make ¾ cup potato mixture.

In a mixer bowl stir together the potato mixture, the yeast mixture, the sugar, shortening, ¼ cup butter or margarine, and salt; beat well. Stir in 1 cup of the flour; beat well. Cover and let rise in a warm place till spongy (30 to 45 minutes). Beat batter down; beat in eggs and remaining flour. Cover; let rise in warm place till almost double (about 45 minutes).

Beat batter down; spread into a greased 15x10x1-inch baking pan. Cover; let rise about 45 minutes or till light. With finger make indentations in the top of the dough at 1½-inch intervals. Fill holes with the ¼ cup melted butter or margarine. Stir together the brown sugar and cinnamon; sprinkle into holes. Bake in a 375° oven for 20 to 25 minutes or till golden. Cool on wire rack. Cut into squares. Serve warm or cooled. Makes 12 to 16 servings.

Lane Cake *pictured on page 30*

Lane Cake is credited to Mrs. Emma Rylander Lane of Clayton, Alabama and has been popular since the late 1800s. This three-layer white cake is filled and topped with a rich fruit mixture and decorated with fluffy white frosting.

3¼ cups all-purpose flour
4½ teaspoons baking powder
1½ teaspoons salt
1¼ cups butter *or* margarine
2¼ cups sugar
2 teaspoons vanilla
1½ cups milk
8 stiff-beaten egg whites
    Lane Cake Filling
    Fluffy White Frosting

Grease and lightly flour three 9x1½-inch round baking pans; set aside. Stir together flour, baking powder, and salt. In a large mixer bowl beat the butter or margarine at medium speed of electric mixer for 30 seconds. Add the sugar; beat till fluffy. Beat in the vanilla. Add the dry ingredients and milk alternately to beaten mixture, beating well after each addition. Fold in egg whites. Turn batter into prepared pans. Bake in a 375° oven about 20 minutes or till done. Cool 10 minutes on wire racks; remove from pans. Cool thoroughly. Spread Lane Cake Filling between layers and on top. Pipe or spread sides and around top edge with Fluffy White Frosting. Serves 16.

Lane Cake Filling: In a saucepan melt ½ cup *butter or margarine.* Stir in 1 cup *sugar,* ⅓ cup *bourbon or brandy, and* ⅓ cup *water.* Bring just to boiling, stirring to dissolve sugar. Stir about *half* of the hot mixture into 9 slightly beaten *egg yolks;* return to hot mixture in saucepan. Cook and stir about 3 minutes or till thickened. Remove from heat. Stir in 1 cup finely chopped *raisins,* ¾ cup chopped *pecans,* ½ cup chopped *maraschino cherries,* ½ cup flaked *coconut,* and ¾ teaspoon *vanilla.* Cover; cool to room temperature.

Fluffy White Frosting: In a saucepan combine 1 cup *sugar,* ⅓ cup *water,* ¼ teaspoon *cream of tartar,* and a dash *salt.* Bring to boiling, stirring till sugar dissolves. In a mixer bowl *very slowly* add the hot mixture to 2 *egg whites* and 1 teaspoon *vanilla,* beating constantly at high speed of electric mixer about 7 minutes or till stiff peaks form.

Les Oreilles de Cochon

Les Oreilles de Cochon (lays o-RAY duh ko-SHOW) is French for "pigs' ears." These pecan-studded pastries are drizzled with cane syrup, which is an amber sugar syrup used in place of maple syrup in parts of the South. You can substitute dark corn syrup mixed with light molasses for the cane syrup in this recipe.

2 cups all-purpose flour
1 teaspoon baking powder
½ teaspoon salt
2 eggs
½ cup butter *or* margarine, melted and cooled
Cooking oil for deep-fat frying
1½ cups cane syrup *or* 1 cup dark corn syrup *plus* ½ cup light molasses
¾ cup coarsely chopped pecans

Stir together flour, baking powder, and salt; set aside. In a deep bowl beat eggs with fork or wire whisk. Gradually beat in cooled butter or margarine. Stir into flour mixture till well combined. Divide dough into 24 balls. On lightly floured surface roll each ball into a paper-thin round 6 inches in diameter. Cover to prevent drying.

In large deep saucepan or deep-fat fryer heat 2 inches of oil to 365°. Place one round of dough in oil; as soon as it rises to the surface, pierce center with long-handled fork and twist fork a quarter turn to give dough pig's ear shape. Press fork and dough against side of the pan to retain shape. Fry 1 to 1½ minutes or till golden. Drain on paper toweling. Keep warm. Repeat with remaining rounds.

In 2-quart saucepan bring cane syrup or syrup-molasses mixture to boiling; attach candy thermometer and cook the syrup to 230° over medium-low heat, stirring frequently. Drizzle hot syrup over hot pastries; sprinkle with pecans. Serve warm or at room temperature. Makes 24.

Coconut Cake

For a special touch, use shredded fresh coconut to sprinkle on the cake.

To get the coconut meat, use an ice pick to punch out the eyes of the coconut shell. Drain out the milk.

Remove the meat from the shell, cutting off and discarding the brown skin. Then, shred enough coconut to measure 2 cups.

2 cups all-purpose flour
1 tablespoon baking powder
1 teaspoon salt
½ cup butter *or* margarine
1½ cups sugar
1 teaspoon vanilla
½ teaspoon almond extract (optional)
3 egg yolks
1 cup milk
3 egg whites
Fluffy Frosting
2 cups coconut

Grease and flour two 9x1½-inch round baking pans. Combine the flour, baking powder, and salt. Beat butter with electric mixer 30 seconds. Add sugar, vanilla, and almond extract if desired, and beat till well blended. Add egg yolks, one at a time, beating 1 minute after each. Add flour mixture and milk alternately to beaten mixture, beating at low speed after each addition just till combined.

Wash beaters thoroughly. Beat egg whites till stiff peaks form. Gently fold into beaten mixture. Turn into prepared pans. Bake in a 375° oven for 20 to 25 minutes or till cakes test done. Cool 10 minutes on wire racks. Remove; cool.

Meanwhile, prepare Fluffy Frosting. Cut cake layers in half horizontally. Spread 1 cake layer with *1 cup* frosting and sprinkle with ¼ *cup* of the coconut. Repeat layers 2 more times. Top with final slice. Frost sides and top with remaining frosting. Sprinkle coconut on top and sides. Serves 12.

Fluffy Frosting: Combine 1½ cups *sugar,* ½ cup *water,* ½ teaspoon *cream of tartar,* and dash *salt.* Cook and stir till bubbly and sugar dissolves. Combine 3 *egg whites* and 1½ teaspoons *vanilla.* Very slowly add hot mixture to unbeaten egg whites while beating constantly at high speed of electric mixer. Beat 7 minutes or till stiff peaks form.

Pictured:
Les Oreilles de Cochon and *Café Brûlot* (see recipe, page 51).

Short'nin' Bread   *pictured on the cover*

The unleavened dough for these rich cookies should be mixed thoroughly by hand or it will be dry and crumbly.

½ cup butter *or* margarine
¼ cup packed brown sugar
1¼ cups all-purpose flour
Powdered sugar (optional)

In a mixer bowl beat butter or margarine and sugar till light and fluffy. Add flour, mixing by hand to form ball. Turn dough out onto lightly floured surface; roll into a 9x6-inch rectangle. Cut with 1½-inch fluted cookie cutters. (Or, cut into 1¼-inch diamonds or squares.) Place on ungreased cookie sheet. Bake in a 325° oven for 20 to 25 minutes or till done. Transfer to wire rack; cool. Sift powdered sugar over tops if desired. Makes 15 to 18 cookies.

Chess Tarts   *pictured on pages 4 and 5*

There are many versions of this dessert, but Southerners say that the best *Chess Tarts* always have a thin top "crust" that rises to the surface of the lemony egg-butter mixture.

Pastry for Double-Crust Pie (see recipe, page 141)
4 slightly beaten eggs
1½ cups sugar
6 tablespoons butter *or* margarine, melted and cooled
¼ cup milk
1 tablespoon cornmeal
¾ teaspoon finely shredded lemon peel
1 tablespoon lemon juice

Prepare and roll out *half* of the pastry at a time to slightly less than ⅛-inch thickness. Cut each half into eight 4-inch circles. Fit into small fluted tart pans, 2½ inches in diameter at top and 1¼ inches deep. (Or, cut 4-inch circles from heavy-duty foil; place one pastry round on each foil circle and shape into tarts.) Set aside.

For filling, in mixing bowl stir together eggs, sugar, butter or margarine, milk, cornmeal, lemon peel, and lemon juice. Place tart pans on baking sheet; divide filling evenly among tart shells. Bake in a 350° oven for 35 to 40 minutes or till knife inserted near center comes out clean. Cool on wire rack. Cover; store in refrigerator. Makes 16 tarts.

Fried Peach Pies

1 8-ounce package dried peaches, cut up
3 cups water
¼ cup sugar
1 teaspoon ground cinnamon (optional)
3 cups all-purpose flour
1½ teaspoons salt
1 cup lard *or* shortening
⅔ to ¾ cup cold water
Cooking oil for deep-fat frying
Powdered sugar (optional)

Rinse the dried peaches. In a saucepan combine the peaches and the 3 cups water. Bring to boiling; reduce heat. Cover and simmer for 20 to 25 minutes or till peaches are tender; drain. Stir together the peaches, sugar, and cinnamon if desired; set aside.

Combine flour and salt. Cut in lard till mixture resembles small peas. Sprinkle *1 tablespoon* of the water over part of the mixture; gently toss with a fork. Push to side of bowl. Repeat till all is moistened. Form into a ball.

On lightly floured surface roll dough to ⅛-inch thickness. Cut into 4-inch circles. Place *1 tablespoon* filling on half of each circle. Fold over into half-moon shape; seal edges with tines of a fork. In a skillet heat ¼ inch cooking oil to 375°. Fry pies for 6 to 8 minutes or till golden, turning once. Drain on paper toweling. Sprinkle with powdered sugar if desired. Makes 18 to 20.

Black Bottom Pie

Black Bottom Pie is appropriately named because of the rich chocolate base topped with a fluffier rum-gelatin mixture. This pie can be made with the chocolate wafer crust or the gingersnap graham crust.

**Chocolate Wafer Crust *or*
Gingersnap-Graham Crust**
½ **cup sugar**
 1 **tablespoon cornstarch**
 2 **cups milk**
 4 **slightly beaten egg yolks**
 1 **teaspoon vanilla**
 1 **6-ounce package (1 cup)
   semisweet chocolate pieces**
 1 **envelope unflavored gelatin**
¼ **cup cold water**
½ **teaspoon rum flavoring *or* 2
   tablespoons light rum**
 4 **egg whites**
½ **cup sugar
   Pecan halves**

Prepare desired crust. In a saucepan combine ½ cup sugar and the cornstarch. Stir in milk and egg yolks. Cook and stir over medium heat till mixture thickens and coats a metal spoon. Remove from heat; stir in vanilla. Stir chocolate into 1¼ *cups* of the thickened mixture till melted; pour into baked shell. Chill.

Meanwhile, soften gelatin in the cold water. Stir into remaining hot thickened mixture till gelatin dissolves. Stir in rum flavoring or rum. Chill to the consistency of corn syrup, stirring occasionally. Immediately beat egg whites till soft peaks form. Gradually add ½ cup sugar, beating till stiff peaks form. When gelatin is partially set (the consistency of unbeaten egg whites), fold in stiff-beaten egg whites. Chill till mixture mounds when spooned. Spread over pie. Chill several hours or till set. Garnish with pecans. Cover; store in refrigerator. Serves 8.

Chocolate Wafer Crust: In a mixing bowl combine 1½ cups finely crushed *chocolate wafers* (25 wafers) and 6 tablespoons *butter or margarine,* melted. Turn the chocolate crumb mixture into a 9-inch pie plate. Spread the crumb mixture evenly in the pie plate. Press onto bottom and sides to form a firm, even crust. Refrigerate about 1 hour or till firm.

Gingersnap-Graham Crust: Toss together ¾ cup finely crushed *gingersnaps* (12 cookies), ½ cup finely crushed *graham crackers* (7 crackers), ¼ cup melted *butter or margarine,* and 2 tablespoons *sugar.* Turn crumb mixture into a 9-inch pie plate. Spread the crumb mixture evenly in the pie plate. Press onto bottom and sides to form a firm, even crust. Bake in a 375° oven for 4 to 5 minutes. Cool thoroughly on wire rack.

Key Lime Pie

Sweetened condensed milk was first manufactured in the 1850s. It was combined with the juice of Florida Key limes to make this sweet creamy pie.

Limes are native to India and it is said they were introduced to Florida in the 1500s. Key limes are small and lemon yellow in color. These limes are strong flavored and very acidic.

Baked Pastry Shell (see recipe, page 141) or Graham Cracker Crust (see recipe, page 140)
6 egg yolks
2 14½-ounce cans Eagle Brand sweetened condensed milk
1 teaspoon finely shredded lime peel
1 cup lime juice
Whipped cream (optional)
Lime slices (optional)

Prepare Baked Pastry Shell or Graham Cracker Crust as directed. In a large mixer bowl beat egg yolks with electric mixer till thick and lemon colored. Stir in the sweetened condensed milk and lime peel. Gradually add lime juice, beating at medium speed till smooth and fluffy.

Turn beaten mixture into pie shell. Cover and refrigerate about 4 hours or till firm. Before serving, top with whipped cream and garnish with lime slices if desired. Makes 8 servings.

Pralines

1½ cups sugar
1½ cups packed brown sugar
1 cup light cream
3 tablespoons butter or margarine
2 cups pecan halves

In a heavy 3-quart saucepan stir together the sugar, brown sugar, and light cream. Bring mixture to boiling over medium heat, stirring constantly. Cook to 234° (soft-ball stage), stirring only as necessary to prevent sticking (mixture should boil gently over entire surface). Remove from heat; add butter or margarine but do not stir. Let mixture stand with thermometer in pan.

Cool, without stirring, to 150° (about 30 minutes). Quickly stir in pecans. Beat candy for 2 to 3 minutes or till slightly thickened and glossy. Drop candy from a tablespoon onto a baking sheet lined with waxed paper. If candy becomes too stiff to drop easily from a spoon, add a few drops hot water and stir. Makes about 30 pralines.

Bananas Foster

This flaming banana dessert is said to have been created more than 30 years ago at Brennan's, a New Orleans restaurant, for a customer named Richard Foster.

4 ripe small bananas
Lemon juice
⅔ cup packed brown sugar
⅓ cup butter or margarine
Dash ground cinnamon
2 tablespoons banana liqueur
3 tablespoons rum
Vanilla ice cream

Peel bananas and cut in half lengthwise and crosswise. Brush bananas with lemon juice to prevent darkening. In a skillet or blazer pan of a chafing dish heat the brown sugar and butter or margarine till mixture melts, stirring occasionally.

Add the bananas; cook, uncovered, for 3 to 4 minutes, turning once. Sprinkle with cinnamon. Drizzle the banana liqueur atop. In a small saucepan heat the rum just till warm. Ignite and pour the rum over the banana mixture. Serve over vanilla ice cream. Makes 6 servings.

Ramos Gin Fizz *pictured on pages 4 and 5*

The *Ramos Gin Fizz,* a famous New Orleans drink, was developed by Henry C. Ramos in his bar in the 1880s.

Orange flower water, a derivative of the orange tree blossom, is traditional in making this drink. However, orange extract can be substituted.

2 **egg whites**
½ **cup light cream**
1½ **ounces gin**
4 **to 5 ice cubes**
2 **tablespoons powdered sugar**
1 **tablespoon lemon juice**
   Few drops orange flower water *or* orange extract

In blender container combine egg whites, light cream, gin, ice cubes, powdered sugar, lemon juice, and orange flower water or extract. Cover and blend till foamy. Pour into 2 tall chilled glasses. Garnish each with an orange slice if desired. Makes 2 (10-ounce) servings.

Mint Julep

½ **ounce Simple Syrup**
2 **to 4 sprigs fresh mint**
  Crushed ice
3 **ounces bourbon**
  Powdered sugar
  Lemon slice
  Mint sprig

Pour ½ ounce Simple Syrup into tall glass. Add fresh mint and crush with back of spoon. Fill glass with crushed ice. Add the bourbon and stir gently. Add more ice to fill glass. Sprinkle with powdered sugar. Garnish with lemon and mint. Makes 1.

Simple Syrup: Pour 1 cup *boiling water* over 1 cup *sugar;* stir till sugar dissolves. Chill. Makes about 1½ cups.

Café Brûlot *pictured on page 47*

  Peel of 1 orange
3 **inches stick cinnamon, broken**
6 **whole cloves**
4 **sugar cubes**
1 **3x¼-inch strip lemon peel, membrane removed**
½ **cup brandy**
2 **cups hot double-strength coffee**

Remove white membrane from orange peel. Cut peel into 3x½-inch strips. In a blazer pan of chafing dish combine the orange peel, cinnamon, cloves, sugar cubes, and lemon peel. In a small saucepan heat brandy till nearly boiling. Remove from heat and ignite; pour over mixture in blazer pan. Place blazer pan over chafing dish burner. Spoon brandy over sugar till cubes melt. Stir in the coffee. Makes 4 (4-ounce) servings.

New Orleans Café au Lait *pictured on the cover*

New Orleans Café au Lait is served for breakfast, lunch, and dinner and is made from French roasted coffee with chicory. Chicory is made from a white chicory root that is dried, roasted, and ground like coffee.

1 **cup ground coffee with chicory**
3 **cups water**
3 **cups light cream *or* milk**

Measure ground coffee into basket of pot. Measure water. *For electric drip coffee makers,* pour cold water into upper compartment. Place pot on heating element; allow water to drip through coffee basket. *For non-electric drip coffee makers,* pour boiling water over coffee grounds in basket. Allow water to drip into bottom section.

When coffee has finished dripping, remove basket; discard grounds. Stir the brewed coffee. Keep warm over low heat.

Meanwhile, heat the light cream or milk over low heat. Beat with a rotary beater till foamy. Transfer heated cream to a warmed serving container. Pour coffee and cream in equal amounts into serving cups. Makes 8 (6-ounce) servings.

THE MIDWEST

The Midwest is the home of the "amber waves of grain" immortalized in the song "America the Beautiful."

Some of the richest farmland lies within these boundaries. The abundant yields from this fertile area can be traced not only to American tables, but to foreign countries as well.

Pork chops, T-bone steaks, corn, soybeans, wheat, oats, popcorn, apples, and cherries are just a few favorites from the Midwest.

The Great Lakes supply freshwater fish such as catfish, whitefish, and bass. Lakes, farm ponds, and rivers scattered throughout the Midwest also are brimming with fish.

Cooking here is best described as savory simplicity. Creative heartland cooks utilized their lavish supply of quality food in recipes that are usually lightly seasoned.

Midwestern specialities are naturally newer than those from the other regions because this area was settled later. European immigrants influenced the cooking in larger metropolitan areas such as Chicago, Milwaukee, St. Louis, Cincinnati, Detroit, and Cleveland. The Scandinavian touch is obvious in the northern section of the Midwest. Special people and special foods are the essence of the Midwestern cuisine.

Recipes pictured: *Apple Cake* (see recipe, page 62), *Twice-Baked Potatoes* (see recipe, page 59).

53

Cornish Beef Pasties

When miners from Cornwall, England came to Wisconsin and Michigan mining towns, they introduced their lunchtime favorite, *Cornish Beef Pasties* (PASS-tees).

Originally, the pastry for these vegetable-meat pies was made tough to survive the trip to work in sacks or hip pockets. Today's pasties have tender, flaky crusts bulging with a variety of savory fillings.

2 cups all-purpose flour
1 teaspoon salt
⅔ cup shortening
5 to 6 tablespoons cold water
1 pound beef round steak, cut into ¼-inch cubes
⅔ cup diced, peeled turnip, carrot, *or* rutabaga
1 medium potato, peeled and coarsely chopped
½ cup finely chopped onion
1 teaspoon salt
¼ teaspoon pepper
Milk
1 tablespoon sesame seed
Catsup (optional)

In a large mixing bowl stir together flour and 1 teaspoon salt. With pastry blender, cut in the shortening till mixture resembles coarse crumbs. Add cold water, a tablespoon at a time, tossing with a fork to moisten. Form into a ball. Cover and chill 1 hour.

Combine beef, turnip, potato, onion, 1 teaspoon salt, and the pepper; set aside. Divide dough into 5 portions. On lightly floured surface roll each portion into a 7-inch circle. Place about ⅔ cup filling in the center of *each* circle; bring sides of pastry over filling. Pinch edges to seal. Cut slits in pastry for steam to escape.

Brush pastry lightly with milk and sprinkle with sesame seed. Carefully transfer pasties to an ungreased baking sheet. Bake in a 375° oven for 35 to 40 minutes or till golden brown. Serve with catsup if desired. Makes 5 servings.

Beef Pot Roast

1 3- to 4-pound beef chuck pot roast
All-purpose flour
¾ cup water, beef broth, dry red *or* white wine, beer, *or* tomato juice
½ teaspoon dried basil *or* thyme, crushed
½ teaspoon Worcestershire sauce
4 medium potatoes, peeled and quartered
4 carrots, cut into 1½-inch pieces
Pot Roast Gravy

Trim excess fat from meat; reserve trimmings. Coat all sides of meat with flour. In a Dutch oven heat trimmings till about 2 tablespoons hot fat accumulate. Discard trimmings. (If necessary, add cooking oil to equal 2 tablespoons fat.)

Cook meat slowly in hot fat about 10 minutes or till brown on all sides. Sprinkle with salt and pepper. Add water or desired liquid, basil or thyme, and Worcestershire. Cover; simmer for 1¼ to 1½ hours.

Add potatoes and carrots. Sprinkle with salt and pepper. Cover; continue cooking about 45 minutes or till meat and vegetables are tender. Add additional water as needed to prevent sticking. (Or, after adding liquid and seasonings, cover and bake in a 325° oven for 1¼ to 1½ hours. Add potatoes and carrots; continue baking, covered, about 45 minutes more or till tender.)

Remove meat and vegetables to a platter; keep warm. Prepare Pot Roast Gravy; serve with meat and vegetables. Makes 8 servings.

Pot Roast Gravy: Pour meat juices and fat into a large glass measure. Skim fat from pan juices (if necessary, add additional liquid to equal 1½ cups). Return juices to Dutch oven. Combine ½ cup *cold water* and ¼ cup all-purpose *flour*. Stir into pan juices. Cook and stir till thickened and bubbly. Cook and stir 1 minute more. If desired, add several drops *Kitchen Bouquet*. Season to taste with salt and pepper.

Chicken Fried Steak with Cream Gravy

Crispy fried chicken is said to have inspired this popular method of cooking less-tender cuts of beef.

After a healthy pounding to tenderize it, the meat is given a crumb coating and quick fry in the skillet till its crust is crisp and golden brown.

1 **pound beef round steak, cut ½ inch thick**
1 **beaten egg**
1 **tablespoon milk**
  Dash pepper
½ **cup finely crushed saltine crackers (14 crackers)**
3 **tablespoons cooking oil**
2 **tablespoons all-purpose flour**
¼ **teaspoon salt**
⅛ **teaspoon pepper**
1¼ **cups milk**

Pound steak to ¼-inch thickness. Cut into 4 serving-size portions. Stir together the egg, milk, and pepper. Dip meat into egg mixture, then into crushed crackers. In a 12-inch skillet brown meat slowly in hot oil for 5 to 6 minutes on each side or till done. Remove steak to platter; keep warm.

For gravy, stir flour, salt, and pepper into drippings in skillet. (If necessary add a little additional oil to skillet.) Add the milk all at once. Cook and stir, scraping up browned particles in skillet, till mixture is thickened and bubbly. Cook and stir 1 minute more. Serve steak with gravy. Makes 4 servings.

Sausage and Kraut

The Midwestern population boasts a large number of citizens with Polish and German ancestry. These sausage-and-sauerkraut-loving people serve this satisfying dish with crusty bread (and lots of pride) to family and guests alike.

4 **slices bacon, cut into 1-inch pieces**
½ **pound lean boneless pork, cut into ½-inch cubes**
1 **small onion, chopped (¼ cup)**
½ **pound Polish sausage, sliced**
2½ **cups water**
¼ **cup dry white wine**
1 **4-ounce can sliced mushrooms**
1½ **teaspoons instant beef bouillon granules**
¾ **teaspoon paprika**
1 **bay leaf**
1 **16-ounce can sauerkraut, drained and snipped**
2 **tablespoons cornstarch**

In 3-quart saucepan cook bacon till crisp; drain bacon, reserving drippings. Set bacon aside. Brown pork cubes and onion in reserved drippings. Stir in bacon, sausage, water, wine, *undrained* mushrooms, bouillon granules, paprika, and bay leaf. Cover; simmer about 1 hour or till pork cubes are tender.

Remove bay leaf. Stir in sauerkraut. Combine cornstarch and ¼ cup *cold water.* Add to sauerkraut mixture; cook and stir till thickened and bubbly. Cook, stirring constantly, 2 minutes more. Makes 4 to 6 servings.

Stuffed Cabbage Rolls

1 **beaten egg**
½ **cup milk**
¼ **cup finely chopped onion**
1 **teaspoon Worcestershire sauce**
½ **pound ground pork** *and* ½ **pound ground beef** *or* 1 **pound ground beef**
¾ **cup cooked rice**
6 **large** *or* 12 **medium cabbage leaves**
1 **10¾-ounce can condensed tomato soup**
1 **tablespoon brown sugar**
1 **tablespoon lemon juice**

In a bowl combine egg, milk, onion, Worcestershire sauce, ¾ teaspoon *salt,* and dash *pepper;* mix well. Add meat and cooked rice; mix well.

Remove center vein of cabbage leaves, keeping each leaf in 1 piece. Immerse leaves in boiling water about 3 minutes or till limp; drain. Place ½ *cup* meat mixture on each large leaf or ¼ *cup* mixture on each medium leaf; fold in sides. Starting at unfolded edge, roll up each leaf, making sure folded sides are included in roll.

Arrange in a 12x7½x2-inch baking dish. Combine soup, brown sugar, and lemon juice; pour over cabbage rolls. Bake, uncovered, in a 350° oven about 1¼ hours, basting twice with sauce. Makes 6 servings.

Pork Stew with Cornmeal Dumplings

The central states are known for their corn-fed pork production. It's no wonder that pork is a popular ingredient in dishes of this region.

This hearty stew topped with double-corn dumplings pays tribute to that tender Midwestern pork, but the robust seasonings also complement beef or lamb.

2 **pounds pork stew meat, cut into 1-inch cubes**
2 **tablespoons cooking oil**
1 **28-ounce can tomatoes, cut up**
1 **12-ounce can (1½ cups) beer**
1 **medium onion, cut into thin wedges**
1 **clove garlic, minced**
1 **tablespoon sugar**
1 **tablespoon Worcestershire sauce**
1 **teaspoon dried thyme, crushed**
2 **bay leaves**
¾ **teaspoon salt**
¼ **teaspoon pepper**
¼ **teaspoon ground nutmeg**
2 **tablespoons all-purpose flour**
  Cornmeal Dumplings
  Paprika (optional)

In 4-quart Dutch oven brown meat cubes, half at a time, in hot cooking oil. Return all meat to pan. Add *undrained* tomatoes, *1 cup* of the beer, onion, garlic, sugar, Worcestershire sauce, thyme, bay leaves, salt, pepper, and nutmeg. Bring to boiling; reduce heat. Cover and simmer, 1 hour or till meat is tender. Spoon off fat.

Combine the remaining beer and flour; stir into stew. Cook and stir till thickened and bubbly. Prepare Cornmeal Dumplings. Drop batter by rounded tablespoons onto boiling stew mixture to make 8 dumplings. Sprinkle tops with paprika if desired. Cover and simmer, *without lifting cover,* for 10 to 12 minutes or till dumplings are done. Makes 8 servings.

Cornmeal Dumplings: In bowl stir together ½ cup all-purpose *flour,* ⅓ cup *yellow cornmeal,* 1½ teaspoons *baking powder,* ¼ teaspoon *salt,* and dash *pepper.* Combine 1 beaten *egg,* 2 tablespoons *milk* and 2 tablespoons *cooking oil.* Add to flour mixture and stir till blended. Stir in one 8¾-ounce can *whole kernel corn,* drained.

Corn-Stuffed Pork Chops

6 **pork loin chops, cut 1½ inches thick**
¼ **cup chopped green pepper**
1 **small onion, chopped (¼ cup)**
1 **tablespoon butter *or* margarine**
1 **beaten egg**
1½ **cups toasted bread cubes**
½ **cup cooked whole kernel corn**
2 **tablespoons chopped pimiento**
½ **teaspoon salt**
¼ **teaspoon ground cumin**
  Dash pepper
2 **tablespoons cooking oil**

Cut a pocket in each chop by cutting from fat side almost to bone edge. Season cavity with a little salt and pepper.

In a small saucepan cook green pepper and onion in butter or margarine till tender but not brown. Combine egg, bread cubes, corn, pimiento, salt, cumin, and pepper. Add green pepper-onion mixture to bread cube mixture; toss lightly. Spoon about ¼ *cup* of the stuffing into each pork chop. Securely fasten pocket opening with wooden picks.

In large oven-going skillet brown chops slowly in hot cooking oil for 10 to 15 minutes; turn once. Drain off fat. Bake, uncovered, in a 350° oven for 45 to 60 minutes or till done. Before serving, remove picks. Makes 6 servings.

Pictured:
Pork Stew with Cornmeal Dumplings and Swedish Limpa (see recipe, page 61).

Pheasant with Wild Rice

The highly prized grain we call wild rice is not rice at all, but the seed of a marsh grass grown in Minnesota.

Wild rice is still harvested from boats in much the same way the Sioux and Chippewa Indians did centuries ago. Much of the chaff remains on the grain; therefore, the rice should be rinsed two or three times before using.

- **1 cup chopped onion**
- **1 cup chopped carrot**
- **1 cup chopped celery**
- **⅓ cup butter *or* margarine**
- **5¼ cups water**
- **1½ cups wild rice, rinsed**
- **1 tablespoon salt**
- **3 cups sliced fresh mushrooms**
- **¾ teaspoon dried sage, crushed**
- **¾ teaspoon dried thyme, crushed**
- **¾ teaspoon dried savory, crushed**
- **2 2- to 3-pound pheasants *or* broiler-fryer chickens**
  Salt (optional)
- **6 slices bacon**

In a saucepan cook onion, carrot, and celery, covered, in butter or margarine till tender but not brown. Add water, wild rice, and salt. Cover; cook 35 to 40 minutes or till rice is nearly tender. Stir in mushrooms, sage, thyme, and savory. Cover and cook 10 minutes more or till water is absorbed.

Rub cavities of birds with salt if desired. Stuff lightly with some of the wild rice mixture. Skewer neck skin to back; tie legs to tail. Twist wings under back. Place, breast up, on a rack in a shallow roasting pan. Lay bacon over birds. Place remaining stuffing in a 1-quart casserole; cover.

Roast birds, uncovered, in a 350° oven for 1½ to 2 hours or till tender. During the last 30 minutes, bake remaining stuffing in covered casserole with birds. Spoon stuffing from casserole onto a platter; top with birds. Serves 6 to 8.

Country Fried Catfish

Fish fanciers in the Midwest know the pleasures of eating *Country Fried Catfish.* The ritual of preparing the fillets always involves dipping them in buttermilk or sour milk, then rolling in cornmeal before frying.

- **1 pound fresh *or* frozen catfish *or* other fish fillets**
- **½ cup buttermilk *or* sour milk**
- **½ cup all-purpose flour**
- **1 beaten egg**
- **⅓ cup all-purpose flour**
- **⅓ cup yellow cornmeal**
- **½ teaspoon salt**
- **⅛ teaspoon pepper**
  Cooking oil for deep-fat frying

Thaw fish, if frozen. Cut fillets into 3x2-inch pieces. Place ¼ *cup* of the buttermilk and ½ cup flour in separate bowls. Combine egg and remaining ¼ cup buttermilk in another bowl. Mix ⅓ cup flour, the cornmeal, salt, and pepper in a fourth bowl. Dip fish in buttermilk, then flour, then egg mixture, and finally in cornmeal mixture to coat.

In saucepan or deep-fat fryer heat 2 inches oil to 365°. Fry 2 or 3 fillets at a time for 5 to 7 minutes or till golden and fish flakes easily when tested with a fork. Drain on paper toweling; keep warm in a 325° oven while frying remainder. Serves 4.

Baked Stuffed Whitefish

Whitefish, a relative of salmon and trout, is available primarily in the states bordering the Great Lakes.

The whitefish in this recipe is stuffed with an herb-seasoned vegetable mixture sparked with a touch of lemon.

- **1 3-pound fresh *or* frozen dressed whitefish *or* other fish, boned**
- **1 small carrot, shredded**
- **¼ cup finely chopped celery**
- **¼ cup finely chopped onion**
- **2 tablespoons butter**
- **2 tablespoons snipped parsley**
- **½ teaspoon dried basil, crushed**
- **¼ teaspoon shredded lemon peel**
- **3 cups dry bread cubes**
- **2 teaspoons lemon juice**
- **¼ to ⅓ cup chicken broth**
  Cooking oil

Thaw fish, if frozen; pat dry with paper toweling. Place in a greased shallow baking pan; sprinkle cavity with salt.

For stuffing, in saucepan cook carrot, celery, and onion in butter 5 minutes or till vegetables are crisp-tender. Remove from heat. Stir in parsley, basil, lemon peel, ¼ teaspoon *salt*, and dash *pepper.* Add bread cubes; toss. Add the lemon juice and enough of the chicken broth to moisten; toss lightly.

Fill fish cavity loosely with stuffing. Brush skin of fish with the oil. Cover loosely with foil. Bake in a 350° oven for 45 to 60 minutes or till fish flakes easily when tested with a fork. Use 2 large spatulas to lift fish to serving platter. Garnish with fresh dill if desired. Serves 6.

Whipped Rutabaga Puff

Rutabaga commonly is used interchangeably with its cousin, the turnip. To substitute turnips in this recipe, cook 1 pound of peeled, cut-up turnips for 10 to 20 minutes in boiling salted water before mashing.

1 medium rutabaga (1 pound), peeled and cut up
1 small onion, chopped (¼ cup)
2 tablespoons butter *or* margarine
1 tablespoon sugar
½ teaspoon salt
Dash pepper
¾ cup soft bread crumbs (1 slice)
2 eggs

In a saucepan cook rutabaga and onion, covered, in a small amount of boiling salted water for 25 to 35 minutes or till tender. Drain. Add butter or margarine, sugar, salt, and pepper; beat well with electric mixer or mash with a potato masher. Add bread crumbs and eggs; beat well. Turn into a lightly greased 1-quart casserole. Bake, uncovered, in a 375° oven for 35 to 40 minutes. Makes 4 to 6 servings.

Twice-Baked Potatoes *pictured on page 53*

4 medium baking potatoes
2 tablespoons butter *or* margarine
Milk
2 slices American cheese, halved diagonally
Paprika (optional)

Scrub potatoes; prick with a fork. Bake in a 425° oven for 40 to 60 minutes or in a 350° oven for 70 to 80 minutes.

Cut a lengthwise slice from the top of each baked potato; discard skin from slice. Reserving potato shells, scoop out the insides and add to potato portions from top slices; mash. Add butter. Beat in enough milk to make of a stiff consistency. Season to taste with salt and pepper.

Pipe or spoon mashed potato mixture into potato shells. Place in a 10x6x2-inch baking dish. Bake in a 425° oven for 20 to 25 minutes or till light brown. Place cheese atop potatoes; sprinkle with paprika if desired. Bake 2 to 3 minutes more or till cheese melts. Makes 4 servings.

Scalloped Tomatoes

1 medium onion, chopped
   (½ cup)
¼ cup butter *or* margarine
3 slices bread, coarsely
   crumbled (2¼ cups)
6 medium tomatoes,
   peeled and sliced
   Salt
   Pepper
   Sugar

Cook onion in butter or margarine till tender but not brown; stir in crumbled bread. In a 1-quart casserole layer *half* of the tomatoes; sprinkle with salt, pepper, and sugar. Cover with *half* of the crumb mixture. Repeat layers. Bake, uncovered, in a 350° oven for 30 minutes. Makes 6 servings.

Wilted Salad

Originally, *Wilted Salad* used whatever greens were grown in the garden, from dandelion greens to endive.

Prepared properly, fresh lettuce or spinach leaves wilt only slightly when tossed with the hot bacon-vinegar dressing.

5 slices bacon, cut up
½ cup sliced green onion
2 tablespoons white wine
   vinegar
1 tablespoon lemon juice
2 teaspoons sugar
½ teaspoon salt
   Few dashes pepper
8 cups torn leaf lettuce *or*
   fresh spinach
1 hard-cooked egg, chopped

In large skillet cook bacon over medium heat till crisp. Add green onion, vinegar, lemon juice, sugar, salt, and pepper. Gradually add lettuce or spinach, tossing just till leaves are coated and wilted slightly. Turn into a salad bowl. Sprinkle with chopped egg. Makes 4 servings.

Corn Relish

Living in the heart of the American Corn Belt, Iowans have a knack for fixing sweet corn in a bushel of ways. *Corn Relish* is a delicious example that starts with either fresh or frozen kernels.

4 fresh ears of corn *or*
   one 10-ounce package
   frozen whole kernel corn
½ cup sugar
1 tablespoon cornstarch
1 teaspoon ground turmeric
½ teaspoon dry mustard
½ cup vinegar
⅓ cup cold water
2 tablespoons finely chopped
   celery
2 tablespoons finely chopped
   green pepper
2 tablespoons chopped
   pimiento
1 tablespoon finely chopped
   onion

Cut fresh corn from cob. In saucepan cook corn, covered, in a small amount of boiling salted water for 12 to 15 minutes or till tender. (Or, cook frozen corn according to package directions.) Drain cooked corn.

In saucepan combine sugar, cornstarch, turmeric, and dry mustard; stir in vinegar and cold water. Stir in drained corn, celery, green pepper, pimiento, and onion. Cook, stirring constantly, till thickened and bubbly; cook and stir 2 minutes more. Cover and chill thoroughly. Makes 2½ cups.

Swedish Limpa *pictured on page 57*

Swedish Limpa is an excellent sample of the flavors Scandinavians brought to our country. This rye bread gets its unique flavor from caraway seed, fennel seed, and orange peel.

3¼ to 3¾ cups all-purpose flour
  2 packages active dry yeast
  1 tablespoon caraway seed
  ½ teaspoon fennel seed (optional)
  2 cups warm water (115° to 120°)
  ½ cup packed brown sugar
  2 tablespoons finely shredded orange peel
  1 tablespoon cooking oil
  1 teaspoon salt
2½ cups rye flour

In a large mixer bowl combine 2½ cups of the all-purpose flour, the yeast, caraway seed, and, if desired, fennel seed. Stir together water, brown sugar, orange peel, cooking oil, and salt. Add to flour mixture. Beat at low speed of electric mixer for 30 seconds, scraping bowl constantly. Beat 3 minutes at high speed.

Stir in rye flour and as much of the remaining all-purpose flour as you can mix in with a spoon. Turn out onto floured surface. Knead in enough of the remaining all-purpose flour to make a moderately stiff dough that is smooth and elastic (6 to 8 minutes total). Place in a greased bowl; turn once to grease surface. Cover; let rise in a warm place till double (1¼ to 1½ hours).

Punch dough down; divide in half. Cover; let rest 10 minutes. Shape into two 4½-inch round loaves on a greased baking sheet. Cover; let rise till nearly double (about 40 minutes). Bake in a 350° oven for 40 to 45 minutes; cover with foil the last 10 minutes, if necessary, to prevent overbrowning. Cool on wire rack. Makes 2 loaves.

Honey-Wheat Muffins

Kansas' bountiful fields of red winter wheat have given the state its title of "the nation's breadbasket." The golden grain is featured in home-style *Honey-Wheat Muffins*.

  1 cup all-purpose flour
  ½ cup whole wheat flour
  2 teaspoons baking powder
  1 beaten egg
  ½ cup milk
  ½ cup honey
  ¼ cup cooking oil
  ½ teaspoon finely shredded lemon peel

In a bowl stir together all-purpose flour, whole wheat flour, baking powder, and ½ teaspoon *salt*. Make a well in center of flour mixture. Combine egg, milk, honey, oil, and lemon peel; add all at once to flour mixture, stirring just till moistened (batter should be lumpy). Fill greased or paper-bake-cup-lined muffin cups ⅔ full. Bake in a 375° oven for 20 minutes. Remove from pan; serve warm. Makes 10 muffins.

Orange-Nut Bread

  1 medium orange
  2 cups all-purpose flour
  ½ cup sugar
  2 teaspoons baking powder
  ½ teaspoon baking soda
  ½ teaspoon salt
  1 beaten egg
  ½ cup water
  2 tablespoons butter *or* margarine, melted
  1 cup pitted dates, chopped
  ¾ cup chopped walnuts

Quarter orange; remove peel and seeds. Discard seeds. Scrape off and discard white membrane from inside of peel. Cut up peel. In blender container place orange pulp and peel; cover and blend till nearly smooth. Set aside.

In mixing bowl stir together flour, sugar, baking powder, baking soda, and salt. Combine egg, water, butter, and orange mixture. Add to flour mixture; stir just till moistened. Fold in dates and nuts.

Pour into three greased 6x3x2-inch loaf pans. Bake in a 350° oven for 35 to 40 minutes. Cool 10 minutes on wire racks. Remove bread from pans. Cool thoroughly. Wrap; store overnight before slicing. Makes 3 loaves.

Walnut Bars

The black walnut is native to the American woodlands. Several Midwestern desserts, including pie, cake, fudge, and *Walnut Bars*, capitalize on the unique flavor of the black walnut. However, these bars are also good with other types of walnuts.

½ **cup butter** *or* **margarine**
¾ **cup packed brown sugar**
¼ **teaspoon salt**
3 **eggs**
1 **teaspoon vanilla**
1½ **cups all-purpose flour**
¾ **cup chopped black walnuts**
¼ **teaspoon cream of tartar**
½ **cup sugar**

For crust, in mixer bowl beat butter for 30 seconds. Add brown sugar and salt; beat till fluffy. Separate egg yolks from whites; set whites aside. Add egg yolks and vanilla to beaten mixture; beat well.

Gradually add flour to beaten mixture, beating constantly. Stir in *half* of the walnuts. Spread mixture in an ungreased 13x9x2-inch baking pan. Bake in a 350° oven for 15 minutes.

Meanwhile, wash beaters well. For meringue, combine egg whites and cream of tartar; beat till soft peaks form. Gradually add the sugar; beat till stiff peaks form. Fold in remaining walnuts. Spread over hot crust. Bake about 20 minutes more or till golden. Cut into bars while warm. Makes 24.

Ozark Pudding

From the hill country of southern Missouri comes an apple dessert called *Ozark Pudding*. It was reportedly a favorite with President and Mrs. Truman.

Be sure to serve it warm with generous dollops of whipped cream.

2 **eggs**
1 **cup sugar**
1 **teaspoon vanilla**
⅓ **cup all-purpose flour**
1 **tablespoon baking powder**
⅛ **teaspoon salt**
2 **cups chopped, peeled apple**
½ **cup chopped walnuts**
Unsweetened whipped cream

Grease and flour a 9x9x2-inch baking pan. In a large mixer bowl beat together the eggs, sugar, and vanilla till light and fluffy. Stir together the flour, baking powder, and salt. Stir into beaten mixture. Fold in apple and walnuts.

Turn mixture into prepared pan. Bake in a 325° oven for 30 to 35 minutes. Spoon into dessert dishes. Serve warm with unsweetened whipped cream. Makes 6 to 8 servings.

Apple Cake

4 **medium cooking apples**
2 **eggs**
1 **teaspoon vanilla**
1 **cup cooking oil**
1½ **cups sugar**
2 **cups all-purpose flour**
1 **teaspoon baking soda**
1 **teaspoon salt**
1 **teaspoon ground cinnamon**
1 **cup finely chopped walnuts**
Powdered Sugar Glaze (see recipe, page 169)

Peel, core, and very finely chop apples. In a large mixer bowl combine eggs and vanilla. Beat with an electric mixer at high speed for 2 minutes or till light. Gradually add oil, beating for 2 minutes or till thick. Gradually beat in sugar.

Combine flour, soda, salt, and cinnamon; add flour mixture, apples, and walnuts alternately to beaten mixture, beating well after each addition. Beat at medium speed for 3 minutes.

Turn batter into a greased and floured 9-inch tube pan. Bake in a 350° oven for 55 to 60 minutes or till cake tests done. Cool in pan for 10 to 15 minutes. Remove from pan; cool on wire rack. Drizzle with Powdered Sugar Glaze. Serves 12.

Pictured:
Cherry Pie (see recipe, page 64), Apple Cake, and Walnut Bars.

Apple Jonathan

If John Chapman, alias Johnny Appleseed, hadn't planted apple seedlings throughout the Ohio River valley in the early 1800s, the apple might not have become the all-American fruit.

Apple Jonathan is one example of the variety of ways mid-America enjoys this versatile fruit.

8 **to 10 tart cooking apples, peeled, cored, and thinly sliced (6 cups)**
½ **cup pure maple syrup *or* maple-flavored syrup**
½ **cup sugar**
¼ **cup butter *or* margarine**
1 **egg**
1 **cup all-purpose flour**
2 **teaspoons baking powder**
1 **teaspoon finely shredded orange peel**
½ **teaspoon salt**
½ **cup orange juice**

In a bowl toss apples with maple syrup till well coated. Spread evenly in a 10x6x2-inch baking dish. Cover; bake in a 350° oven for 25 minutes.

Meanwhile, in a small mixer bowl beat together sugar and butter or margarine till light. Beat in egg. Stir together flour, baking powder, orange peel, and salt; add flour mixture and orange juice alternately to beaten mixture, beating well after each addition.

Uncover baking dish. Spread batter over hot apples. Return to oven; bake 25 to 30 minutes more or till cake tests done. Serve warm or cool. Dollop with unsweetened whipped cream if desired. Makes 6 to 8 servings.

Cherry Pie   *pictured on page 63*

4 **cups fresh *or* frozen pitted tart red cherries (20 ounces)**
1 **cup sugar**
3 **tablespoons quick-cooking tapioca**
1 **teaspoon finely shredded lemon peel**
1 **tablespoon cherry brandy (optional)**
 Pastry for Double-Crust Pie (see recipe, page 141)

In large bowl combine cherries, sugar, tapioca, lemon peel, and ⅛ teaspoon *salt.* Stir in brandy if desired. Let stand 20 minutes, stirring occasionally.

Prepare and roll out pastry. Line a 9-inch pie plate with *half* of the pastry; trim to ½ inch beyond edge of pie plate. Fill with cherry mixture. Cut remaining pastry into strips ½ inch wide. Weave strips atop filling to make lattice crust; flute edges high. Cover edge of pie with foil.

Bake in a 375° oven for 25 minutes. Remove foil and bake 30 to 35 minutes more or till crust is golden. Cool on wire rack. Makes 8 servings.

Brown Sugar-Rhubarb Pie

Technically a vegetable but used like a fruit, rhubarb has acquired the name "pieplant" over the years. Its long-standing popularity in pies and tarts is undoubtedly the reason.

You won't end up with an extra egg yolk or egg white when you make this pie. The filling uses three egg yolks and the meringue requires three whites.

**Pastry for Single-Crust Pie
(see recipe, page 141)**
- 1 **to 1¼ cups packed brown
  sugar**
- ¼ **cup all-purpose flour**
- ¼ **teaspoon salt**
- 1 **pound rhubarb, diced (4 cups)**
- 3 **egg yolks**
- 1 **tablespoon lemon juice
  Meringue (see recipe,
  page 139)**

Prepare and roll out pastry. Line a 9-inch pie plate. Trim pastry to ½ inch beyond edge of pie plate. Flute edge; *do not prick pastry*. Bake in a 450° oven for 5 minutes. Cool.

To prepare filling, combine brown sugar, flour, and salt; stir in rhubarb. Let stand 15 minutes. Beat egg yolks slightly. Stir beaten yolks and lemon juice into rhubarb mixture.

Turn rhubarb filling into pastry shell. To prevent overbrowning, cover edge of pie with foil. Bake in a 375° oven for 25 minutes. Remove foil; bake 20 to 25 minutes more or till nearly set. (Pie appears soft in center but becomes firm after cooling.)

Prepare Meringue. Spread Meringue over filling; seal to edge. Bake in a 350° oven for 12 to 15 minutes. Cool on wire rack. Cover; refrigerate to store. Makes 8 servings.

Fruit Cobbler

Peach Filling or Rhubarb Filling
- 1 **cup all-purpose flour**
- 2 **tablespoons sugar**
- 1½ **teaspoons baking powder**
- ¼ **teaspoon salt**
- ¼ **cup butter or margarine**
- 1 **slightly beaten egg**
- ¼ **cup milk**

Prepare Peach or Rhubarb Filling; keep warm. For biscuit topper, stir together flour, sugar, baking powder, and salt. Cut in butter or margarine till mixture resembles coarse crumbs. Combine egg and milk; add all at once to flour mixture. Stir just to moisten. Turn hot filling into a 1½-quart casserole. Immediately spoon biscuit topper in 8 mounds over hot filling. Bake in a 400° oven about 20 minutes. Serve warm. Makes 8 servings.

Peach Filling: Combine ½ cup packed *brown sugar*, 4 teaspoons *cornstarch*, and ¼ teaspoon ground *nutmeg*. Stir in ½ cup *water*. Cook and stir till thickened and bubbly. Stir in 4 cups sliced, peeled, fresh *peaches* (8 medium); 1 tablespoon *lemon juice*; and 1 tablespoon *butter or margarine*. Heat through.

Rhubarb Filling: Combine 1 cup *sugar*, 2 tablespoons *cornstarch*, and ¼ teaspoon ground *cinnamon*. Stir in 4 cups *fresh rhubarb* cut into 1-inch pieces (or one 18-ounce package *frozen rhubarb*, thawed) and ¼ cup *water*. Cook and stir till thickened and bubbly. Stir in 1 tablespoon *butter*.

THE SOUTHWEST

This four-state region has a colorful background filled with cowboy folklore, tales of the dust bowl days in Oklahoma, and the effect of sudden wealth when oil was discovered.

The American Indians, the Spanish, and the Mexicans have all left their mark on the foods of the Southwest. For example, Southwestern Indian tribes introduced the settlers to green and red chili peppers, pinto beans, and pine nuts, as well as unfamiliar forms of preserved corn such as chicos (sun-dried roasted corn) and blue cornmeal.

Flavorings which crossed the Rio Grande include coriander, anise, cumin, mint, black sage, and wild celery.

The settlers in turn anglicized Indian and Spanish recipes such as chili, enchiladas, and blue corn bread.

Texans adopted Indian and Mexican cooking techniques for barbecuing meats such as beef brisket, spareribs, and cabrito (young goat). Its vast grazing land makes the Southwest a leader in cattle and sheep production and the ideal meat supplier for the ever-popular jumbo-size Texas barbecues.

This same region, known for its plains, plateaus, Painted Desert, and Grand Canyon, also is the birthplace of the distinctive Tex-Mex cuisine. This style of cooking is a marriage between American and Mexican foods. The major difference between the Mexican and Tex-Mex cuisines is that the latter is more generous with meat and cheese in its recipes.

Recipes pictured: *Stuffed Sopaipillas* (see recipe, page 69) and *Avocado-Grapefruit Salad* (see recipe, page 76).

Tacos

Ever since *Tacos* crossed the border from Mexico, they've topped the list of favorite American foods.

Perhaps the endless number of fillings possible and the pleasure of custom-making these crisp tortilla sandwiches account for their popularity.

Observe one rule of etiquette when serving tacos — provide two paper napkins per taco.

12 **Corn Tortillas (see recipe, page 76)** *or* **taco shells Cooking oil**
 1 **pound ground beef, bulk chorizo,** *or* **bulk Italian sausage**
 1 **medium onion, chopped**
 1 **clove garlic, minced**
1½ **to 2 teaspoons chili powder**
 ¼ **teaspoon ground cumin**
 2 **medium tomatoes, chopped Shredded lettuce**
 1 **medium onion, chopped (½ cup)**
 1 **cup shredded sharp cheddar cheese (4 ounces) Red Chili Sauce (see recipe below)** *or* **bottled taco sauce**

If using corn tortillas, in a heavy skillet heat ¼ inch cooking oil. Fry each tortilla 10 seconds or till limp. With tongs, fold tortilla in half and continue frying, holding edges apart. Cook 1¼ to 1½ minutes more or till crisp, turning once. Drain on a paper-toweling-lined baking sheet; keep warm in a 250° oven while preparing meat mixture. (Or, warm taco shells in a 250° oven.)

In a skillet cook ground beef or sausage, 1 medium onion, and garlic till meat is brown. Drain off fat. Season meat mixture with the chili powder, cumin, and ¾ teaspoon *salt*. (Omit salt if using sausage.) Stir in ¼ cup *water*; cook about 5 minutes or till most of the water is evaporated. Fill each taco shell with some of the meat mixture, tomatoes, lettuce, 1 medium onion, and cheese; pass Red Chili Sauce or taco sauce. Serves 6.

Red Chili Sauce

Legend claims chili peppers aid digestion and clarify the blood. But it is their fiery flavor that has made bowls of chili sauce commonplace on Southwestern tables.

Oils in chilies can irritate your skin and eyes. Always wash your hands thoroughly with soap and water after working with these potent peppers.

 6 **dried ancho** *or* **pasilla chilies** *or* **1½ teaspoons crushed red pepper**
 4 **small tomatoes (1 pound)** *or* **one 16-ounce can whole peeled tomatoes**
 2 **cloves garlic, minced**
 1 **tablespoon olive oil** *or* **cooking oil**
 2 **teaspoons sugar**
 ½ **teaspoon dried oregano, crushed**
 ¼ **teaspoon ground cumin**

If using dried chilies, cut chilies open. Discard stems and seeds. Cut chilies into small pieces with scissors or a knife. Place in a bowl; add 2 cups *boiling water*. Let stand for 1 hour. Drain.

To peel fresh tomatoes, dip in boiling water for 30 seconds; plunge into cold water. Slip skins off. Quarter tomatoes. Place quartered fresh or *undrained* canned tomatoes in blender container or food processor bowl. Cover; blend till smooth.

Add drained chilies or crushed red pepper and the garlic. Cover; blend till smooth. Combine tomato mixture, oil, sugar, oregano, cumin, and ¾ teaspoon *salt*. Bring to boiling; reduce heat. Simmer 15 minutes or till slightly thickened. Makes 2 cups.

Tamale Pie

2¼ **cups cold water**
 ¾ **cup yellow cornmeal**
 ½ **teaspoon salt**
 1 **tablespoon lard** *or* **butter**
 1 **pound ground beef**
 1 **cup chopped onion**
 1 **cup chopped green pepper**
 1 **clove garlic, minced**
 1 **15-ounce can tomato sauce**
 1 **12-ounce can whole kernel corn, drained**
 ½ **cup sliced pitted ripe olives**
 2 **to 3 teaspoons chili powder**
 ¾ **cup shredded cheddar cheese**

In saucepan combine cold water, cornmeal, and salt. Bring just to boiling; reduce heat. Stir in lard or butter. Cook over low heat 10 minutes, stirring often. Remove from heat.

In skillet cook beef, onion, green pepper, and garlic till meat is brown; drain. Stir in tomato sauce, corn, olives, chili powder, and ¾ teaspoon *salt*. Bring to boiling; reduce heat. Simmer 20 to 25 minutes or till thickened, stirring often.

Spread *three-fourths* of the cornmeal mixture on bottom and up sides (to about 1 inch from top) of a greased 2-quart casserole. Spoon in meat mixture. Carefully spoon remaining cornmeal mixture atop. Bake in a 350° oven for 30 minutes. Sprinkle with cheese; bake 5 minutes. Serves 6.

Picadillo

Also called Spanish hash, *Picadillo* (pee-kah-DEE-yo) is a sweet, spicy meat mixture popular in Texas.

It is served as an entrée, as an hors d'oeuvre with large corn chip dippers, or as a filling for tacos, enchiladas, empanadas, or green chili peppers.

1 **pound ground beef** *or*
  ½ **pound ground beef** *and*
  ½ **pound ground pork**
1 **medium onion, chopped (½ cup)**
2 **cloves garlic, minced**
1 **16-ounce can tomatoes, cut up**
½ **cup raisins**
¼ **cup slivered almonds**
1 **tablespoon vinegar**
1 **teaspoon sugar**
½ **teaspoon ground cinnamon**
¼ **teaspoon ground cumin**
  Dash ground cloves
1 **bay leaf**

In a 10-inch skillet cook ground meat, onion, and garlic till meat is brown and onion is tender; drain off fat. Stir in *undrained* tomatoes, raisins, almonds, vinegar, sugar, cinnamon, cumin, cloves, bay leaf, ½ teaspoon *salt*, and ⅛ teaspoon *pepper*. Simmer, uncovered, for 20 to 25 minutes. Remove bay leaf. Makes 4 servings or 3½ cups.

Stuffed Sopaipillas *pictured on page 67*

Main-dish *Stuffed Sopaipillas* (so-pah-PEE-yas) are not as well known as honey-drizzled sopaipillas, but they are just as much a Southwestern specialty. According to one source, sopaipillas originated in Albuquerque some 300 years ago.

The secret to deep-frying a puffy sopaipilla is to spoon the hot fat over the circle of dough as soon as it rises to the surface of the hot fat.

1 **package active dry yeast**
¾ **cup lukewarm water (110° to 115°)**
1 **tablespoon cooking oil**
2 **cups all-purpose flour**
½ **teaspoon salt**
½ **teaspoon baking powder**
  Shortening *or* **cooking oil for deep-fat frying**
  Fresh Chili Sauce (Salsa)
  Sausage Filling *or* **Chicken Filling**
1 **cup shredded cheddar** *or* **Monterey Jack cheese**
½ **cup sliced green onion**
  Sliced, peeled avocado

Dissolve yeast in water. Add 1 tablespoon oil; set aside. In a mixing bowl stir together the flour, salt, and baking powder. Add yeast mixture, stirring with fork till moistened.

Turn out onto lightly floured surface; knead gently 15 to 20 strokes. Divide into 12 equal portions; shape into balls. Cover and let rest, with balls of dough not touching, for 10 minutes.

On lightly floured surface roll one ball of dough at a time into a 4-inch circle. (Keep remaining dough covered while working.) Place one circle at a time in deep hot fat (365°). When dough rises to surface, *immediately* spoon hot fat over top till dough puffs. Continue frying, turning once, till golden (2 to 3 minutes total). Drain on paper toweling. Repeat with remaining dough.

Prepare Fresh Chili Sauce and desired filling. Cut off about ¼ of sopaipilla to expose pocket. Fill with desired warm filling. Pass Fresh Chili Sauce, cheese, onion, and avocado. Makes 12.

Fresh Chili Sauce (Salsa): Combine 3 medium *tomatoes*, finely chopped, *or* one 16-ounce can *tomatoes*, drained and chopped; one 4-ounce can chopped *green chili peppers*, drained; ½ cup finely chopped *onion*; 1 tablespoon *vinegar*; 1 teaspoon *sugar*; and ⅛ teaspoon *salt*. Let stand 15 minutes.

Sausage Filling: Cook 1½ pounds bulk or link (casing removed) *chorizo* or *Italian sausage* till done. Drain. Stir in ¾ cup *Red Chili Sauce* (see recipe, page 68) or *taco sauce*.

Chicken Filling: Melt 3 tablespoons *butter*; stir in ¼ cup all-purpose *flour* and 1 teaspoon *salt*. Add 1 cup *chicken broth*. Cook and stir till thickened and bubbly; cook and stir 1 minute more. Add 1 tablespoon snipped *parsley*, 1 tablespoon *lemon juice*, 1 teaspoon *grated onion*, and dash each *paprika*, ground *nutmeg*, and *pepper*. Stir in 1½ cups diced cooked *chicken*; heat.

Posole

Originally, this hearty Mexican soup was made from the head of a pig and was served on New Year's Day for good luck.

Today, *Posole* (poh-SOH-leh) is made with more-common cuts of pork. It is served with an assortment of crisp vegetable garnishes for sprinkling over the hot soup.

1½ **pounds lean boneless pork, cut into 1-inch cubes**
2 **tablespoons cooking oil**
1 **medium onion, chopped (½ cup)**
2 **cloves garlic, minced**
4 **cups chicken broth**
1½ **teaspoons dried oregano, crushed**
¼ **teaspoon ground cumin**
2 **14½-ounce cans hominy, drained**
1 **4-ounce can chopped green chili peppers**
Sliced radishes (optional)
Sliced cabbage (optional)
Sliced green onion (optional)

In a large saucepan or Dutch oven brown *half* of the pork cubes in hot oil; remove meat and set aside. Add remaining meat, the onion, and garlic; cook till meat is brown. Return all meat to saucepan. Stir in chicken broth, oregano, and cumin. Bring to boiling; reduce heat. Cover and simmer for 1 hour.

Stir in drained hominy and chopped green chili peppers. Cover and simmer 30 minutes more. Skim off fat. Ladle into bowls. Serve with sliced radishes, shredded cabbage, and sliced green onion if desired. Makes 6 to 8 servings.

Texas-Style Chili

There are two unbreakable rules that must be followed in making authentic *Texas-Style Chili* or "bowl of red." Never use ground meat. And never add beans to the meat mixture. Serve the beans alongside the chili or not at all.

2½ **pounds venison steak *or* beef round steak, cut into ½-inch cubes**
3 **tablespoons cooking oil**
1 **medium onion, chopped (½ cup)**
1 **clove garlic, minced**
1 **10½-ounce can condensed beef broth**
1 **soup can (1⅓ cups) water**
2 **teaspoons sugar**
2 **teaspoons dried oregano, crushed**
2 **teaspoons cumin seed, crushed**
½ **to ¾ teaspoon ground red pepper**
½ **teaspoon paprika**
2 **bay leaves**
1 **4-ounce can chopped green chili peppers**
2 **tablespoons cornmeal**
Hot cooked rice
Hot cooked pinto beans

In a large saucepan or Dutch oven brown *half* of the venison or beef cubes in hot oil; remove meat and set aside. Add remaining meat, the onion, and garlic; cook till meat is brown. Return all meat to saucepan. Stir in beef broth, water, sugar, oregano, cumin seed, ground red pepper, paprika, and bay leaves. Bring to boiling; reduce heat. Simmer, uncovered, about 1¼ hours or till meat is tender.

Stir in chopped green chili peppers and cornmeal. Simmer 20 minutes more, stirring occasionally. Remove bay leaves. Serve with hot cooked rice and beans. Makes 6 to 8 servings.

Pictured:
Texas-Style Chili and Blue Corn Bread (see recipe, page 77).

Sour Cream Chicken Enchiladas

Enchiladas are shaped differently depending on where in the Southwest they are served. In Arizona, the tortillas are typically rolled around the filling. In New Mexico, the tortillas and filling are stacked in alternating layers.

1½ cups chicken broth
3 tablespoons all-purpose flour
2 8-ounce cartons dairy sour cream
2 tablespoons snipped parsley
⅛ teaspoon pepper
1 medium onion, finely chopped (½ cup)
2 tablespoons butter *or* margarine
3 cups chopped cooked chicken
2 4-ounce cans chopped green chili peppers, drained
2 tablespoons cooking oil
12 corn tortillas (see recipe, page 76) *or* purchased corn tortillas
1 cup shredded Monterey Jack cheese (4 ounces)
Sliced pitted ripe olives (optional)
Pimiento strips (optional)

In a saucepan gradually stir chicken broth into flour. Cook and stir till thickened and bubbly. Cook and stir 1 minute more. Remove from heat; stir some of the hot mixture into sour cream, parsley, and pepper. Return all to hot mixture in saucepan. Set aside.

In a skillet cook onion in butter or margarine about 5 minutes or till tender but not brown. Remove from heat. Stir in chicken, chili peppers, and *1 cup* of the sour cream mixture.

In another skillet heat cooking oil. Dip tortillas, one at a time, into the hot oil for 10 seconds or just till limp, adding more oil if needed. Drain on paper toweling.

Spoon chicken mixture on tortillas; roll up. Place seam side down in a greased 12x7½x2-inch baking dish. Pour remaining sour cream mixture atop. Cover; bake in a 350° oven about 30 minutes or till heated through.

Remove foil; sprinkle with shredded cheese. Return to oven; bake 2 to 3 minutes more or till cheese melts. Top with sliced olives and pimiento strips if desired. Makes 6 servings.

Bean and Cheese Burritos

Roll a flour tortilla around a filling of refried beans and cheese or meat, and you've made a burrito.

Fry the burrito in hot fat till the tortilla is crisp and you've got a chimichanga. This cousin to the burrito, with a name that doesn't mean anything, is a relatively new sensation in the evolving cuisine of the Southwest.

12 Flour Tortillas (see recipe, page 77) *or* purchased flour tortillas
1 large onion, chopped (1 cup)
2 tablespoons cooking oil
4 cups Refried Beans (see recipe, page 74) *or* two 16-ounce cans refried beans
3 cups shredded Monterey Jack *or* cheddar cheese (12 ounces)
Shredded lettuce
Green Chili Sauce (see recipe, page 73)

Wrap stack of tortillas tightly in foil; heat in a 350° oven for 15 minutes to soften. In skillet cook onion in oil till tender but not brown. Add refried beans; cook and stir till heated through.

Spoon about ¼ *cup* bean mixture onto *each* tortilla near one edge. Top *each* with ¼ *cup* shredded cheese. Fold edge nearest filling up and over filling just till mixture is covered. Fold in two sides envelope fashion, then roll up.

Arrange on a baking sheet; bake in a 350° oven about 10 minutes or till heated through. Serve burritos surrounded by shredded lettuce. Pass Green Chili Sauce. Makes 6 servings.

• **Beef Burritos:** Prepare Bean and Cheese Burritos as above, *except* substitute 2 cups (10 ounces) *chopped cooked beef* for *half* of the refried beans. Continue as directed.

• **Chimichangas:** Prepare Bean and Cheese Burritos or Beef Burritos as above. Fry the bean- or beef-filled tortillas in deep hot fat (365°) about 2 minutes on each side or till golden brown. Drain on paper toweling. Keep warm in 300° oven while frying remaining chimichangas. Serve as directed for burritos *or* with shredded *lettuce, dairy sour cream,* and *Guacamole* (see recipe, page 81).

Huevos Rancheros

Huevos Rancheros (WAY-vohs ran-CHAIR-rohs) or "ranch-style eggs" traditionally is made with fried eggs, but poached or scrambled eggs may also be used.

Not just a breakfast dish, *Huevos Rancheros* makes fine lunch and supper fare when served with re-fried beans.

Green Chili Sauce (see recipe below)
4 **Corn Tortillas (see recipe, page 76)** *or* **Flour Tortillas (see recipe, page 77)** *or* **purchased tortillas**
1 **to 2 tablespoons cooking oil**
8 **eggs**
1 **cup shredded Monterey Jack cheese (4 ounces)**

Prepare Green Chili Sauce; keep warm. Meanwhile, wrap the stack of tortillas tightly in foil. Heat in a 350° oven for 15 minutes. In a 12-inch skillet heat cooking oil. Carefully break eggs into the skillet one at a time. When the whites are set and edges cooked, add 1 tablespoon *water.* Cover skillet. Cook eggs to desired doneness.

Unwrap warm tortillas. Place a tortilla on each of 4 oven-proof serving plates; top each tortilla with two fried eggs. Spoon some of the warm Green Chili Sauce atop eggs. Sprinkle with some of the cheese. Return to 350° oven and bake for 2 to 3 minutes or till cheese is melted. Serves 4.

Green Chili Sauce

1 **medium onion, chopped (½ cup)**
1 **clove garlic, minced**
1 **tablespoon olive oil** *or* **cooking oil**
2 **medium tomatoes, peeled and chopped (1¼ cups)**
1 **4-ounce can chopped green chili peppers, drained**
1 **tablespoon snipped parsley** *or* **cilantro**
½ **teaspoon salt**
Dash pepper

In a skillet cook onion and garlic in hot oil till onion is tender but not brown. Stir in tomatoes, chili peppers, parsley or cilantro, salt, and pepper. Simmer for 10 to 15 minutes or till slightly thickened. Makes about 1½ cups.

Chiles Rellenos

In *Chiles Rellenos* (CHEE-lays ray-YAY-nohs), the chili peppers must be peeled to allow the soufflé-like batter to adhere to the peppers. To do this, the peppers first are broiled till they blister. Then, they are sealed in a bag for 10 minutes to make peeling even easier.

6 large poblano *or* mild green
    California chili peppers *or*
    two 4-ounce cans whole
    green chili peppers
6 ounces Monterey Jack *or* mild
    cheddar cheese
4 egg whites
4 egg yolks
3 tablespoons all-purpose flour
¼ teaspoon salt
    Cooking oil for shallow-fat
    frying
    Red Chili Sauce (see recipe,
    page 68) *or* Green Chili
    Sauce (see recipe, page 73)
    (optional)

Broil fresh peppers 2 inches from heat about 15 minutes till all sides are blistered, turning often. Place in paper or plastic bag. Close bag tightly; let stand 10 minutes. Peel peppers. Make a slit at stem end and remove seeds. (Or, rinse, seed, and drain canned chilies. Pat dry.)

Cut cheese into 6 pieces to fit peppers. Stuff each pepper with a piece of cheese, being careful not to split peppers. In large mixer bowl beat egg whites till soft peaks form. In small mixer bowl beat egg yolks 4 to 5 minutes or till thick; beat in flour and salt. Stir some of the egg whites into yolk mixture. Fold yolk mixture into whites.

In a large heavy skillet heat ½ inch cooking oil to 375°. Spoon a scant ¼ *cup* batter into hot oil. Spread batter into a circle or oval a little larger than the pepper. Fry 3 at a time. As batter begins to set, carefully top mound of batter with stuffed pepper. Cover with another scant ¼ *cup* batter. Continue cooking 2 to 3 minutes per side or till golden. Drain on paper toweling; keep warm while frying remainder. Serve with Red Chili Sauce or Green Chili Sauce if desired. Makes 3 servings.

Refried Beans

These beans are called "refried" whether they're fried once or several times.

Refried Beans may be served as a side dish (garnish with shredded cheddar or Monterey Jack cheese, if you like) or used as a filling for tacos, burritos, or enchiladas.

1 pound dry pinto beans
    (2½ cups)
¼ cup lard *or* bacon drippings
2 cloves garlic, minced
1½ teaspoons salt

In a Dutch oven combine beans and 6 cups *water.* Bring to boiling. Reduce heat; simmer 2 minutes. Remove from heat. Cover; let stand 1 hour. (Or, soak beans in water overnight in a covered pan.) Drain.

In same Dutch oven combine drained beans and *4 cups* more water. Bring to boiling. Cover and simmer 2 hours or till beans are very tender.

In a large heavy skillet melt lard; add beans with liquid, garlic, and salt. Using a potato masher or fork, mash beans completely. Cook, uncovered, for 10 to 15 minutes or till thick, stirring often. Makes 6 to 8 side-dish servings or about 5 cups.

Summer Vegetables

3 fresh ears of corn
1 medium onion, chopped
1 clove garlic, minced
2 tablespoons butter
1 pound zucchini, thinly sliced
3 medium tomatoes, peeled
    and chopped (2 cups)

With a sharp knife cut kernels from ears of corn to measure 1½ cups; *do not scrape cob.* In a skillet cook onion and garlic in butter till onion is tender but not brown. Stir in corn, zucchini, tomatoes, 1 teaspoon *salt,* and ¼ teaspoon *pepper.* Cover and cook over low heat about 15 minutes or just till vegetables are tender. Serves 4 to 6.

Pictured clockwise:
Summer Vegetables, Avocado-Grapefruit Salad (see recipe, page 76), and Flour Tortillas (see recipe, page 77).

Garbanzo Salad

The garbanzo bean closely follows the pinto bean as the favorite dried legume in the Southwest. The two differ enough that it is acceptable to serve *Garbanzo Salad* at a meal featuring pinto beans.

1 15-ounce can garbanzo beans, drained
1 medium tomato, chopped
¼ cup chopped onion
¼ cup chopped green pepper
2 tablespoons chopped canned green chili peppers
¼ cup olive oil *or* cooking oil
3 tablespoons wine vinegar
  Dash pepper
  Lettuce

In a bowl combine drained garbanzo beans, chopped tomato, onion, green pepper, and chopped green chili peppers. Stir together cooking oil, vinegar, and pepper. Add to bean mixture; mix well. Cover and refrigerate several hours or overnight, stirring occasionally. Turn into a lettuce-lined salad bowl. Makes 6 servings.

Avocado-Grapefruit Salad *pictured on pages 67 and 75*

1 grapefruit
2 medium avocados
  Bibb *or* leaf lettuce leaves
1 medium red onion, thinly sliced
½ cup French salad dressing
¾ teaspoon chili powder

Peel grapefruit. Working over a bowl to save juice, slice each grapefruit section away from the membrane; discard membrane. Cut avocados in half lengthwise; remove and discard seeds and peel. Slice avocados into bowl containing the grapefruit juice. Toss gently to coat.

Place lettuce leaves in a salad bowl or on individual salad plates. Arrange avocado slices and grapefruit sections on lettuce. Top with onion rings. Combine salad dressing and chili powder. Drizzle atop salad. Makes 4 to 6 servings.

Corn Tortillas

At first, *Corn Tortillas* were made by grinding meal into masa on a stone mortar and pestle called a metate. The stone gradually would grind off into the moist mash, prompting the Spanish saying that a man is ready to die when he's eaten two whole metates.

Today, *Corn Tortillas* are commonly made with dehydrated masa available in Mexican markets and some supermarkets.

Use these tortillas to make tacos, enchiladas, huevos rancheros, or tostaditas, or serve them warm, buttered, and rolled up.

2 cups Masa Harina tortilla flour
1¼ cups warm water

In a mixing bowl combine tortilla flour and warm water. Mix with hands till dough is firm but moist. (Add more water if needed.) Let stand 15 minutes. Divide dough into 12 equal portions; shape into balls about 2 inches in diameter.

Using a tortilla press, rolling pin, or flat baking dish, press each ball of dough between 2 moistened sheets of waxed paper into a 7-inch round. Carefully peel off top sheet of waxed paper. Place tortilla, paper side up, on a medium-hot ungreased griddle or skillet.

As the tortilla begins to heat, gently peel off remaining sheet of waxed paper. Cook, turning occasionally, for 2 to 2½ minutes or till tortilla is dry and light brown (tortilla should still be soft). Makes 12 tortillas.

• **Tostaditas:** Mix together, shape, and cook Corn Tortillas as above. (Or, use purchased corn tortillas.) In a large skillet heat 1 inch *cooking oil* to 375.° Cut each tortilla into 6 wedges. Fry a few at a time about 1 minute or till crisp and light brown, turning occasionally. Drain on paper toweling. Sprinkle tostaditas lightly with salt if desired.

Flour Tortillas *pictured on page 75*

Like corn tortillas, home-made *Flour Tortillas* are simple to make and fresher than the frozen, refrigerated, or canned tortillas at the store. Serve *Flour Tortillas* buttered and rolled up as a bread or use them to make bur-ritos, chimichangas, or huevos rancheros.

2 cups all-purpose flour
1 teaspoon salt
1 teaspoon baking powder
2 tablespoons lard *or* shortening
½ to ¾ cup warm water

In a mixing bowl stir together flour, salt, and bak-ing powder. Cut in lard till mixture resembles cornmeal. Gradually add warm water and mix till dough can be gathered into a ball. Knead the dough 15 to 20 times. Let stand 15 minutes.

Divide dough into 12 equal portions; shape into balls. On a lightly floured surface or between 2 pieces of waxed paper, roll each ball into a 7-inch round. Cook on a medium-hot ungreased griddle or skillet about 20 seconds or till puffy. Turn and cook about 20 seconds more or till edges curl up slightly. Makes 12 tortillas.

Blue Corn Bread *pictured on page 70*

Blue Corn Bread gets its color and nutlike flavor from blue corn-meal, a Southwestern exclusive. The Navajo version of this bread contains and is baked in juniper ashes.

1 cup all-purpose flour
1 cup blue *or* yellow cornmeal
¼ cup sugar
4 teaspoons baking powder
¾ teaspoon salt
2 beaten eggs
1 cup milk
¼ cup cooking oil

In mixing bowl stir together flour, cornmeal, sugar, baking powder, and salt. Add eggs, milk, and cooking oil. Beat just till smooth (do not overbeat). Turn into a greased 9x9x2-inch baking pan. Bake in a 425° oven 20 to 25 minutes. Serves 8 or 9.

Pueblo Bread

The shape of *Pueblo Bread* has been de-scribed as resembling a bear claw, sunrays, and the petals of a flower. There is no de-bate, however, among those who have tasted it that this crusty French-like bread has a wonderful texture and flavor.

Indians in New Mexico bake *Pueblo Bread* in adobe ovens, but your conventional gas or electric oven will produce equally delicious results.

1 package active dry yeast
¼ cup warm water (110° to 115°)
2 tablespoons lard, melted and cooled, *or* cooking oil
1 teaspoon salt
3¼ to 3½ cups all-purpose flour
1 cup warm water

Soften yeast in the ¼ cup warm water about 5 minutes. In a large mixing bowl combine melted lard or oil, salt, and softened yeast. Alternately add most of the flour (about 3 cups) and the 1 cup warm water, a little at a time, beating thoroughly by hand after each addition.

Turn out onto a lightly floured surface. Knead in enough of the remaining flour to make a dough that is smooth and elastic (6 to 8 minutes total). Shape into a ball. Place in a greased bowl, turn-ing once to grease surface. Cover; let rise in a warm place till double (about 1 hour).

Punch down dough; turn out onto lightly floured surface and knead for 3 minutes. Cover; let rest 10 minutes. Divide in half. Roll each half into an oval 10 inches long and 5 inches wide. Make a crease 3½ inches from one narrow end. Fold smaller por-tion over. Place on a greased baking sheet.

With kitchen shears make 3 cuts in top fold of dough, cutting ⅔ of the way inward toward fold to make 4 petal-like sections. Cover; let rise till nearly double (30 to 40 minutes). Bake in a 400° oven for 20 to 25 minutes or till done. Makes 2 loaves.

Indian Feast Day Cookies

These cookies are served on the Feast Day of St. John the Baptist, a celebration combining Catholic rituals and Indian ceremonies.

Whole wheat flour and pine nuts go into the dough, which is cut and hand-shaped into designs as shown at left.

1½ cups sugar
1 cup shortening
1 beaten egg
¼ cup milk
1 teaspoon vanilla
2 cups all-purpose flour
1 cup whole wheat flour
½ cup finely chopped pine nuts
1 teaspoon baking powder
¼ teaspoon salt

Beat together sugar and shortening 5 to 6 minutes. Mix egg, milk, and vanilla. Combine remaining ingredients; add flour mixture and egg mixture alternately to beaten mixture, beating after each addition. Divide in half. On lightly floured surface roll half of the dough into a 12x6-inch rectangle. Cut into 2-inch squares. With sharp knife make cuts in squares; shape into designs with fingers. Repeat with remaining dough. Bake on ungreased cookie sheet in a 350° oven 15 to 16 minutes. Makes 36.

Flan

⅓ cup sugar
2 beaten eggs
1 13-ounce can (1⅔ cups) evaporated milk
¼ cup sugar
1 teaspoon vanilla
Dash salt

In small skillet heat and stir the ⅓ cup sugar over medium heat till sugar melts and becomes golden brown. Quickly pour the sugar mixture into a 3½-cup ring mold or four 6-ounce custard cups, tilting to coat bottom and sides.

Combine eggs, milk, sugar, vanilla, and salt. Pour into caramel-coated mold or cups; set in baking pan on oven rack. Pour hot water around mold or cups in pan to depth of 1 inch. Bake in a 325° oven for 50 to 55 minutes (35 to 40 minutes for custard cups) or till knife inserted halfway between center and edge comes out clean. Chill. Loosen custard from sides; invert onto platter or serving plates. Serves 4.

Buñuelos

The American way to make *Buñuelos* (boon-WAY-lohs) is paper-thin and crispy. Sprinkled with cinnamon sugar or drizzled with cinnamon-flavored syrup, they're a wonderful finger food dessert.

Be sure to serve the syrup warm, as it hardens when cooled and is difficult to reheat. Start to make the syrup while the balls of dough rest.

1⅔ cups all-purpose flour
2 teaspoons sugar
½ teaspoon baking powder
¼ teaspoon salt
2 tablespoons butter *or* margarine
1 beaten egg
¼ cup milk
Cooking oil for deep-fat frying
Cinnamon Sugar *or* Cinnamon-Sugar Syrup

In bowl combine flour, sugar, baking powder, and salt. Cut in butter till mixture resembles coarse crumbs. Combine egg and milk. Stir egg mixture into flour mixture; mix well. On lightly floured surface knead dough about 3 minutes or till smooth. Divide into 16 equal portions; shape into balls. Let stand 10 minutes.

In large heavy skillet heat about 1 inch of cooking oil to 375°. Roll each ball into a 6-inch circle. Fry in hot oil for 30 to 45 seconds per side or till golden. Drain on paper toweling. Sprinkle with Cinnamon Sugar or drizzle with Cinnamon-Sugar Syrup. Makes 16.

Cinnamon Sugar: Stir together ¼ cup *sugar* and ¼ teaspoon ground *cinnamon.*

Cinnamon-Sugar Syrup: In a saucepan combine 1 cup *sugar,* ½ cup packed *brown sugar,* ½ cup *water,* 2 tablespoons *dark corn syrup,* and 3 inches stick *cinnamon* or dash ground *cinnamon.* Bring mixture to boiling. Reduce heat; boil gently without stirring about 20 minutes or till thick. Discard cinnamon stick.

Pictured:
Indian Feast Day Cookies.

SOUTHWEST

Fruit-Filled Empanadas

Empanadas (em-pah-NAH-das) are turnovers that may contain a variety of fillings. They even may be filled with a meat mixture such as Picadillo (see recipe, page 69).

To make miniature turnovers or empanaditas, cut the pastry in this recipe into 3-inch circles. Prepare only half of the desired filling and use only 1 teaspoon filling for each turnover. This recipe will make 36 empanaditas.

**Cinnamon-Apricot,
  Pineapple-Sweet Potato,
  or Pumpkin-Raisin Filling
Pastry for Double-Crust Pie
  (see recipe, page 141)
Milk
Sugar**

Prepare desired filling. Prepare pastry; roll out to slightly less than ⅛-inch thickness. Cut into 6-inch circles. Spoon 3 to 4 tablespoons desired filling on center of each. Moisten edges with water; fold in half, sealing edges with fork. Place on ungreased baking sheet. Brush with milk; sprinkle with sugar. Bake in a 400° oven about 15 minutes. Makes 12.

Cinnamon-Apricot Filling: In a saucepan combine 8 ounces *dried apricots*, rinsed, and enough water to cover. Bring to boiling; reduce heat. Cover; simmer 20 minutes. Drain. In blender container blend apricots, 1 cup *sugar*, 1 teaspoon ground *cinnamon*, ½ teaspoon ground *nutmeg*, and ¼ teaspoon *salt* till smooth.

Pineapple-Sweet Potato Filling: Combine one 15½-ounce can *crushed pineapple*, well drained; 1 cup mashed, cooked *sweet potatoes*; ½ cup chopped *walnuts*; 2 tablespoons *sugar*; and ½ teaspoon *salt*.

Pumpkin-Raisin Filling: Combine one 16-ounce can *pumpkin*, 1 cup packed *brown sugar*, ½ cup *raisins*, ½ cup chopped *walnuts*, 1 teaspoon ground *cinnamon*, and ¼ teaspoon ground *cloves*.

New Mexican Chocolate

To make a frothy top on this hot drink, Mexicans whip the mixture with a carved tool called a molinillo. You can achieve the same effect with a rotary beater.

½ **cup sugar**
⅓ **cup unsweetened cocoa
   powder**
 2 **tablespoons all-purpose flour**
 1 **teaspoon ground cinnamon**
1½ **cups cold water**
 6 **cups milk**
 1 **tablespoon vanilla**

In a 3-quart saucepan combine sugar, cocoa powder, flour, cinnamon, and ¼ teaspoon *salt*. Stir in water. Bring to boiling, stirring constantly. Reduce heat; simmer about 4 minutes, stirring often.

Gradually stir in milk. Heat almost to boiling; *do not boil.* Remove from heat; add vanilla. Beat till frothy. Serve in mugs. If desired, garnish with cinnamon stick and whipped cream. Serves 10.

Ceviche

Ceviche (seh-VEE-cheh) is an appetizer made with raw fish that is "cooked" without the use of heat. The fish is marinated several hours in lime or lemon juice, giving the fish a texture and flavor similar to poached fish.

1 pound fresh *or* frozen haddock fillets *or* other fish fillets
1 cup fresh lime *or* lemon juice
1 small onion
¼ cup olive oil *or* cooking oil
2 or 3 pickled serrano *or* jalapeño peppers, rinsed, seeded, and cut into strips
¾ teaspoon salt
¼ teaspoon dried oregano, crushed
⅛ teaspoon pepper
2 medium tomatoes
Snipped cilantro *or* snipped parsley *or* avocado slices

Thaw fish, if frozen. Cut fish fillets into ½-inch cubes. In a nonmetal bowl cover cubed fish with lime or lemon juice. Cover and refrigerate 4 hours or overnight or till fish is opaque, turning fish occasionally.

Thinly slice the onion; separate into rings. Add onion to fish with olive oil or cooking oil, pickled peppers, salt, oregano, and pepper. Toss gently to combine well; chill.

Peel and chop tomatoes; toss with chilled fish mixture. Garnish with snipped cilantro, parsley, or avocado slices. Makes 10 to 12 appetizer servings.

Guacamole

Authentic *Guacamole* (guah-kah-MO-leh) has a coarse, chunky texture. Purists say the flavors are milder when mashed by hand than when pureed.

The myth of keeping the avocado seed in the guacamole to prevent the mixture from discoloring is not as effective as covering the guacamole during storage.

2 medium avocados
1 tablespoon lime *or* lemon juice
1 small tomato, peeled and finely chopped (½ cup)
2 tablespoons finely chopped onion
2 tablespoons finely chopped canned green chili peppers
1 clove garlic, minced
½ teaspoon snipped cilantro (optional)
¼ teaspoon salt
Tostaditas (see recipe, page 76) *or* large corn chips

Cut the avocados in half lengthwise. Remove seeds and scoop flesh into a mixing bowl. Mash with a fork or potato masher; add lime juice or lemon juice and mix well.

Stir in tomato, onion, chilies, garlic, cilantro if desired, and salt; mix well. Serve as a dip with Tostaditas or corn chips or serve as a sauce with main dishes. Makes 2 cups.

Chili con Queso

1 medium onion, finely chopped (½ cup)
1 clove garlic, minced
1 tablespoon butter *or* margarine
2 medium tomatoes, peeled and chopped
1 4-ounce can chopped green chili peppers, drained
¼ teaspoon salt
1 cup shredded American cheese (4 ounces)
1 cup shredded Monterey Jack cheese (4 ounces)
Light cream *or* milk
Tostaditas (see recipe, page 76) *or* large corn chips

In a medium saucepan cook onion and garlic in butter or margarine till onion is tender but not brown. Stir in tomatoes, chili peppers, and salt. Simmer, uncovered, for 10 minutes.

Add cheeses, a little at a time, stirring just till melted. Stir in a little light cream if mixture becomes too thick. Serve warm in a chafing dish with Tostaditas or corn chips. Makes about 2¼ cups.

THE WEST

Wild game, fish, seafood, countless fruits and vegetables, and other foods are available from this seemingly endless horn of plenty — the West.

Characterized by the rugged Rocky Mountains, the Pacific Ocean, and the forest of the Northwest, this area offers a diversified style of cooking molded by an equally diverse population.

It was the California Gold Rush that drew speculators from around the world in search of instant wealth and a new life. Russians, Chinese, Japanese, Germans, Portuguese, Italians, and Mexicans all brought with them cooking heritages that helped create the Western cuisine. Included in the West are the last two states to be admitted to the union — Alaska and Hawaii.

A good portion of Alaska's territory could still be considered a wilderness. Wild game and hefty produce abound in this rugged climate. Alaskan king crab, venison, game birds, blueberries, and cranberries are just a sample.

The Hawaiian Islands, in contrast, are a tropical paradise with palm trees and exotic foods.

Recipes pictured: *Sourdough Bread* (see recipe, page 91), *Crab Louis* (see recipe, page 86), and *Macadamia Nut Pie* (see recipe, page 93).

Beef Teriyaki with Pineapple

Hawaiian food has been influenced by the different people who settled the islands — Hawaiians, Tahitians, Portuguese, Chinese, Japanese, Europeans, and mainland Americans.

Here the American steak takes on the flavor of the Hawaiian teriyaki marinade. It's a combination of oil, soy sauce, lemon juice, garlic, dry sherry, brown sugar, and gingerroot.

¼ **cup peanut oil** *or* **cooking oil**
¼ **cup soy sauce**
2 **tablespoons lemon juice**
2 **tablespoons dry sherry**
1 **tablespoon brown sugar**
1½ **teaspoons grated fresh gingerroot** *or* ½ **teaspoon ground ginger**
1 **clove garlic, minced**
1 **pound beef sirloin steak, cut into 1-inch cubes**
1 **green pepper, cut into 1-inch pieces**
1 **8¼-ounce can pineapple chunks, drained**

For marinade, combine peanut oil or cooking oil, soy sauce, lemon juice, sherry, brown sugar, gingerroot or ginger, and garlic. Place beef in plastic bag set in a deep bowl or shallow baking dish. Pour marinade over meat. Close bag; refrigerate for 4 hours or overnight, turning bag or spooning marinade over meat occasionally.

Drain, reserving marinade. If desired, cook green pepper pieces in boiling water about 2 minutes. Drain. On 4 skewers alternately thread steak pieces, green pepper pieces, and pineapple chunks. Place kabobs on rack of unheated broiler pan. Broil kabobs 3 inches from heat for 8 to 10 minutes. Turn kabobs occasionally and brush frequently with reserved marinade. (*Or,* grill kabobs over *medium* coals for 17 to 19 minutes for medium-rare. Turn kabobs occasionally and brush frequently with reserved marinade.) Serves 4.

Chop Suey

Chop Suey (chop SOO-ee) is a blend of the American and Chinese cuisines. This flavorful stew served with rice and soy sauce was said to have developed in San Francisco during the 19th century.

1 **cup sliced onion**
1 **cup sliced fresh mushrooms**
¾ **cup bias-sliced celery**
½ **cup sliced water chestnuts**
½ **cup chopped green pepper**
2 **tablespoons cooking oil**
2 **cups cooked pork** *or* **chicken cut into bite-sized strips**
1 **16-ounce can bean sprouts, drained**
¾ **cup chicken broth**
2 **tablespoons soy sauce**
1 **tablespoon cornstarch**
Hot cooked rice

In a heavy skillet or wok stir-fry onion, mushrooms, celery, water chestnuts, and green pepper in hot cooking oil for 3 minutes. Add cooked pork or chicken, bean sprouts, and chicken broth. Cook till heated through. Combine the soy sauce and cornstarch. Add the soy sauce mixture to the vegetable mixture. Cook and stir till thickened and bubbly. Cook and stir 2 minutes more. Serve over hot cooked rice. Pass additional soy sauce if desired. Makes 4 or 5 servings.

Mormon Split Pea Soup

1 **pound dry green split peas (2 cups)**
6 **cups water**
1 **large onion, chopped (1 cup)**
½ **cup chopped celery**
2 **teaspoons salt**
½ **teaspoon dried marjoram, crushed**
1 **pound ground pork**
1 **teaspoon ground sage**
¾ **teaspoon salt**
3 **medium potatoes, peeled and diced (3 cups)**

Rinse the dry split peas. In a large kettle or Dutch oven combine the split peas, water, onion, celery, the 2 teaspoons salt, marjoram, and ¼ teaspoon *pepper.* Bring the mixture to boiling. Reduce heat; cover and simmer the mixture about 1 hour or till the peas are tender.

Meanwhile, combine the ground pork, the sage, ¾ teaspoon salt, and dash *pepper;* mix well. Shape mixture into 1-inch meatballs. Add the meatballs and diced potatoes to soup mixture; return soup to boiling. Reduce heat; cover and simmer 20 minutes more. Season to taste with salt and pepper. Makes 8 servings.

Marinated Venison Chops   *pictured on page 87*

4 **venison chops** *or* **steaks, cut
   ¾ inch thick (about 1 pound)**
¼ **cup red wine vinegar**
¼ **cup cooking oil**
¼ **cup catsup**
1 **tablespoon Worcestershire
   sauce**
1 **clove garlic, minced**
½ **teaspoon salt**
½ **teaspoon dry mustard
   Dash pepper**

Place venison chops or steaks in a plastic bag set in a deep bowl or shallow baking dish. For marinade, combine the wine vinegar, cooking oil, catsup, Worcestershire sauce, garlic, salt, dry mustard, and pepper. Pour marinade over meat in the plastic bag; close bag. Refrigerate for 6 hours or overnight, turning bag occasionally.

Drain venison, reserving marinade; pat dry. Place marinated chops on the rack of an unheated broiler pan. Broil 4 inches from heat for 6 to 8 minutes; brush with marinade. Turn and continue broiling to desired doneness. Brush with marinade just before serving. (Allow about 12 minutes total time for medium-rare, 14 minutes for medium, and 16 minutes for well-done.) Place broiled chops or steaks on serving platter. Heat remaining marinade and skim off fat; serve with chops. Makes 4 servings.

Grilled Elk Burgers

1 **beaten egg**
3 **tablespoons catsup**
1 **teaspoon Worcestershire sauce**
¼ **cup soft bread crumbs**
1 **small onion, finely chopped
   (¼ cup)**
1 **teaspoon prepared
   horseradish**
1½ **pounds ground elk** *or*
   ground buffalo
6 **slices sourdough bread, cut
   1 inch thick and toasted
   Cranberry Catsup (see recipe,
   page 90) (optional)**

In bowl combine the egg, catsup, and Worcestershire sauce. Stir in the bread crumbs, onion, horseradish, and ½ teaspoon *salt*. Add the ground meat; mix well. Shape into six ½-inch-thick burgers. Grill over *medium* coals till desired doneness, turning once (about 15 minutes total time for medium doneness). Serve burgers on toasted sourdough bread. Spoon some Cranberry Catsup atop if desired. Makes 6 servings.

Abalone Steaks

Native abalone is found along the California coast. The ear-shaped shell of this seafood is a common sight in Western curio shops. Its beautiful iridescent shell once held the flavorful white abalone meat.

1 **pound fresh** *or* **frozen abalone**
2 **eggs**
2 **tablespoons milk**
¾ **cup fine dry bread crumbs**
¼ **cup sesame seed, toasted**
½ **teaspoon salt**
⅛ **teaspoon ground red pepper**
½ **cup all-purpose flour**
¼ **cup butter** *or* **margarine
   Lemon wedges**

Thaw abalone, if frozen. Cut into 4 serving-size portions. If necessary, pound each portion to ⅓-inch thickness. Pat abalone dry with paper toweling. In bowl combine eggs and milk. In another bowl combine the bread crumbs, sesame seed, salt, and ground red pepper.

Dip abalone in the flour; dip in the egg mixture, then the bread crumb mixture. In a skillet cook coated abalone, half at a time, in *2 tablespoons* of the hot butter or margarine about 2 minutes on each side or till golden. Repeat with remaining abalone and butter or margarine. Serve with lemon wedges. Makes 4 servings.

Cioppino   *pictured on cover*

A delectable fish stew with an Italian name and ingredients, *Cioppino* (cha-PEE-no) supposedly originated on the Monterey peninsula and was popularized at Fisherman's Wharf in San Francisco.

1 **pound fresh *or* frozen fish fillets**
1 **small green pepper, cut into ½-inch squares**
2 **tablespoons finely chopped onion**
1 **clove garlic, minced**
1 **tablespoon cooking oil**
1 **16-ounce can tomatoes, cut up**
1 **8-ounce can tomato sauce**
½ **cup dry white *or* dry red wine**
3 **tablespoons snipped parsley**
½ **teaspoon salt**
¼ **teaspoon dried oregano, crushed**
¼ **teaspoon dried basil, crushed Dash pepper**
1 **12-ounce package frozen shelled shrimp *or* two 4½-ounce cans shrimp, drained, *or* one 12-ounce package frozen crab meat**
1 **7½-ounce can minced clams**

Partially thaw fish fillets, if frozen. Remove and discard skin from fillets. Cut fillets into 1-inch pieces; set aside. In a 3-quart saucepan cook green pepper, onion, and garlic in hot cooking oil till onion is tender but not brown.

Add the *undrained* tomatoes, tomato sauce, white or red wine, parsley, salt, oregano, basil, and pepper. Bring to boiling. Reduce heat; cover and simmer 20 minutes. Add fish pieces, shrimp or crab meat, and *undrained* clams to tomato mixture. Bring just to boiling. Reduce heat; cover and simmer for 5 to 7 minutes or till fish flakes easily when tested with a fork and shrimp are done. Makes 6 servings.

Crab Louis   *also pictured on page 83*

When the Metropolitan Opera Company played in Seattle in the early 1900s, it was said that Enrico Caruso gave *Crab Louis* rave reviews. He named the main-dish salad after the chef who created it.

¼ **cup whipping cream**
1 **cup mayonnaise *or* salad dressing**
¼ **cup chili sauce**
2 **tablespoons finely chopped onion**
1 **teaspoon lemon juice**
¼ **teaspoon salt Dash ground red pepper**
1 **large head lettuce, shredded**
2 **to 3 cups cooked crab meat, chilled, *or* two 7-ounce cans crab meat, chilled and drained**
2 **small tomatoes, cut into wedges**
1 **medium avocado, halved, seeded, peeled, and sliced**
2 **hard-cooked eggs, sliced**

For dressing, whip cream till soft peaks form. Fold in mayonnaise or salad dressing, chili sauce, finely chopped onion, lemon juice, salt, and ground red pepper. Cover and refrigerate till thoroughly chilled.

Arrange shredded lettuce on a serving plate or 4 individual salad plates. If necessary, remove cartilage from crab meat. Arrange crab meat atop shredded lettuce.

Arrange tomato wedges, avocado slices, and egg slices around crab meat. Pour chilled dressing over salad. Makes 4 servings.

Pictured clockwise:
Sourdough Bread (see recipe, page 91), Marinated Venison Chops (see recipe, page 85), and Crab Louis

Barley-Stuffed Trout

Trout, a popular game and table fish in the United States, thrive in the cold western lakes, streams, and rivers.

Adult trout weigh from about ½ pound to the record 120 pounds. You'll find most trout sold in ½- to 4-pound sizes.

4 fresh or frozen dressed trout (with head and tail) (about 5 ounces each)
½ cup quick-cooking barley
½ cup sliced fresh mushrooms
½ cup shredded carrot
1 small onion, chopped (¼ cup)
2 tablespoons butter or margarine
1¼ cups chicken broth
¼ cup snipped parsley
½ teaspoon dried oregano, crushed
2 tablespoons butter or margarine, melted

Thaw trout, if frozen. In a saucepan cook barley, mushrooms, carrot, and onion in the 2 tablespoons butter or margarine till barley is golden, stirring often. Stir in chicken broth, parsley, oregano, ¼ teaspoon *salt,* and dash *pepper.* Bring to boiling; reduce heat. Cover and simmer for 10 to 12 minutes or till barley is tender.

Sprinkle fish cavities with salt. Fill cavities with barley mixture. Keep any remaining barley mixture warm. Brush some of the 2 tablespoons melted butter over fish. Place fish on rack of unheated broiler pan. Broil 5 inches from heat for 5 minutes. Turn; brush with butter and broil about 5 minutes more or till fish flakes easily when tested with a fork. Serve fish with remaining barley mixture. Garnish with fresh dill if desired. Makes 4 servings.

Grilled Salmon Steaks

4 fresh or frozen salmon steaks or other fish steaks
⅓ cup cooking oil
3 tablespoons lemon juice
2 tablespoons snipped parsley
1 teaspoon dried dillweed
¼ teaspoon salt
¼ teaspoon dry mustard
Dash pepper

Thaw fish, if frozen. For marinade, in shallow dish combine oil, lemon juice, parsley, dillweed, salt, dry mustard, and pepper. Add fish; cover and let stand at room temperature for 2 hours, turning occasionally. (Or, marinate fish in refrigerator for 4 to 6 hours.) Drain, reserving marinade.

Place steaks in a well-greased wire grill basket. Grill over *medium-hot* coals for 5 to 8 minutes or till light brown. Brush with marinade and turn; grill 5 to 8 minutes more or till fish flakes easily when tested with a fork, brushing often. Makes 4 servings.

Seattle Clam Hash

It's said that settlers who came from New England to the Northwest substituted clams for the beef in their traditional corned beef hash. This interesting side dish can be made with fresh or canned clams.

3 medium potatoes
⅓ cup chopped onion
1 tablespoon butter or margarine
1 pint shucked clams, chopped, or two 6½-ounce cans minced clams, drained
¼ cup light cream or milk
½ teaspoon salt
¼ teaspoon pepper
¼ cup butter or margarine

Cook potatoes in boiling salted water about 30 minutes or till tender. Cool; peel and finely chop potatoes. Cook onion in 1 tablespoon butter or margarine till tender. In mixing bowl combine the chopped potatoes, cooked onion, clams, light cream or milk, salt, and pepper.

In a 10-inch skillet melt the ¼ cup butter or margarine; remove from heat. With a spatula, pat the potato-clam mixture into the skillet, leaving a ½-inch space around edge. Cook over medium heat for 6 to 8 minutes or till brown. Turn hash in large portions; brown for 4 to 5 minutes more. Makes 4 to 6 servings.

Artichokes with Citrus Butter Sauce

Castroville, California, south of San Francisco, is known as the artichoke center of the world.

To eat a cooked artichoke, pull off one leaf at a time and dip the base in a sauce. Turn the leaf upside down and draw it through your teeth, eating only the tender flesh. Discard the remainder of the leaf. Continue removing leaves until the fuzzy "choke" appears. Scoop out and discard the "choke." Eat the remaining heart with a fork, dipping each piece in sauce.

2 **artichokes (about 10 ounces each)**
¼ **cup butter** or **margarine**
1 **tablespoon snipped parsley**
1 **tablespoon lemon juice**

Wash artichokes, trim stems and remove loose outer leaves. Cut off 1 inch of tops; snip off sharp leaf tips. Add the artichokes to boiling salted water. Reduce heat; cover and simmer for 20 to 30 minutes or till a leaf pulls out easily. Drain cooked artichokes upside down.

For sauce, in saucepan melt the butter or margarine. Stir in parsley and lemon juice. After draining artichokes upside down, turn right side up and serve with the butter sauce. Makes 2 servings.

Lentil Casserole

1 **cup dry lentils**
1 **14½-ounce can chicken broth**
¾ **cup water**
1 **bay leaf**
1 **medium onion, chopped (½ cup)**
2 **tablespoons catsup**
1 **tablespoon molasses**
¼ **teaspoon dry mustard**
¼ **teaspoon Worcestershire sauce**
1 **slice bacon, crisp-cooked, drained, and crumbled**

Rinse lentils. In a 2-quart saucepan combine the lentils, chicken broth, water, and the bay leaf. Bring mixture to boiling; reduce heat. Cover and simmer 30 minutes. Discard bay leaf.

Stir in onion, catsup, molasses, dry mustard, and Worcestershire sauce. Turn mixture into a 1½-quart casserole. Cover and bake in a 350° oven for 40 minutes. Sprinkle with crumbled bacon. Return to oven and bake, uncovered, about 10 minutes more. Makes 6 servings.

Basque Potatoes

California, Nevada, Idaho, and Colorado proved to be good settling grounds for the Basque sheepherders who immigrated from Europe to the United States. They started arriving at about the time of the California gold rush in 1849.

Basque Potatoes is just one example of their hearty fare.

3 **medium potatoes, peeled and thinly sliced**
2 **tablespoons bacon drippings**
1 **small onion, finely chopped (¼ cup)**
Salt
Pepper
2 **eggs**
1 **tablespoon snipped parsley**
½ **teaspoon dried thyme, crushed**

In a 10-inch skillet cook potatoes in bacon drippings, covered, for 10 minutes. Uncover; add onion and cook over medium heat till potatoes are brown, turning potatoes occasionally. Season with salt and pepper.

Beat together the eggs, parsley, and thyme; pour over potato mixture in skillet. Cover and cook about 3 minutes or till eggs are set. Serves 4.

Cranberry Catsup

In Alaska, cranberries accompany many meals. Two types of cranberries grow in the state — the highbush cranberry, which has a red currant-like fruit, and the lingonberry or lowbush cranberry. Both are used interchangeably in Alaskan recipes.

Cranberry Catsup is actually a relish that combines the cranberry with onion, vinegar, cinnamon, allspice, celery seed, and cloves. Serve it with meat or game.

8 cups cranberries
1 large onion, finely chopped (1 cup)
1 cup water
4 cups sugar
⅔ cup white vinegar
2 teaspoons ground cinnamon
2 teaspoons ground allspice
2 teaspoons celery seed
2 teaspoons salt
1 teaspoon pepper
½ teaspoon ground cloves

In a 5-quart Dutch oven combine cranberries, onion, and the water. Bring mixture to boiling. Reduce heat; cover and simmer about 10 minutes or till berries are easily mashed. Pour cranberry mixture into blender container, half at a time. Cover and blend till smooth. Push mixture through a sieve.

In the Dutch oven stir together the cranberry mixture, sugar, vinegar, cinnamon, allspice, celery seed, salt, pepper, and cloves. Bring to boiling; boil gently, uncovered, about 5 minutes or till mixture is the consistency of catsup. (Mixture will thicken when cooled.) Remove mixture from heat. Ladle the mixture into hot ½-pint canning jars leaving ½-inch headspace. Adjust lids. Process jars in boiling water bath for 5 minutes (start timing when water boils). Serve with game, beef, pork, or lamb. Makes 7 half-pints.

Caesar Salad

1 egg
1 tablespoon olive oil
1 tablespoon butter *or* margarine
1 clove garlic, minced
1 cup cubed French bread
2 tablespoons lemon juice
3 tablespoons olive oil
6 cups torn romaine
¼ cup grated Parmesan cheese
3 anchovy fillets, cut up
Freshly ground pepper

Allow egg to come to room temperature. For croutons, in medium skillet heat the 1 tablespoon olive oil, butter or margarine, and garlic. Add bread cubes; cook over medium-low heat 3 to 4 minutes or till brown, stirring occasionally. Remove from heat; set aside.

To coddle egg, place whole egg in small saucepan of boiling water; remove from heat and let stand 1 minute. Cool slightly. Place lemon juice in a large salad bowl. Add the 3 tablespoons olive oil and egg; mix till creamy. Add romaine; toss to coat. Sprinkle salad with croutons, Parmesan, anchovies, and pepper; toss gently. Serves 6.

Sourdough Starter

Sourdough starter made its way west with the pioneers. It was used as a leavener for breads and other leavened foods when there was no source of yeast. Stories are told of how prospectors journeyed across Alaska carrying the sourdough starter with them.

Here *Sourdough Starter* is used to make *Blueberry Sourdough Pancakes* and bread reminiscent of the famous San Francisco *Sourdough Bread.*

Prepare *Sourdough Starter* at least 5 days before preparing the bread or pancakes. Store the starter in the refrigerator in a jar covered with cheese-cloth. Follow recipe directions to replenish the starter after each use and to add sugar or honey during storage.

1 package active dry yeast
2½ cups warm water (110° to 115°)
2 cups all-purpose flour
1 tablespoon sugar *or* honey

Dissolve yeast in ½ *cup* of the water. Stir in remaining 2 cups water, the flour, and sugar or honey. Beat till smooth. Cover with cheesecloth. Let stand at room temperature for 5 to 10 days or till bubbly; stir 2 to 3 times each day. (A warmer room hastens the fermentation process.)

To store, transfer Sourdough Starter to a jar and cover with cheesecloth; refrigerate. *Do not cover jar tightly with a metal lid.* To use starter, bring desired amount to room temperature.

To replenish starter after using, stir ¾ cup *all-purpose flour,* ¾ cup *water,* and 1 teaspoon *sugar or honey* into remaining amount. Cover; let stand at room temperature 1 day or till bubbly. Refrigerate for later use.

If the starter isn't used within 10 days, stir in 1 teaspoon *sugar or honey.* Repeat every 10 days or till the starter is used.

Sourdough Bread   *pictured on pages 82 and 87*

1 cup Sourdough Starter
1 package active dry yeast
1½ cups warm water (110° to 115°)
6 to 6½ cups all-purpose flour
2 teaspoons salt
2 teaspoons sugar
½ teaspoon baking soda

Bring Sourdough Starter to room temperature. Dissolve yeast in water. Stir in 2½ *cups* flour, salt, sugar, and starter. Combine another 2½ *cups* flour and soda; stir into yeast mixture. Stir in as much remaining flour as you can mix in with a spoon. Turn out onto floured surface. Knead in enough remaining flour to make a stiff dough that is smooth and elastic (8 to 10 minutes total). Shape into a ball in greased bowl; turn once. Cover; let rise in warm place till double (1½ hours).

Punch down; divide in half. Cover; let rest 10 minutes. Shape each half into a 6-inch round loaf on greased baking sheet. Brush with water. Slash tops in diamond pattern. Cover; let rise till nearly double (about 1 hour). Place a shallow baking pan with boiling water on bottom rack of a 400° oven. Bake bread on top rack 35 minutes; cover with foil after 20 minutes. Cool on rack. Makes 2.

Blueberry Sourdough Pancakes

1 cup Sourdough Starter
1¼ cups all-purpose flour
2 tablespoons sugar
1 teaspoon baking powder
½ teaspoon baking soda
1 beaten egg
1 cup milk
1 tablespoon cooking oil
1 cup fresh *or* frozen blueberries, thawed

Bring Sourdough Starter to room temperature. Combine flour, sugar, baking powder, soda, and ½ teaspoon *salt.* Combine egg, milk, oil, and starter. Add to flour mixture; stir till blended but slightly lumpy. Pour about ¼ cup batter onto hot, lightly greased griddle or heavy skillet for each pancake. Sprinkle *each* pancake with *1 tablespoon* blueberries. When pancakes have a bubbly surface and slightly dry edges, turn to cook other side. Serve with butter and maple-flavored syrup if desired. Makes 12.

Fig Bread   *pictured on pages 4 and 5*

It's said that figs were introduced to the United States in 1520 by the Spaniards. Today, California produces the largest volume of figs in the country.

Figs add a distinctive flavor to this quick bread that has a fine cakelike texture.

1¾ **cups all-purpose flour**
2 **teaspoons baking powder**
½ **teaspoon salt**
⅓ **cup shortening**
⅔ **cup sugar**
2 **eggs**
2 **teaspoons finely shredded lemon peel**
2 **tablespoons lemon juice**
1 **teaspoon vanilla**
⅔ **cup milk**
¾ **cup finely snipped dried figs**
½ **cup chopped pecans *or* walnuts**

Grease and lightly flour an 8x4x2-inch loaf pan; set aside. Stir together the flour, baking powder, and salt. In mixer bowl beat shortening with electric mixer at medium speed for 30 seconds. Add the sugar and beat till fluffy. Add eggs, one at a time, beating 1 minute after each addition. Beat in the lemon peel, lemon juice, and vanilla. Add the dry ingredients and milk alternately to the beaten mixture, beating on low speed after each addition just till combined.

Stir in the figs and pecans or walnuts. Turn mixture into prepared pan. Bake in a 350° oven for 60 to 65 minutes or till wooden pick inserted near center comes out clean. Cool on wire rack for 10 minutes. Remove from pan; cool thoroughly on wire rack. For easier slicing, wrap baked loaf in foil and store overnight. Makes 1 loaf.

Macadamia Nut Pie   *also pictured on page 83*

Although native to Australia, the macadamia nut tree was planted in Hawaii about 100 years ago. Today, commercial quantities of this shiny round nut are grown in the Hawaiian islands.

To prepare macadamia nuts for use, crack open their shells and roast the kernels in coconut oil.

Pastry for Single-Crust Pie (see recipe, page 141)
4 **beaten eggs**
1 **cup light corn syrup**
⅔ **cup sugar**
¼ **cup butter *or* margarine, melted**
2 **tablespoons all-purpose flour**
1 **teaspoon vanilla**
Dash salt
¾ **cup chopped macadamia nuts**

Prepare and roll out pastry. Line a 9-inch pie plate. Trim pastry to ½ inch beyond edge of pie plate. Flute edge; *do not prick pastry.*

Stir together the eggs, corn syrup, sugar, melted butter, flour, vanilla, and salt. Beat till smooth. Pour into prepared pastry shell. Sprinkle with nuts.

To prevent overbrowning, cover edge of pie with foil. Bake in a 350° oven for 25 minutes. Remove foil; bake about 25 minutes more or till a knife inserted near center comes out clean. Cool. Cover; refrigerate to store. Makes 10 servings.

Fresh Fruit Salad   *pictured on the cover*

1 **pineapple**
2 **cups fresh strawberries**
2 **oranges, peeled and sectioned**
2 **cups honeydew melon balls**
2 **kiwi, peeled and sliced**
⅓ **cup pomegranate seeds**
Lettuce leaves
Honey-Poppy Seed Dressing

Rinse pineapple. Twist off the crown and cut off the base. Slice off strips of rind lengthwise; then cut out and discard eyes. Slice the fruit into spears; cut off hard core. Cover spears; chill. Rinse and drain strawberries; cover and chill. Cover and chill orange sections, melon, kiwi, and pomegranate.

On a large lettuce-lined platter arrange the pineapple, strawberries, oranges, melon, and kiwi. Sprinkle with pomegranate seeds. Serve with Honey-Poppy Seed Dressing. Makes 8 servings.

Honey-Poppy Seed Dressing: In small mixer bowl beat together ½ cup *honey,* ¼ teaspoon finely shredded *lemon peel,* ¼ cup *lemon juice,* and ¼ teaspoon *salt.* Gradually add ¾ cup *salad oil,* beating with an electric mixer or rotary beater till thickened. Beat in 2 teaspoons *poppy seed.* Cover and refrigerate till chilled. Makes 1½ cups.

Pictured:
Grapefruit Chiffon Loaf Cake (see recipe, page 94) and Macadamia Nut Pie

93

Prune Cake

Prunes are dried plums, and it's said that more than 75 percent of the world's supply of prunes and plums is grown in California. The Santa Clara Valley of California became the center of prune production in the 1850s.

1½ cups pitted, dried prunes (8 ounces)
1½ cups all-purpose flour
1 teaspoon baking soda
¼ teaspoon salt
¼ cup butter *or* margarine
¼ cup shortening
1 cup sugar
1 teaspoon vanilla
2 eggs
¾ cup chopped walnuts
Whipped cream

Rinse dried prunes. Cover with water 1 inch above fruit. Bring to boiling. Reduce heat; cover and simmer for 15 minutes. Cool to room temperature. Drain prunes, reserving 1 cup liquid. Chop prunes.

Grease and flour a 13x9x2-inch baking pan. Combine the flour, baking soda, and salt. Beat butter and shortening with electric mixer for 30 seconds. Add sugar and vanilla and beat till fluffy.

Add eggs, one at a time, beating 1 minute after each. Add dry ingredients and reserved prune liquid alternately to beaten mixture, beating after each addition just till combined. Stir in prunes and nuts. Spread batter into prepared pan. Bake in a 350° oven for 30 to 35 minutes. Serve topped with whipped cream. Makes 12 servings.

Grapefruit Chiffon Loaf Cake   *pictured on page 92*

1 cup all-purpose flour
¾ cup sugar
1½ teaspoons baking powder
¼ teaspoon salt
¼ cup cooking oil
3 egg yolks
3½ teaspoons finely shredded grapefruit peel
⅓ cup grapefruit juice
4 egg whites
¼ teaspoon cream of tartar
1 cup sifted powdered sugar
½ teaspoon vanilla
1 to 2 tablespoons grapefruit juice

Combine flour, sugar, baking powder, and salt. Make a well in center of dry ingredients. Add oil, egg yolks, *1½ teaspoons* of the grapefruit peel, and the ⅓ cup grapefruit juice. Beat with electric mixer till smooth. Wash beaters thoroughly. Beat egg whites and cream of tartar till stiff peaks form (tips stand straight).

Gradually pour batter in a thin stream over entire surface of egg whites, folding in lightly. Pour into an ungreased 9x5x3-inch loaf pan. Bake in a 350° oven about 35 minutes or till cake tests done. Invert; cool in pan. Loosen edges; remove from pan. Combine powdered sugar, remaining grapefruit peel, vanilla, and enough of the 1 to 2 tablespoons juice to make of drizzling consistency. Spread over top of cake. Makes 12 servings.

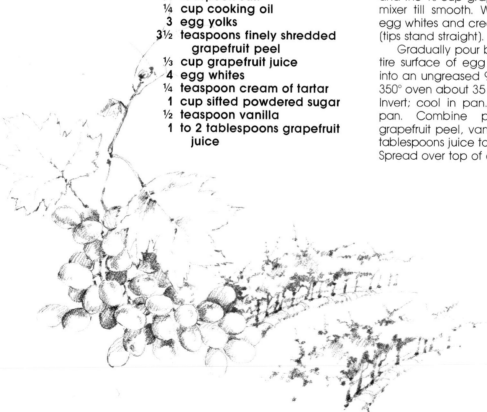

Apricot-Pineapple Pie

**Pastry for Double-Crust Pie
(see recipe, page 141)**
2 **cups dried apricots**
¾ **cup sugar**
2 **tablespoons all-purpose flour**
1 **20-ounce can crushed
pineapple**
1 **tablespoon butter or
margarine**

Prepare and roll out the pastry. Line a 9-inch pie plate with *half* of the pastry. Trim pastry to edge of plate. Rinse and halve apricots. In large saucepan cover apricots with water; bring to boiling. Cover and simmer for 15 to 20 minutes or till tender. Drain. In mixing bowl combine sugar and flour; add drained apricots and *undrained* pineapple. Toss to mix thoroughly.

Turn fruit mixture into the pastry-lined pie plate; dot with butter or margarine. Cut remaining pastry into ½-inch-wide strips with pastry wheel or sharp knife. Weave strips atop filling to make lattice crust. Seal and flute edge. To prevent overbrowning, cover edge of pie with foil. Bake in a 375° oven for 25 minutes. Remove foil; bake 20 to 25 minutes more. Cool on wire rack. Makes 8 servings.

Lomi Lomi Salmon

Lomi in Hawaiian means massage. *Lomi Lomi Salmon* is salted salmon that has been chopped into fine pieces.

It is served as an appetizer in the traditional luau and is eaten with the fingers. Try it as a topper on assorted crackers.

1 **3⅔-ounce can sliced smoked
red salmon (lox), drained
and finely chopped**
1 **medium tomato, peeled and
finely chopped (¾ cup)**
¼ **cup finely chopped
green onion**
2 **tablespoons finely chopped
green pepper**
Shredded lettuce
Assorted crackers

In small bowl combine salmon, tomato, green onion, and green pepper. Mash or chop till well blended. Cover and refrigerate till thoroughly chilled. Stir before serving. Serve atop shredded lettuce with assorted crackers. Makes 1⅓ cups.

California Cooler *pictured on the cover*

1 **cup orange juice**
¼ **cup honey**
1 **750-milliliter bottle dry
white or rosé wine**
2 **tablespoons lemon juice**
2 **cups carbonated water,
chilled**
Ice cubes

In a saucepan heat orange juice and honey together just till honey is blended. Cool to room temperature. Stir in wine and lemon juice. Cover and refrigerate till chilled. Just before serving, slowly add carbonated water, stirring with up-and-down motion. Serve in tall glasses over ice. Garnish with orange slices if desired. Makes 6 (8-ounce) servings.

Mai Tai

1½ **ounces orange juice**
1½ **ounces unsweetened
pineapple juice**
1 **ounce light rum**
1 **ounce dark rum**
1 **ounce sweetened lime juice**
½ **ounce orange liqueur**
Cracked ice

In a tall glass mix the orange juice, pineapple juice, light rum, dark rum, lime juice, and orange liqueur. Add enough cracked ice to fill the glass; stir. If desired, garnish the glass with a thin slice of lime and some fresh mint. Makes 1 serving.

ALL·AMERICAN RECIPES

This chapter of All-American Recipes encompasses new and old classics that can't be claimed by a particular region of the United States.

This collection epitomizes American cuisine — a combination of old cooking methods and new food technology. You'll find a mélange of made-from-scratch recipes that start with basic ingredients, as well as updated recipes that incorporate convenience products such as canned or packaged foods.

Of course, many of these recipes are not native

American creations. Pizza, spaghetti, and lasagna are Italian dishes that have been Americanized.

Other recipes are distinctly American in origin. For example, a California insurance salesman is credited with creating the chiffon cake in 1927. This culinary invention combines the lightness of angel cake with the richness of a shortening cake. His secret — the use of cooking oil instead of solid shortening, and stiffly beaten egg whites for additional leavening.

Another American first was the potato chip. According to legend, this now-popular snack was a happy accident caused when an irate chef over-cooked fried potatoes after a complaining customer

continued to return them to the kitchen because they weren't crisp enough.

Recipes in this chapter reflect this American creativity, be they original or borrowed.

Recipes pictured: *Chocolate Milk Shake* (see recipe, page 158), *Spinach, Bacon, and Mushroom Salad* (see recipe page 121), and *Submarine Sandwiches* (see recipe, page 105).

Herbed Meat-Vegetable Kabobs

When primitive man skewered meat on his weapons and held them over a fire to cook, he created the first kabob. Natives of the Near East popularized the concept skewering lamb, a mainstay in their diet.

Today, Americans combine a variety of meats, seafood, and vegetables on their skewers. This recipe uses beef that has been marinated in a blend of oil, lemon juice, and herbs.

½ **cup cooking oil**
1 **medium onion, chopped (½ cup)**
¼ **cup snipped parsley**
¼ **cup lemon juice**
1 **teaspoon dried marjoram, crushed**
1 **teaspoon dried thyme, crushed**
1 **clove garlic, minced**
2 **pounds boneless beef or lamb, cut into 1-inch cubes**
4 **medium onions, cut into wedges**
3 **green or sweet red peppers, cut into 1-inch squares**

In a bowl combine oil, the chopped onion, parsley, lemon juice, marjoram, thyme, garlic, 1 teaspoon *salt*, and ½ teaspoon *pepper*; stir in meat cubes. Cover; refrigerate 6 to 8 hours, stirring occasionally. Drain meat, reserving marinade. Cook onion wedges in water till tender; drain.

Thread eight skewers with meat cubes, onion wedges, and green or sweet red pepper squares. Grill over *hot* coals about 15 minutes, turning and brushing once with reserved marinade. (Or, place kabobs on rack of unheated broiler pan. Broil 3 to 4 inches from heat for 10 to 12 minutes, turning and brushing once with reserved marinade.) Serves 8.

Basic Beef Stew   *pictured on page 102*

1½ **pounds beef stew meat, cut into 1-inch cubes**
2 **tablespoons cooking oil**
1 **large onion, chopped (1 cup)**
1 **clove garlic, minced**
1 **tablespoon instant beef bouillon granules**
2 **teaspoons Worcestershire sauce**
1 **teaspoon salt**
1 **teaspoon dried thyme, crushed**
¼ **teaspoon pepper**
3 **medium potatoes, peeled and cut into 1-inch cubes**
3 **large carrots, sliced ½ inch thick**
1 **stalk celery, sliced**
¼ **cup all-purpose flour**

In a large saucepan or Dutch oven brown meat, half at a time, in hot cooking oil. Return all meat to saucepan; add onion, garlic, bouillon granules, Worcestershire sauce, salt, thyme, pepper, and 3 cups *water*. Bring to boiling; reduce heat. Cover and simmer mixture 1¼ hours.

Add potatoes, carrots, and celery; cover and simmer about 30 minutes more or till meat and vegetables are tender. Skim off fat if necessary. Combine flour and ½ cup *water*. Stir into stew. Cook and stir till thickened and bubbly. Cook and stir 1 minute more. Makes 6 servings.

Steak Sandwiches   *pictured on the cover*

⅔ **cup beer**
⅓ **cup cooking oil**
1 **teaspoon salt**
¼ **teaspoon garlic powder**
¼ **teaspoon pepper**
1½ **pounds beef flank steak**
2 **tablespoons butter or margarine**
½ **teaspoon paprika**
3 **cups sliced onions**
12 **slices French bread, toasted**
1 **cup dairy sour cream**
½ **teaspoon prepared horseradish**

Combine beer, oil, salt, garlic powder, and pepper. Place steak in a shallow baking dish. Pour beer mixture over steak. Cover; refrigerate overnight, turning once or twice.

Drain steak; pat dry with paper toweling. Broil steak 3 inches from heat to desired doneness. (Allow 5 to 7 minutes per side for medium-rare.) In a 10-inch skillet melt butter; stir in paprika and dash *salt*. Add onion; cook till tender.

Thinly slice steak on the diagonal across grain. For each serving, arrange steak atop 2 slices toasted bread. Top with onions. Heat sour cream just till warm. Stir in horseradish; spoon over onions. Sprinkle with paprika if desired. Serves 6.

Old-Fashioned Fresh Vegetable-Beef Soup

3 **pounds beef shank crosscuts**
8 **cups water**
4 **teaspoons salt**
½ **teaspoon dried oregano, crushed**
¼ **teaspoon dried marjoram, crushed**
5 **whole black peppercorns**
2 **bay leaves**
4 **fresh ears of corn** or **1 10-ounce package frozen whole kernel corn**
3 **tomatoes, peeled and cut up**
2 **medium potatoes, peeled and cubed (2 cups)**
1 **cup fresh cut green beans** or ½ **of a 9-ounce package frozen cut green beans**
2 **medium carrots, sliced (1 cup)**
2 **stalks celery, sliced (1 cup)**
1 **medium onion, chopped (½ cup)**

In a large kettle or Dutch oven combine beef crosscuts, water, salt, oregano, marjoram, peppercorns, and bay leaves. Bring mixture to boiling. Reduce heat; cover and simmer about 2 hours.

Remove the beef. When cool enough to handle, cut meat from bones; chop meat. Strain broth; skim off fat. Return broth to kettle. Cut fresh corn from cobs. Add the chopped meat, fresh or frozen corn, tomatoes, potatoes, fresh or frozen green beans, carrots, celery, and onion. Cover and simmer about 1 hour. Season to taste with salt and pepper. Makes 10 to 12 servings.

Corned Beef Hash

You can adjust the proportion of beef to potatoes in *Corned Beef Hash* depending on personal taste and what you have on hand. Just be sure that the meat and potatoes are chopped, not ground or processed in a food processor.

2 **tablespoons butter** or **margarine**
3 **cups finely chopped cooked corned beef (¾ pound)**
2 **cups finely chopped cooked potatoes**
1 **medium onion, finely chopped**
¼ **cup light cream** or **milk**
1 **teaspoon Worcestershire sauce**
⅛ **teaspoon pepper**
Catsup or **chili sauce (optional)**

In a 10-inch skillet melt butter or margarine. Stir in corned beef, potatoes, onion, light cream or milk, Worcestershire sauce, and pepper. Cook, stirring occasionally, till light brown. Serve with catsup or chili sauce if desired. Makes 4 servings.

• **Roast Beef Hash:** Prepare Corned Beef Hash as above, *except* substitute 3 cups chopped cooked *roast beef* for the 3 cups corned beef and add ¼ teaspoon *salt*. Continue as directed.

Reubens

A restaurant cook from Omaha, Nebraska won the National Sandwich Idea Contest in 1956 when he introduced the Reuben. The overwhelming popularity of the sandwich confirms that the award was well deserved.

12 **slices rye** or **pumpernickel bread**
½ **cup thousand island salad dressing**
6 **slices Swiss cheese**
1 **8-ounce can sauerkraut, well drained**
1 **pound thinly sliced cooked corned beef**
⅓ **cup butter** or **margarine, softened**

Spread *half* of the rye or pumpernickel bread slices with the thousand island dressing. Top each with 1 slice of Swiss cheese. Place sauerkraut atop cheese slices. Top with corned beef and another slice of bread. Butter both sides of sandwiches. Cook on both sides till golden brown and cheese is melted. Makes 6 servings.

Stuffed Peppers

Versatile green peppers function as edible serving containers in *Stuffed Peppers*. Whether you precook the peppers or use them raw, their walls are sturdy enough to hold one serving of stuffing. In addition, the peppers impart their flavor to the meat mixture during baking.

- **6 large green peppers**
- **1 pound ground beef**
- **⅓ cup chopped onion**
- **1 8-ounce can whole kernel corn, drained**
- **1 8-ounce can tomato sauce**
- **¾ cup cooked rice**
- **½ cup shredded cheddar cheese**
- **2 tablespoons chili sauce**
- **1 teaspoon Worcestershire sauce**
- **½ teaspoon chili powder**
- **¾ cup soft bread crumbs**
- **1 tablespoon butter *or* margarine, melted**

Cut tops from peppers; discard seeds and membranes. (Reserve tops for another use.) If desired, cook peppers in large amount of boiling salted water for 3 to 5 minutes. Invert to drain. Sprinkle insides lightly with salt.

In a 10-inch skillet cook ground beef and onion till meat is brown; drain off fat. Stir in corn, tomato sauce, rice, cheese, chili sauce, Worcestershire sauce, chili powder, and ¾ teaspoon *salt*. Spoon mixture into peppers.

Place in an 8x8x2-inch baking dish. Combine bread crumbs and melted butter; sprinkle atop peppers. Bake, uncovered, in a 350° oven about 35 minutes or till heated through. Makes 6 servings.

Taco Salad

- **1 pound ground beef**
- **½ envelope (¼ cup) *regular* onion soup mix**
- **¾ cup water**
- **Few dashes bottled hot pepper sauce**
- **1 small head lettuce, torn into bite-sized pieces (4 cups)**
- **1 large tomato, cut into wedges**
- **1 cup shredded sharp cheddar cheese (4 ounces)**
- **½ cup sliced pitted ripe olives**
- **¼ cup chopped green pepper *or* chopped canned green chili peppers**
- **2 cups corn chips**
- **Taco sauce (optional)**

In a medium skillet brown beef. Drain off fat. Sprinkle dry onion soup mix over meat; stir in water. Simmer mixture, uncovered, about 10 minutes or till water cooks away. Stir in hot pepper sauce.

Meanwhile, in salad bowl combine lettuce, tomato, cheese, olives, and green pepper or green chili peppers; toss well. Place lettuce mixture on individual salad plates if desired. Spoon meat mixture over lettuce; garnish with corn chips. Pass taco sauce if desired. Makes 4 to 6 servings.

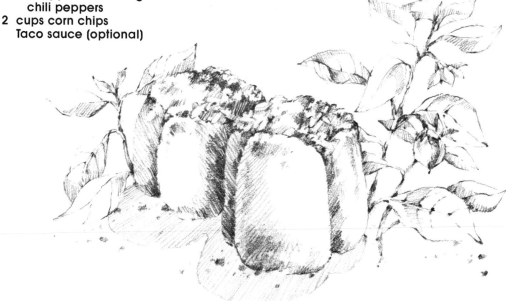

Sloppy Joes

Though it may take the challenge out of eating this sandwich, you can eat *Sloppy Joes* open-faced with a knife and fork.

1 pound ground beef
1 medium onion, chopped
   (½ cup)
1 stalk celery, chopped
   (½ cup)
¼ cup chopped green pepper
1 8-ounce can tomato sauce
⅓ cup chili sauce
1 teaspoon Worcestershire sauce
½ teaspoon salt
⅛ teaspoon pepper
4 to 6 hamburger buns, split
   and toasted

In a 10-inch skillet cook beef, onion, celery, and green pepper till meat is brown. Drain off fat. Stir in tomato sauce, chili sauce, Worcestershire sauce, salt, and pepper. Bring to boiling. Reduce heat and simmer, uncovered, 5 to 10 minutes or to desired consistency. Serve on toasted buns. Makes 4 to 6 servings.

Stuffed Burgers

2 beaten eggs
¼ cup milk
¾ cup soft bread crumbs
   (1 slice)
2 tablespoons snipped parsley
2 teaspoons Worcestershire
   sauce
¾ teaspoon salt
   Dash pepper
1½ pounds ground beef
   **Bacon-Mushroom Stuffing,
   Vegetable Stuffing, Blue
   Cheese Stuffing,** *or*
   **Oriental Stuffing
   Hamburger buns (optional)**

In a large mixing bowl combine eggs and milk; stir in bread crumbs, parsley, Worcestershire sauce, salt, and pepper. Add beef; mix well. Shape meat mixture into twelve ¼-inch-thick patties. Place about 2 tablespoons of desired stuffing atop *each* of *six* of the patties to within ½ inch of edge. Top with remaining patties; seal edges.

Place on rack of unheated broiler pan. Broil 3 inches from heat to desired doneness, turning once (allow 10 to 12 minutes total time for medium). Serve burgers on hamburger buns if desired. Makes 6 servings.

Bacon-Mushroom Stuffing: In a skillet cook 4 slices *bacon* till crisp. Drain, reserving 1 tablespoon drippings. Crumble bacon; set aside. Cook 2 tablespoons *each* finely chopped *celery* and chopped *onion* in reserved drippings in skillet till tender. Stir in the crumbled bacon and one 3-ounce can chopped *mushrooms*, drained. Makes about ¾ cup stuffing.

Vegetable Stuffing: In a skillet cook ½ cup shredded *potato,* ¼ cup chopped *onion,* and ¼ cup shredded *carrot* in 2 tablespoons *butter or margarine* till vegetables are tender. Combine the cooked vegetables; ⅓ cup soft *bread crumbs;* 1 beaten *egg;* ½ teaspoon *salt;* ⅛ teaspoon dried *marjoram,* crushed; and dash *pepper.* Mix well. Makes about ¾ cup.

Blue Cheese Stuffing: In a bowl combine one 5-ounce jar *blue cheese spread,* 2 tablespoons *mayonnaise* or *salad dressing,* 2 teaspoons *Worcestershire sauce,* and ¼ teaspoon *dry mustard;* mix well. Makes about ¾ cup.

Oriental Stuffing: In a bowl combine ½ cup *bean sprouts;* ¼ cup *water chestnuts,* chopped; 2 *green onions,* sliced; 1 tablespoon *soy sauce;* and ⅛ teaspoon ground *ginger.* Toss together lightly. Makes about ¾ cup.

Apple-Stuffed Rib Roast

1 **4-pound pork loin center rib roast, backbone loosened**
Salt
Pepper
1 **20-ounce can sliced apples**
1 **pound ground pork**
9 **slices dry raisin bread, cut into ½-inch cubes**
1 **teaspoon ground cinnamon**
¾ **teaspoon salt**
½ **teaspoon ground cardamom**
¼ **teaspoon ground allspice**
Dash pepper
Fresh sage (optional)

Place roast rib side down. Cut pockets in roast from meaty side between rib bones. Season with salt and pepper. Drain apples, reserving juice. Finely chop apples and set aside. Add water to reserved juice to make 1 cup liquid; set aside.

In a skillet cook ground pork till brown; drain off fat. Stir in chopped apples, bread cubes, cinnamon, ¾ teaspoon salt, cardamom, allspice, and dash pepper. Add reserved apple liquid; toss to moisten. Spoon about ½ cup stuffing into each pocket of roast. (Spoon remaining stuffing into a 1-quart casserole; cover and refrigerate.)

Place roast, rib side down, in shallow roasting pan. Insert meat thermometer in meat so it doesn't touch bone. Roast meat in a 325° oven for 1½ hours or till meat begins to brown. Remove from oven; cover loosely with foil to prevent stuffing from overbrowning. Roast 1 to 1½ hours more or till meat thermometer registers 170°. Bake stuffing in casserole, uncovered, with roast the last 40 minutes of roasting. Garnish roast with fresh sage if desired. Makes 8 servings.

Lasagna

Strictly speaking, *Lasagna* is the broad flat noodle used in many Italian dishes. To most Americans, however, it is a casserole layered with this widest of pasta noodles, meat sauce, and cheese.

Lasagna is ideal to serve when entertaining. It can be made ahead, refrigerated or frozen, and reheated before serving.

1 **pound bulk pork sausage** *or* **ground beef**
1 **medium onion, chopped (½ cup)**
1 **clove garlic, minced**
1 **16-ounce can tomatoes, cut up**
1 **8-ounce can tomato sauce**
1 **6-ounce can tomato paste**
2 **teaspoons dried basil, crushed**
1 **teaspoon salt**
1 **tablespoon cooking oil**
8 **ounces lasagna noodles**
2 **beaten eggs**
2½ **cups ricotta** *or* **cream-style cottage cheese**
¾ **cup grated Parmesan** *or* **Romano cheese**
2 **tablespoons dried parsley flakes**
1 **teaspoon salt**
½ **teaspoon pepper**
1 **pound mozzarella cheese, thinly sliced**

In a skillet cook meat, onion, and garlic till meat is brown. Drain off fat. Stir in the *undrained* tomatoes, tomato sauce, tomato paste, basil, and 1 teaspoon salt. Cover; simmer 15 minutes, stirring often. Meanwhile, add the cooking oil to large amount of boiling salted water; cook noodles in the water for 10 to 12 minutes or just till tender. Drain and rinse the cooked lasagna noodles.

Combine eggs, ricotta or cottage cheese, ½ cup of the Parmesan cheese, the parsley, 1 teaspoon salt, and the pepper. Layer *half* of the noodles in a 13x9x2-inch baking dish; spread with *half* of the ricotta mixture. Add *half* of the mozzarella cheese and *half* of the meat sauce. Repeat layers. Sprinkle remaining Parmesan cheese atop.

Bake in a 375° oven for 30 to 35 minutes or till heated through. (Or, assemble ahead and refrigerate; bake in a 375° oven about 45 minutes.) Let stand 10 minutes before serving. Makes 10 servings.

Pictured clockwise:
Basic Beef Stew (see recipe, page 98), Submarine Sandwiches (see recipe, page 105), and Apple-Stuffed Rib Roast.

Spaghetti and Meat Sauce

Though we cannot take credit for originating *Spaghetti and Meat Sauce,* it's still an American favorite.

Thomas Jefferson introduced America to spaghetti when he returned from Italy with a die for making the pasta. But not until the early 1900s, when the wheat needed for pasta production was grown here, was spaghetti commercially produced in this country.

¾ **pound bulk Italian sausage**
½ **pound ground beef**
1 **medium onion, chopped (½ cup)**
¼ **cup chopped green pepper**
2 **cloves garlic, minced**
2 **16-ounce cans tomatoes, cut up**
1 **6-ounce can tomato paste**
⅔ **cup dry red wine**
1 **4-ounce can mushroom stems and pieces (optional)**
1 **teaspoon sugar**
1 **teaspoon dried Italian seasoning, crushed**
1 **pound hot cooked spaghetti Grated Parmesan or Romano cheese**

In a Dutch oven cook the sausage, ground beef, onion, green pepper, and garlic till meats are brown. Drain off fat. Stir in *undrained* tomatoes, tomato paste, red wine, *undrained* mushrooms if desired, sugar, Italian seasoning, ¾ cup *water,* and 1 teaspoon *salt.* Simmer, uncovered, about 50 minutes or to desired consistency, stirring occasionally. Serve over hot spaghetti. Pass cheese. Makes 6 servings.

Pizza

Pizza is second only to the hamburger on America's list of favorite foods. This is quite remarkable considering that it didn't catch on until after World War II. When American GIs returned from Italy with fond memories of the bubbling hot Italian specialty, the pizza craze began. The ever-increasing demand for pizza is certain to continue as long as there are appetites to satisfy.

2¾ **to 3¼ cups all-purpose flour**
1 **package active dry yeast**
1 **teaspoon salt**
1 **cup warm water (115° to 120°)**
2 **tablespoons cooking oil Cornmeal**
1 **15-ounce can tomato sauce**
1 **large onion, chopped (1 cup)**
1 **clove garlic, minced**
1 **teaspoon dried Italian seasoning, crushed**
3 **cups shredded mozzarella cheese (12 ounces)**
½ **pound bulk Italian sausage, cooked and drained, or sliced pepperoni**
1½ **cups sliced green pepper, cooked sliced mushrooms, and/or sliced pitted ripe olives**
⅓ **cup grated Parmesan cheese**

In a mixer bowl combine *1¼ cups* of the flour, the yeast, and salt. Stir in the warm water and oil. Beat with electric mixer at low speed for ½ minute, scraping bowl constantly. Beat 3 minutes at high speed. Stir in as much of the remaining flour as you can mix in with a spoon. Turn out onto a lightly floured surface. Knead in enough of the remaining flour to make a moderately stiff dough that is smooth and elastic (6 to 8 minutes total).

For a thick crust, place in greased bowl; turn once. Cover; let rise till double (about 1 hour). Punch down. Divide in half. Cover; let rest 10 minutes. Sprinkle 2 greased 9x9x2-inch baking pans or 10-inch oven-going skillets with cornmeal; with greased fingers pat dough into the bottom and halfway up the sides. Cover; let rise till nearly double (30 to 45 minutes). Bake in a 375° oven for 20 to 25 minutes or till light brown.

For thin crust, divide dough in half after kneading. Cover; let rest 10 minutes. Sprinkle 2 greased 12-inch pizza pans with cornmeal. On lightly floured surface roll out each dough half into a 13-inch circle; transfer to pizza pans. Build up edges. Bake in a 425° oven about 12 minutes or till light brown.

Meanwhile, for sauce, in a 2-quart saucepan combine tomato sauce, onion, garlic, and Italian seasoning. Bring to boiling; simmer, uncovered, 5 minutes. Sprinkle *1½ cups* of the mozzarella over crusts. Spread sauce over cheese. Sprinkle each with the sausage and desired vegetables. Top with remaining mozzarella and the Parmesan cheese.

For *thick*-crust pizza, bake in a 375° oven 20 to 25 minutes or till bubbly. For *thin* crust, bake in a 425° oven 10 to 15 minutes. Makes 2.

Sausage Sandwiches

1 pound bulk Italian sausage
½ pound ground beef
1 medium onion, chopped
   (½ cup)
1 15-ounce can tomato sauce
1 7½-ounce can tomatoes,
   cut up
1 teaspoon dried oregano,
   crushed
⅛ teaspoon pepper
4 individual French rolls
   (about 8 inches long)
1 6-ounce package (4 slices)
   mozzarella cheese slices

In a 10-inch skillet cook sausage, beef, and onion till meat is brown; drain off fat. Stir in tomato sauce, *undrained* tomatoes, oregano, pepper, and ¾ teaspoon *salt.* Bring to boiling. Reduce heat and simmer, uncovered, about 25 minutes or till thick, stirring frequently.

Slice the rolls lengthwise, cutting almost all the way through. Spoon in meat mixture. Top with cheese. Place rolls on a 15x10x1-inch baking pan. Bake in a 400° oven 6 to 8 minutes or till cheese is melted. Cut rolls in half crosswise. Serves 8.

Submarine Sandwiches *pictured on pages 97 and 102*

Down through the years, *Submarine Sandwiches* have been called grinders, heroes, hoagies, poor boys, and torpedoes. All describe a substantial sandwich made by piling layers of meats, cheeses, onion, and tomato on long split rolls.

4 individual French rolls
   (about 8 inches long)
⅓ cup mayonnaise *or*
   salad dressing
¼ cup dairy sour cream
1 tablespoon prepared mustard
   or Dijon-style mustard
   Butter *or* margarine, softened
6 ounces boiled ham slices
6 ounces sliced salami
6 ounces sliced cooked chicken
   or turkey
4 ounces sliced Swiss cheese
4 ounces sliced cheddar cheese
2 medium tomatoes, sliced
1 large green pepper, seeded
   and cut into rings
1 large onion, sliced (optional)

Split French rolls lengthwise. Scoop out some of the center. Combine mayonnaise, sour cream, and mustard; spread generously on top halves of rolls. Spread bottom halves with butter or margarine. Layer remaining ingredients in order atop roll bottoms. Sprinkle lightly with salt and pepper. Add roll tops. Cut rolls in half crosswise. Makes 8 servings.

Chef's Salad

1 clove garlic, halved
6 cups torn lettuce
3 cups torn romaine
8 ounces Swiss *or* cheddar
   cheese
6 ounces fully cooked ham *or*
   cooked beef
6 ounces cooked chicken *or*
   turkey
4 hard-cooked eggs, sliced
3 medium tomatoes, cut into
   wedges
2 small green peppers, cut into
   rings and quartered
   Salad dressing (see recipes,
   page 121)

Rub 6 large individual salad bowls with the cut surface of garlic clove; discard garlic. Place torn lettuce and romaine in the salad bowls. Cut cheese, ham or beef, and chicken or turkey into julienne strips. Arrange cheese, meats, eggs, tomatoes, and green peppers over the greens. Serve with your choice of salad dressing. Makes 6 servings.

Chicken Fricassee

A fricassee consists of cut-up pieces of meat stewed in a gravy. In the past, spent old hens were used in *Chicken Fricassee*, and the dish was considered rather commonplace. Today, the use of young chickens, cream, and a discreet blend of seasonings have rescued *Chicken Fricassee* from its previous humble state.

1 3- to 3½-pound broiler-fryer chicken, cut up
2 tablespoons cooking oil
1 medium onion, chopped
2 cups water
1 stalk celery with leaves, cut up
3 parsley sprigs
2 teaspoons instant chicken bouillon granules
½ teaspoon salt
½ teaspoon dried thyme, crushed
¼ teaspoon pepper
1 bay leaf
1 cup light cream
2 tablespoons all-purpose flour
2 beaten egg yolks
   Hot cooked rice, noodles, *or* hot biscuits

In a Dutch oven brown chicken on one side in hot cooking oil. Turn chicken; add onion and brown chicken on other side. Drain off fat. Add water, celery, parsley, chicken bouillon granules, salt, thyme, pepper, and bay leaf. Bring to boiling; reduce heat. Cover and simmer 45 minutes or till chicken is tender.

Remove chicken pieces to large serving bowl; cover and keep warm. Strain broth; skim off fat. Return 1½ cups of the broth to the Dutch oven. Combine light cream and flour; stir into broth. Cook and stir till thickened and bubbly. Cook and stir 1 minute more.

Stir about 1 cup of the hot mixture into beaten egg yolks; return to mixture in the Dutch oven. Cook and stir just till mixture comes to boiling. Pour over chicken. Serve with rice, noodles, or biscuits. Makes 6 servings.

Chicken Pies

   Pastry for Double-Crust Pie (see recipe, page 141)
   Beaten egg
1 medium onion, chopped (½ cup)
⅓ cup butter *or* margarine
½ cup all-purpose flour
½ teaspoon salt
3 cups chicken broth
3 cups cubed cooked chicken
1 10-ounce package frozen peas and carrots, cooked and drained
¼ cup chopped pimiento

Prepare pastry. Roll out on lightly floured surface to ¼-inch thickness. Cut to fit tops of six 10-ounce casseroles, cutting out design in dough if desired. Brush with beaten egg. Bake pastry on ungreased baking sheet in a 450° oven for 10 to 12 minutes.

Meanwhile, in a 3-quart saucepan cook onion in butter till tender but not brown. Stir in flour and salt. Add broth all at once. Cook and stir till thickened and bubbly; cook and stir 1 minute more.

Heat oven-proof casseroles in warm oven or heat other casseroles by rinsing with hot water. Stir chicken, peas and carrots, and pimiento into broth mixture. Heat till bubbly. Pour into heated casseroles. Place pastry atop hot filling just before serving. Serves 6.

Chicken Tetrazzini

Luisa Tetrazzini, a famous opera star of the early 1900s, was known for her outstanding voice as well as for her excessive fondness of food, especially pasta. This creamy chicken and spaghetti composition honors the great soprano for whom the recipe is named.

3 tablespoons butter *or* margarine
1½ cups sliced fresh mushrooms
¼ cup chopped green pepper
¼ cup all-purpose flour
¼ teaspoon salt
1½ cups light cream
1 cup chicken broth
2½ cups cubed cooked chicken
6 ounces spaghetti, cooked and well drained
2 tablespoons dry sherry
¼ cup grated Parmesan cheese
¼ cup sliced almonds

In a large saucepan melt butter or margarine; add mushrooms and green pepper. Cook and stir till tender; stir in flour and salt. Add light cream and broth; cook and stir till thickened and bubbly. Cook and stir 1 minute more. Stir in chicken, spaghetti, and sherry. Heat through.

Turn into a 12x7½x2-inch baking dish. Sprinkle with Parmesan cheese and sliced almonds. Bake in a 400° oven for 10 to 15 minutes. Serves 5 or 6.

Pictured clockwise:
Broccoli-Stuffed Cornish Hens (see recipe, page 109), Chicken Pies, and Turkey Frame Soup (see recipe, page 108).

Elegant Chicken a la King

This American dish was created around the turn of the century at the Brighton Beach Hotel outside New York City. It was not inspired by royalty, as the name suggests, but by Charles E. King II, the owner of the hotel.

- **1 cup sliced fresh mushrooms**
- **¼ cup chopped green pepper**
- **¼ cup butter *or* margarine**
- **2 tablespoons all-purpose flour**
- **½ teaspoon paprika**
- **2¼ cups light cream *or* milk**
- **2 beaten egg yolks**
- **3 cups cubed cooked chicken**
- **2 tablespoons chopped pimiento**
- **2 tablespoons dry sherry**
- **1 teaspoon lemon juice**
- **1 teaspoon onion juice *or* ⅛ teaspoon onion powder**
- **Toast points *or* baked patty shells**

In a large saucepan cook mushrooms and green pepper in butter or margarine till tender but not brown. Stir in flour, paprika, and ¾ teaspoon *salt.* Stir in light cream or milk; cook and stir till thickened and bubbly. Cook and stir 1 minute more. Stir about 1 cup of the hot mixture into beaten egg yolks; return to mixture in saucepan. Cook and stir 1 minute over medium heat. Stir in chicken, pimiento, sherry, lemon juice, and onion juice or onion powder; heat through. Serve over toast points or patty shells. Makes 6 servings.

Chicken Salad

- **3 cups cubed cooked chicken**
- **1 8¼-ounce can crushed pineapple, drained**
- **¾ cup chopped celery**
- **½ cup chopped walnuts**
- **⅓ cup mayonnaise *or* salad dressing**
- **⅓ cup dairy sour cream**
- **2 teaspoons lemon juice**
- **½ teaspoon salt**
- **Dash pepper**
- **6 lettuce cups**

Combine chicken, pineapple, celery, and walnuts. Stir together mayonnaise or salad dressing, sour cream, lemon juice, salt, and pepper; toss lightly with chicken mixture. Chill. Serve in lettuce cups. Makes 6 servings.

Tuna Salad: Prepare the Chicken Salad as directed above, *except* substitute one 12½-ounce can *tuna,* drained and flaked, for the chicken.

Turkey Frame Soup *pictured on page 107*

Most people don't realize there's another meal hiding in a carved turkey carcass. Use the bones to make delicious *Turkey Frame Soup.* Part of the satisfaction of eating this soup comes from knowing that absolutely none of the turkey went to waste.

- **1 meaty turkey frame**
- **3 quarts water (12 cups)**
- **1 onion, quartered**
- **2 teaspoons salt**
- **1 16-ounce can tomatoes, cut up**
- **1 tablepoon instant chicken bouillon granules**
- **1½ teaspoons dried oregano, crushed**
- **1 teaspoon dried thyme, crushed**
- **⅛ teaspoon pepper**
- **4 cups fresh vegetables (any combination of sliced celery, sliced carrot, chopped onion, chopped rutabaga, sliced mushrooms, chopped broccoli, *and* cauliflower flowerets)**
- **1½ cups medium noodles**

Break turkey frame or cut in half with kitchen shears; place in a large Dutch oven with water, onion, and salt. Bring to boiling; reduce heat. Cover; simmer for 1½ hours.

Remove turkey frame; when cool enough to handle, cut off meat and coarsely chop. Discard bones. Strain broth; discard solids. Return broth to the Dutch oven. Stir in cut-up turkey meat, *undrained* tomatoes, bouillon granules, oregano, thyme, and pepper. Stir in fresh vegetables.

Bring to boiling; reduce heat. Cover; simmer for 45 minutes. Stir in uncooked medium noodles; simmer, uncovered, for 8 to 10 minutes or till noodles are tender. Season to taste with salt and pepper. Makes 10 servings.

Broccoli-Stuffed Cornish Hens *pictured on page 107*

Cornish game hens are the smallest members of the chicken family. Often called Rock Cornish hens, they are a crossbreed between the white Plymouth Rock female chicken and the English Cornish male chicken. Specially selected females are fed a high-fat diet, producing Cornish game hens with a tender white meat similar in flavor to chicken.

1 **10-ounce package frozen chopped broccoli**
¼ **cup chopped onion**
1 **cup cooked long grain rice**
½ **cup shredded process Swiss cheese (2 ounces)**
2 **tablespoons butter *or* margarine, melted**
½ **teaspoon salt**
   Dash pepper
4 **1- to 1½-pound Cornish game hens**
   Melted butter *or* margarine
⅓ **cup orange marmalade**
   Cooked broccoli spears (optional)

Cook chopped broccoli according to package directions, *except* omit salt and add the chopped onion; drain well. Combine with cooked rice, shredded Swiss cheese, the 2 tablespoons butter or margarine, salt, and pepper.

Rinse birds; pat dry with paper toweling. Lightly salt cavities. Stuff birds with broccoli mixture. Secure neck skin to back with small skewers. Tie legs to tail. Twist wing tips under back.

Place on rack in a large roasting pan. Brush birds with a little melted butter or margarine. Cover loosely with foil and roast in a 375° oven for 30 minutes. Uncover; roast about 1 hour or till done, brushing with additional melted butter or margarine every half hour. In a saucepan melt marmalade. Brush hens with marmalade during the last 5 minutes of roasting. Serve hens on platter with broccoli spears if desired. Makes 8 servings.

Oven-Fried Fish

Oven-Fried Fish, like fish in a skillet, is golden brown outside and moist and tender inside. The main difference between the two methods is that you won't have to contend with spattering fat when the fish "fries" in a hot oven.

1 **pound fresh *or* frozen fish fillets *or* steaks *or* three 10- to 12-ounce fresh *or* frozen pan-dressed trout *or* other fish**
1 **beaten egg**
½ **cup fine dry bread crumbs**
   Salt
   Pepper
¼ **cup butter *or* margarine, melted**
1 **tablespoon lemon juice**
   Tartar Sauce (see recipe below) (optional)

Thaw fish if frozen. If using a fillet block, cut block into 3 portions. Dip fish into beaten egg, then into bread crumbs. Place coated fish in a well-greased, shallow baking pan. Sprinkle with salt and pepper.

Combine melted butter or margarine and lemon juice; drizzle over fish. Bake in a 500° oven until fish is golden and flakes easily when tested with a fork. (Allow 5 to 6 minutes for each ½ inch of thickness.) Serve with Tartar Sauce if desired. Makes 3 servings.

Tartar Sauce

1 **cup mayonnaise *or* salad dressing**
¼ **cup finely chopped sweet pickle**
1 **tablespoon finely chopped onion**
1 **tablespoon snipped parsley**
1 **tablespoon chopped pimiento**
1 **teaspoon lemon juice**

Combine mayonnaise or salad dressing, chopped sweet pickle, onion, snipped parsley, pimiento, and lemon juice. Chill thoroughly to blend flavors. Makes about 1 cup sauce.

ALL·AMERICAN RECIPES
Main Dishes

Fish and Chips

In the middle 1800s, vendors on the streets of London sold fried fish and baked potatoes. The baked potatoes soon were replaced by fried, sliced potatoes or "chips" because they were easier to eat. Although Americans don't buy their fish and chips wrapped in newspapers the way Londoners do, we're as fond of this fried seafood-vegetable duo as they are.

 1 **pound fresh** *or* **frozen fish fillets**
 3 **medium potatoes, peeled (1 pound)**
   Shortening *or* **cooking oil for deep-fat frying**
 1 **cup all-purpose flour**
 ½ **teaspoon salt**
 ½ **cup milk**
 1 **egg**
 2 **tablespoons cooking oil**
   Salt (optional)
   Malt vinegar (optional)

Thaw fish if frozen. Cut into 4 serving-size portions. Pat fish dry with paper toweling. Cut potatoes lengthwise into ⅜-inch-wide strips. Fry potatoes, about ¼ at a time, in deep hot fat (375°) for 7 to 8 minutes or till golden brown. Remove potatoes; drain and keep warm while preparing fish.

Stir together ½ *cup* of the flour and the ½ teaspoon salt. Add milk, egg, and the 2 tablespoons oil; beat till smooth. Dip fish into remaining ½ cup flour, then into batter.

Fry fish in the deep hot fat (375°) about 2 minutes on each side or till golden brown. Drain. Sprinkle fish and chips with salt and malt vinegar if desired. Makes 4 servings.

Salmon Patties

 1 **15½-ounce can salmon**
 ¼ **cup finely chopped onion**
 3 **tablespoons butter** *or* **margarine**
 1½ **cups soft bread crumbs (2 slices)**
 2 **beaten eggs**
 ¼ **cup snipped parsley**
 2 **teaspoons lemon juice**
   Dash pepper
 2 **tablespoons cooking oil**
 2 **tablespoons all-purpose flour**
 ¼ **teaspoon salt**
 ¾ **cup light cream** *or* **milk**
 ¼ **cup dry white wine**
 ½ **teaspoon dried tarragon, crushed**

Drain salmon, reserving 2 tablespoons liquid. Remove skin and bones; flake meat. Cook onion in *1 tablespoon* of the butter till tender. Remove from heat. Stir in reserved liquid, ¾ *cup* of the bread crumbs, the eggs, *half* of the parsley, the lemon juice, and pepper. Add salmon; mix well. Shape into 4 patties ¾ inch thick; coat with remaining bread crumbs.

In a skillet heat oil. Add patties; cook over medium-low heat about 6 minutes or till brown, turning once. Keep warm. For sauce, in saucepan melt remaining 2 tablespoons butter; stir in flour, salt, and dash *pepper.* Add light cream or milk. Cook and stir till thickened and bubbly. Cook and stir 1 minute more. Add dry white wine, tarragon, and remaining parsley. Heat through. Serve over salmon patties. Makes 4 servings.

Tuna-Noodle Casserole

It wasn't until the early 1900s that tuna became popular with Americans. When food was scarce during World War I, the population learned to appreciate tuna because it was nutritious and economical. The proverbial *Tuna-Noodle Casserole* that once fed our nation during a crisis has maintained its popularity today.

4 ounces medium noodles
½ cup finely chopped celery
⅓ cup finely chopped carrot
⅓ cup finely chopped onion
2 tablespoons butter *or* margarine
1 10¾-ounce can condensed cream of mushroom soup
½ cup cheese spread with pimiento
⅓ cup milk
1 9¼-ounce can tuna, drained and flaked
1 cup crushed potato chips

Cook noodles according to package directions; drain and set aside. In a saucepan cook celery, carrot, and onion in butter or margarine till tender but not brown. Stir in soup, cheese spread, and milk. Heat and stir till cheese is melted. Remove from heat. Stir in cooked noodles; fold in tuna. Turn into a 1½-quart casserole. Sprinkle with crushed chips. Bake, uncovered, in a 350° oven for 30 to 35 minutes. Makes 4 to 6 servings.

Macaroni and Cheese

6 ounces elbow macaroni (1½ cups)
¼ cup finely chopped onion
3 tablespoons butter *or* margarine
2 tablespoons all-purpose flour
½ teaspoon salt
Dash pepper
2 cups milk
2 cups cubed American cheese
1 medium tomato, sliced

Cook macaroni according to package directions; drain. For cheese sauce, in a saucepan cook onion in butter or margarine till tender but not brown. Stir in the flour, salt, and pepper. Add milk all at once; cook and stir till thickened and bubbly. Cook and stir 1 minute more. Add cubed cheese; stir till melted.

Stir macaroni into cheese sauce. Turn into a 1½-quart casserole. Arrange tomato slices atop macaroni; sprinkle with a little salt. Bake in a 350° oven for 30 to 35 minutes or till heated through. Makes 6 servings.

Sourdough Cheese Puff *pictured on page 112*

Sourdough Cheese Puff is a type of strata or layered casserole. It consists of sourdough bread, two kinds of cheese, and an egg mixture that soaks into the bread before baking. As it bakes, it puffs and turns a marvelous golden brown.

This is an ideal make-ahead dish because it yields two casseroles, one you can freeze and one to refrigerate for up to 24 hours before baking.

⅓ cup chopped onion
1 16-ounce loaf sourdough bread, cut into 1-inch strips
4 cups shredded Monterey Jack cheese (16 ounces)
1 cup grated Parmesan cheese
6 eggs
4 cups milk
¼ cup snipped parsley
4 teaspoons prepared mustard
½ teaspoon salt
¼ teaspoon pepper

In a small saucepan cook onion in a small amount of boiling unsalted water till tender; drain. Arrange *one-fourth* of the bread strips in bottom of *each* of two greased 9x9x2-inch baking pans. Sprinkle the Monterey Jack cheese, Parmesan cheese, and onion atop bread in pans. Top *each* casserole with *half* of the remaining bread.

Beat together eggs, milk, parsley, mustard, salt, and pepper; slowly pour *half* of the egg mixture over the bread in *each* pan. Wrap in foil, label, and freeze one pan. Cover and refrigerate remaining pan for 1 to 24 hours. Bake chilled casserole, covered, in a 350° oven for 30 minutes. Uncover; bake 20 to 25 minutes more or till puffy and light brown. Cut into squares to serve.

For frozen casserole, bake frozen foil-wrapped casserole in a 350° oven for 1¼ hours. Unwrap; bake 15 minutes more. Makes 2 casseroles, 6 servings each.

Shallot Soufflé with Mushroom Sauce

Because the soufflé will puff above the dish, you need to fit the dish with a foil collar.

To make the collar, measure enough foil to go around the dish with a 2- to 3-inch over-lap. Fold the foil into thirds lengthwise. Lightly butter one side. With the buttered side in, position the foil around the outside of the dish, letting the collar extend 2 inches above the top of the dish. Secure the foil with tape.

1 tablespoon butter *or* margarine
2 tablespoons grated Parmesan cheese
¼ cup finely chopped shallots *or* green onions
¼ cup butter *or* margarine
¼ cup all-purpose flour
½ teaspoon salt
1 cup milk
2 dashes bottled hot pepper sauce
1 cup shredded cheddar cheese (4 ounces)
4 egg yolks
4 egg whites
Mushroom Sauce

Spread the 1 tablespoon butter over bottom and sides of a 1-quart soufflé dish. Sprinkle with the Parmesan cheese. Fit the soufflé dish with a lightly buttered foil collar; set aside.

In a saucepan cook shallots or onions in the ¼ cup butter or margarine till tender but not brown; stir in flour and salt. Add milk and hot pepper sauce; cook and stir till thickened and bubbly. Cook and stir 1 minute more. Remove from heat. Stir in cheddar cheese till melted.

Beat egg yolks with an electric mixer at high speed about 5 minutes or till thick and lemon-colored. Slowly add cheese mixture, stirring constantly; cool slightly.

Wash beaters thoroughly; beat egg whites till stiff peaks form (tips stand straight). Gradually pour cheese-yolk mixture over beaten whites, folding to blend. Turn into prepared dish. Bake in a 300° oven about 1¼ hours or till knife inserted near center comes out clean. Remove foil collar. Serve immediately with Mushroom Sauce. Serves 4.

Mushroom Sauce: In a medium skillet cook 1½ cups sliced fresh *mushrooms* (4 ounces) and 2 tablespoons finely chopped *shallots or green onions* in 2 tablespoons *butter or margarine* over medium-high heat for 4 to 5 minutes or till tender. Stir in 2 teaspoons all-purpose *flour*, ⅛ teaspoon *salt*, and dash *pepper*. Add ¾ cup *milk* all at once. Cook and stir till thickened and bubbly. Cook and stir 1 to 2 minutes more. Makes 1 cup.

Eggs Benedict

There are two colorful yet vastly different versions of how *Eggs Benedict* had its beginning. One account claims that the dish was invented in the Vatican kitchens for Pope Benedict III. Another says a Waldorf Hotel chef created it for a hungover Mr. Benedict. Regardless of its history, this classic egg dish is known for its elegant simplicity.

6 eggs
6 slices Canadian-style bacon (6 ounces)
4 egg yolks
2 tablespoons lemon juice
⅛ teaspoon salt
Dash white pepper
½ cup butter *or* margarine
3 English muffins, split, toasted, and buttered, *or* 6 rusks, buttered
Fresh oregano *or* paprika (optional)

In a 10-inch skillet heat 1 inch of water to boiling. Break egg into small dish; slide egg into water, tipping dish toward edge of pan. Repeat with remaining eggs. Reduce heat; cover and simmer till eggs are just soft-cooked, about 3 minutes. Remove with slotted spoon; place in pan of warm water to keep warm. In a 12-inch skillet cook bacon over medium heat for 3 minutes on each side. Cover; keep warm.

For sauce, in top of double boiler beat the 4 egg yolks slightly; stir in lemon juice. Place over boiling water (upper pan should not touch water). Add the salt and pepper. Add butter, a little at a time, stirring constantly with wooden spoon till mixture thickens.

Top each English muffin half or rusk with a bacon slice and an egg; spoon on sauce. Garnish with fresh oregano or paprika if desired. Serves 6.

Pictured:
Eggs Benedict and Sourdough Cheese Puff (see recipe, page 111).

Eggs Florentine

1 **10-ounce package frozen chopped spinach**
1 **tablespoon butter** *or* **margarine**
⅛ **teaspoon ground nutmeg**
½ **cup grated Parmesan cheese**
8 **eggs**
¼ **cup light cream** *or* **milk**

Cook spinach according to package directions; drain well. Stir in butter or margarine and nutmeg. Spoon into four 10-ounce custard cups or casseroles; spread evenly on bottom and about ⅔ of the way up sides. Sprinkle each with *1 tablespoon* of the Parmesan cheese.

Break 2 eggs into each dish. Spoon 1 tablespoon light cream or milk over eggs in each dish. Sprinkle with remaining cheese. Bake in a 350° oven for 18 to 22 minutes or till the eggs are set. Makes 4 servings.

Egg Salad Sandwiches

6 **hard-cooked eggs, chopped**
¼ **cup finely chopped celery**
¼ **cup finely chopped sweet pickle**
2 **green onions, thinly sliced**
2 **tablespoons chopped pimiento**
¼ **cup mayonnaise** *or* **salad dressing**
1 **tablespoon prepared mustard**
  Dash bottled hot pepper sauce
  Butter *or* **margarine, softened**
8 **slices bread**
4 **tomato slices**
4 **lettuce leaves**

Combine eggs, celery, pickle, green onions, and pimiento. Stir together mayonnaise or salad dressing, mustard, pepper sauce, and ½ teaspoon *salt;* toss with egg mixture. If necessary, add a little more mayonnaise to moisten. Cover and chill.

To serve, butter the bread slices. Spread *half* of the bread slices with egg mixture; top each with a tomato slice, lettuce leaf, and another bread slice. Makes 4 servings.

Peanut Butter Sandwiches

In 1890, a St. Louis physician who was seeking an easily digested form of protein for his patients prepared the first peanut butter in this country. The new food caught on with the general public and has enjoyed widespread popularity ever since. Millions of *Peanut Butter Sandwiches* are eaten every day, including favorite variations like the ones to the right.

8 **slices white** *or* **whole wheat bread**
⅔ **cup creamy** *or* **chunk-style peanut butter**
  Topping *or* **Addition (optional)**

Spread *half* of the bread slices with peanut butter, adding Topping or Addition if desired. Top with remaining bread slices. Makes 4 servings.

Topping: Top creamy or chunk-style peanut butter with one of the following —
 • ½ cup of your favorite jelly, jam, *or* marmalade
 • ⅓ cup cream cheese mixed with 1 tablespoon honey
 • a combination of ¼ cup raisins and ¼ cup shredded carrot
 • 8 slices crisp-cooked bacon
 • 2 medium apples, peeled and sliced
 • ¼ cup drained crushed pineapple and ¼ cup whole cranberry sauce

Addition: Stir one of the following into the peanut butter before spreading onto bread —
 • ¼ cup orange juice
 • ¼ cup cottage cheese
 • 1 tablespoon mayonnaise *or* salad dressing and 2 tablespoons sweet pickle relish

Green Bean Casserole

Since it was introduced in the sixties, *Green Bean Casserole* has been well received at American dinner tables, particularly at family gatherings and potluck dinners. Its typical French-fried onion topping provides a crunchy contrast to the creamy vegetable mixture.

2 **9-ounce packages frozen cut green beans *or* two 16-ounce cans cut green beans**
1 **10¾-ounce can condensed cream of mushroom soup**
¼ **cup milk**
2 **tablespoons chopped pimiento**
1 **teaspoon lemon juice**
⅛ **teaspoon pepper**
1 **3-ounce can French-fried onions**

Cook frozen beans according to package directions; drain. (Or, drain canned beans.) Combine the beans, mushroom soup, milk, pimiento, lemon juice, and pepper; stir in *half* of the onions. Turn into a 1½-quart casserole. Bake, uncovered, in a 350° oven for 35 to 40 minutes. Sprinkle with remaining onions. Bake, uncovered, 5 minutes more. Makes 6 servings.

• **Sour Cream Green Bean Casserole:** Prepare Green Bean Casserole as above, *except* substitute ¼ cup dairy *sour cream* for the milk.

• **Green Beans Chow Mein:** Prepare Green Bean Casserole as above, *except* substitute condensed *cream of onion soup* for the mushroom soup and 3 ounces *chow mein noodles* for the French-fried onions.

• **Cheesy Green Bean Casserole:** Prepare Green Bean Casserole as above, *except* substitute condensed *cheddar cheese soup* for the mushroom soup and ¼ cup chopped *green pepper* or sliced *water chestnuts* for the pimiento.

Green Beans Amandine   *pictured on the cover*

1 **pound green beans *or* two 9-ounce packages frozen French-style green beans**
2 **tablespoons slivered almonds**
2 **tablespoons butter *or* margarine**
1 **teaspoon lemon juice**

Cut fresh beans French-style, slicing end to end. Cook fresh beans in a small amount of boiling salted water for 10 to 12 minutes or till crisp-tender. (Or, cook frozen beans according to package directions.) Drain and keep warm. Cook almonds in butter over low heat till golden, stirring occasionally. Remove from heat; stir in lemon juice. Toss mixture with beans. Makes 6 servings.

Potatoes Au Gratin

The term "au gratin" is frequently misused to describe any cooked dish that has cheese as an ingredient. It is actually a French phrase indicating that bread crumbs or grated cheese is sprinkled on top of the food before baking or broiling to produce a golden brown crust.

2 **tablespoons butter *or* margarine**
1 **tablespoon all-purpose flour**
¼ **teaspoon dry mustard**
1 **cup milk**
½ **teaspoon Worcestershire sauce**
½ **cup shredded American *or* shredded process Swiss cheese (2 ounces)**
3 **medium potatoes, peeled and thinly sliced (3 cups)**
1 **2-ounce jar sliced pimiento, drained and chopped, *or* one 2-ounce can mushroom stems and pieces, drained**
2 **green onions, sliced**
¾ **cup soft bread crumbs (1 slice)**

In a 2-quart saucepan melt *1 tablespoon* of the butter or margarine; stir in the flour, mustard, ½ teaspoon *salt*, and dash *pepper*. Add milk and Worcestershire sauce; cook and stir till thickened and bubbly. Remove from heat; add cheese, stirring till melted.

Stir in potatoes, pimiento or mushrooms, and green onions. Turn into a 1½-quart casserole. Cover and bake in a 350° oven for 45 minutes.

Melt remaining 1 tablespoon butter or margarine; toss with bread crumbs. Uncover potatoes; sprinkle crumbs atop. Bake, uncovered, 30 minutes more or till potatoes are tender. Serves 6.

Hashed Brown Potatoes

Hashed Brown Potatoes is an American favorite that complements breakfast bacon and eggs as well as a broiled sirloin steak.

The chopped onion or green onion can be omitted from this recipe if desired.

3 **medium potatoes**
3 **tablespoons butter *or* margarine**
¼ **cup finely chopped onion *or* green onion**
½ **teaspoon salt**
Dash pepper

In a saucepan cook whole potatoes, covered, in boiling salted water for 20 to 25 minutes or till almost tender. Drain and chill. Peel potatoes; shred to make about 3 cups.

In a medium skillet melt butter or margarine. Combine potatoes, onion, salt, and pepper; pat into skillet. Cook over low heat for 15 to 20 minutes or till underside is crisp. Cut with a spatula to make 4 wedges; turn. Cook about 5 minutes more or till other side is golden. Makes 4 servings.

French Fries

"French fry" is an American phrase for the method of cooking food in deep hot fat until it's crisp and golden brown.

French Fries and *French-Fried Onion Rings* are two foods cooked this way. These popular side dishes often are coupled with the all-American hamburger and served with catsup.

Baking potatoes, peeled
Shortening *or* cooking oil for deep-fat frying
Salt

Cut potatoes lengthwise into ⅜-inch-wide strips. Fry potatoes a few at a time, in the deep hot fat (360°) for 6 to 7 minutes or till crisp and golden. Drain on paper toweling. (For crisper French fries, fry potatoes at 360° about 5 minutes. Drain on paper toweling and cool. Just before serving, return French fries to fat at 360° for 2 minutes more.) Sprinkle immediately with salt. Serve at once.

French-Fried Onion Rings

6 **medium Bermuda *or* mild white onions, sliced ¼ inch thick**
1 **slightly beaten egg**
1 **cup milk**
3 **tablespoons cooking oil**
1 **cup plus 2 tablespoons all-purpose flour**
Shortening *or* cooking oil for deep-fat frying

Separate onions into rings; set aside. In a bowl combine egg, milk, the 3 tablespoons oil, flour, and ½ teaspoon *salt*. Beat just till well moistened. Using a fork, dip onion rings into batter; drain off excess batter. Fry onion rings, a few at a time, in deep hot fat (375°) for 2 to 3 minutes or till golden, stirring once with a fork to separate rings. Remove from fat and drain on paper toweling. Sprinkle with salt and serve. Makes 6 to 8 servings.

French Onion Soup

This soup is said to have originated in France. It was first made with beef stock, but modern versions typically use canned condensed beef broth as the base.

1½ **pounds onions, thinly sliced**
¼ **cup butter *or* margarine**
3 **10½-ounce cans condensed beef broth**
1 **teaspoon Worcestershire sauce**
6 **to 8 slices French bread, toasted**
Shredded Swiss cheese

Cook onions, covered, in butter about 20 minutes. Add broth, Worcestershire, ¼ teaspoon *salt*, and dash *pepper*; bring to boiling. Place bread on baking sheet; sprinkle with cheese. Broil till cheese is light brown. Ladle soup into bowls and float bread atop. (Or, place bread slice on soup in each broiler-proof soup bowl; sprinkle with cheese. Broil till light brown.) Serves 6 to 8.

Pictured:
Spinach, Bacon, and Mushroom Salad (see recipe, page 121) and French Onion Soup.

Scalloped Potatoes

Irish immigrants in New Hampshire are credited with establishing potatoes as a major crop in the United States in the early 1700s. According to superstition, potatoes should be planted at night during a new moon so that the plants will thrive.

Contrary to popular belief, the potato is not extremely fattening. A medium potato has no more calories than a large apple.

  1 **small onion, chopped (¼ cup)**
  ¼ **cup butter *or* margarine**
  ¼ **cup all-purpose flour**
1½ **teaspoons salt**
  ⅛ **teaspoon pepper**
2½ **cups milk**
  5 **large potatoes, peeled and thinly sliced (5 cups)**

For sauce, cook onion in butter or margarine till tender but not brown. Stir in flour, salt, and pepper. Add milk. Cook and stir till thickened and bubbly. Cook and stir 1 minute more. Remove from heat. Place *half* of the sliced potatoes in a greased 2-quart casserole. Cover with *half* of the sauce. Repeat layers. Cover and bake in a 350° oven for 45 minutes, stirring once. Uncover and bake about 30 minutes more or till potatoes are tender. Makes 4 to 6 servings.

• **Cheesy Scalloped Potatoes:** Prepare Scalloped Potatoes as above, *except* reduce salt to *1 teaspoon* and stir ¾ cup shredded *American cheese* into thickened sauce till melted.

Potato Pancakes with Pizzazz

  4 **slices bacon**
  3 **cups grated potatoes**
  1 **small onion, finely chopped (¼ cup)**
  ¼ **cup finely shredded carrot**
  2 **beaten eggs**
  3 **tablespoons all-purpose flour**
  1 **teaspoon salt**
  ¼ **teaspoon poultry seasoning**
    Dash pepper
    Sour Cream Topper
    Bacon, crisp-cooked, drained, and crumbled (optional)

In a large skillet cook 4 slices bacon till crisp; drain, reserving 2 tablespoons drippings in the skillet. Crumble bacon. In large bowl stir together bacon, potatoes, onion, carrot, eggs, flour, salt, poultry seasoning, and pepper. Mix well.

Return reserved bacon drippings to the skillet; heat. For each pancake pour about ¼ *cup* batter into skillet. Spread the batter slightly. Fry potato pancakes 3 or 4 minutes per side or till brown. Keep pancakes warm as more are fried. Prepare Sour Cream Topper. Serve warm pancakes with Sour Cream Topper. Garnish with additional bacon if desired. Makes 6 to 8 servings.

Sour Cream Topper: Stir together 1 cup dairy *sour cream,* 2 teaspoons *prepared mustard,* and 1 teaspoon *lemon juice.*

Potato Cheese Soup

  3 **medium potatoes, peeled and cut up (about 1 pound)**
  1 **cup water**
  1 **small onion, finely chopped (¼ cup)**
  ¾ **teaspoon salt**
2½ **cups milk**
  2 **tablespoons all-purpose flour**
  ⅛ **teaspoon pepper**
  1 **cup shredded Swiss *or* cheddar cheese**
  2 **tablespoons snipped parsley**

In a 3-quart saucepan combine the cut-up potatoes, water, onion, and salt. Bring to boiling; reduce heat. Cover and simmer about 20 minutes or till the potatoes are tender. Mash slightly but do not drain. In a screw-top jar combine ½ *cup* of the milk, the flour, and pepper. Cover and shake well.

Add milk mixture to the potato mixture along with remaining milk. Cook and stir till mixture is thickened and bubbly. Cook and stir 1 minute more. Add shredded Swiss or cheddar cheese and the parsley; stir till cheese is partially melted. Serve immediately. Makes 6 to 8 servings.

New Potatoes and Peas

New potatoes are the early potatoes that are shipped directly from the field. They're often served with a narrow strip of the peel removed from around the center, as in *New Potatoes and Peas*.

1½ **pounds tiny new potatoes (about 15)**
1 **10-ounce package frozen peas**
¼ **cup sliced green onion**
2 **tablespoons butter** *or* **margarine**
1 **tablespoon all-purpose flour**
¼ **teaspoon salt**
  Dash white pepper
1 **cup milk**

Scrub potatoes; remove a narrow strip of peel around center of each. Cook potatoes, covered, in boiling salted water for 10 to 15 minutes or till tender; drain. Meanwhile, cook frozen peas according to package directions; drain. Cook onion in butter or margarine till tender. Stir in flour, salt, and pepper. Add milk. Cook and stir till thickened and bubbly. Cook and stir 1 minute more. Stir together the cooked potatoes, cooked peas, and the onion mixture. Makes 4 to 6 servings.

Marinated Three-Bean Salad

Marinated Three-Bean Salad is the ideal make-ahead side dish. Store it in the refrigerator for 8 to 24 hours before serving.

Try using different beans as suggested in the recipe note. For other variations, add sliced pimiento, chopped carrot, sliced celery, or sliced canned mushrooms.

1 **16-ounce can lima beans, drained**
1 **16-ounce can cut green beans, drained**
1 **15½-ounce can red kidney beans, drained**
2 **mild medium onions, sliced and separated into rings**
¾ **cup chopped green pepper**
1 **cup vinegar**
⅔ **cup salad oil**
⅓ **cup sugar**
1½ **teaspoons celery seed**

In a large bowl combine lima beans, green beans, red kidney beans, onion rings, and green pepper. In a screw-top jar combine vinegar, salad oil, sugar, and celery seed; cover and shake well. Pour vinegar mixture over vegetables and stir lightly. Cover and refrigerate 8 hours or overnight, stirring occasionally. Drain before serving. Serves 8.

Recipe note: For easy variations, prepare Marinated Three-Bean Salad as above, *except* substitute one of the following cans of beans, drained, for one of those listed above: one 15-ounce can garbanzo beans, one 15-ounce can great northern beans, one 16-ounce can cut wax beans, one 16-ounce can butter beans, *or* one 15-ounce can pinto beans.

Spicy Bacon-Bean Pot

1 **28-ounce can pork and beans in tomato sauce**
1 **15-ounce can red kidney beans, drained**
1 **12-ounce can whole kernel corn, drained**
5 **slices bacon, crisp-cooked, drained, and crumbled**
1 **medium onion, chopped (½ cup)**
½ **cup chopped sweet red pepper** *or* **green pepper**
2 **tablespoons smoke-flavored barbecue sauce**
1 **teaspoon chili powder**
  Dash garlic powder
¼ **cup shredded sharp cheddar cheese (1 ounce)**

In a large Dutch oven stir together pork and beans in tomato sauce, kidney beans, corn, bacon, onion, red or green pepper, barbecue sauce, chili powder, and garlic powder. Cover and cook over medium heat about 35 minutes or to desired consistency, stirring occasionally. Just before serving, top with cheese. Makes 10 servings.

Herbed Fresh Tomato Soup

Spanish explorers knew that Indians ate tomatoes, but until the early 1880s, much of Europe and the New World didn't accept the tomato as anything but an ornamental plant.

The tomato, which is actually a fruit and not a vegetable, was called a "love apple" during colonial times. "If the tomato doesn't poison you, it will make you fall in love," colonists said.

Once the folklore began to fade, the tomato quickly became a favorite, especially as an ingredient in soups and salads.

 2 **tablespoons butter *or* margarine**
 2 **tablespoons olive oil *or* cooking oil**
 2 **medium onions, thinly sliced**
 6 **medium tomatoes, peeled and quartered (about 2 pounds)**
 1 **6-ounce can tomato paste**
 2 **tablespoons snipped fresh basil *or* 2 teaspoons dried basil, crushed**
 4 **teaspoons snipped fresh thyme *or* 1 teaspoon dried thyme, crushed**
 1 **tablespoon instant chicken bouillon granules**
 ½ **teaspoon sugar (optional)**
 2½ **cups water**
 1 **teaspoon salt**
 ⅛ **teaspoon pepper**

In a large saucepan heat butter or margarine and oil till butter melts. Add onions; cook till tender but not brown. Stir in tomatoes, tomato paste, basil, thyme, bouillon granules, and sugar if desired; mash tomatoes slightly. Stir in water; bring to boiling. Reduce heat. Cover; simmer 40 minutes.

Press mixture through food mill. (Or, place about 2 cups at a time in blender container or food processor bowl; cover and blend till smooth. Repeat with remaining mixture.) Strain mixture. Return to the saucepan; stir in salt and pepper. Heat through. Pour into soup tureen or ladle into individual soup bowls. Garnish with chopped celery tops if desired. Makes 8 servings.

Glazed Carrots   *pictured on pages 4 and 5*

 1 **pound carrots, bias-sliced ¼ inch thick *or* cut into julienne strips**
 2 **tablespoons butter *or* margarine**
 2 **tablespoons sugar**
 ⅛ **teaspoon ground cinnamon *or* ground ginger**
 ⅓ **cup raisins (optional)**

In a saucepan cook carrots in a small amount of boiling salted water for 8 to 10 minutes or till tender; drain in colander. In same saucepan combine butter or margarine, sugar, and cinnamon or ginger. Cook and stir 1 minute. Add carrots; cook over low heat about 5 minutes or till carrots are shiny and well glazed, stirring often. Stir in raisins if desired. Makes 4 servings.

Spanish Rice

 6 **slices bacon**
 1 **medium onion, finely chopped (½ cup)**
 1 **small green pepper, finely chopped (½ cup)**
 1 **28-ounce can tomatoes, cut up**
 1 **cup water**
 ¾ **cup long grain rice**
 1 **tablespoon brown sugar**
 1 **tablespoon Worcestershire sauce**
 1 **teaspoon salt**
 1 **teaspoon chili powder**
 ⅛ **teaspoon pepper**
    Dash bottled hot pepper sauce
    Shredded cheddar cheese (optional)

In a 10-inch skillet cook bacon till crisp. Remove and drain on paper toweling; crumble and set aside. Drain drippings, reserving 2 tablespoons in the skillet. Cook onion and green pepper in reserved bacon drippings till tender. Stir in *undrained* tomatoes, water, uncooked rice, brown sugar, Worcestershire sauce, salt, chili powder, pepper, and hot pepper sauce.

Cover and simmer about 30 minutes or till the rice is done and most of the liquid is absorbed. Top with the crumbled bacon. Sprinkle with shredded cheddar cheese if desired. Makes 6 servings.

Spinach, Bacon, Mushroom Salad *pictured on pages 97 and 117*

6 slices bacon
¼ cup salad oil *or* bacon drippings
2 tablespoons wine vinegar *or* lemon juice
1 clove garlic, minced
¼ teaspoon salt
¼ teaspoon dry mustard
  Few dashes freshly ground pepper
4 cups torn spinach
1 cup sliced fresh mushrooms
2 tablespoons sliced green onions

In a skillet cook bacon till crisp. Remove and drain on paper toweling; crumble and set aside. (If desired, reserve ¼ *cup* drippings for dressing.) Meanwhile, to make dressing, in a screw-top jar combine salad oil or reserved bacon drippings, wine vinegar or lemon juice, minced garlic, salt, dry mustard, and pepper. Cover and shake well.

In a salad bowl place spinach, mushrooms, onions, and crumbled bacon; toss lightly. Shake dressing again and pour over spinach mixture. Toss lightly to coat. Serve immediately. Serves 4 to 6.

Vinaigrette

1 cup salad oil
⅔ cup vinegar
1 teaspoon salt
½ teaspoon freshly ground pepper

In a screw-top jar combine oil, vinegar, salt, and pepper. cover and shake well. Serve over assorted torn greens. Makes about 1½ cups.
  • **Herbed Vinaigrette:** Prepare Vinaigrette as directed above, *except* add 1 tablespoon snipped *fresh herb* (basil, dillweed, oregano, tarragon, or thyme) *or* 1 teaspoon *dried herb*, crushed.
  • **Garlic Vinaigrette:** Prepare Vinaigrette as above, *except* add 1 clove *garlic*, minced.

Mayonnaise

Probably the most popular salad in the United States today is the tossed green salad. Spark up your salad making by combining greens that have different flavors and textures.

After rinsing and drying the salad greens, tear them into bite-sized pieces. Tearing exposes the interior and allows the greens to absorb the salad dressing.

Place torn greens in a salad bowl, cover them with a damp paper towel, and refrigerate until serving time. Just before serving, toss with your choice of dressing.

1 teaspoon salt
½ teaspoon dry mustard
¼ teaspoon paprika
  Dash ground red pepper
2 egg yolks
2 tablespoons vinegar
2 cups salad oil
2 tablespoons lemon juice *or* vinegar

Combine salt, dry mustard, paprika, and red pepper. Add yolks and 2 tablespoons vinegar; beat with electric mixer till blended. Add ¼ cup of the oil, 1 teaspoon at a time, beating constantly. While continuing to beat, add remaining oil in a thin, steady stream, alternating the last ½ cup oil with the 2 tablespoons lemon juice or vinegar. Store in a tightly covered jar in refrigerator for up to 4 weeks. Makes 2 cups.
  • **Thousand Island Dressing:** Prepare Mayonnaise as above. (*Or*, use 2 cups purchased mayonnaise.) Stir in ⅓ cup *chili sauce*; 2 hard-cooked *eggs*, chopped; ¼ cup finely chopped *green pepper*; 2 tablespoons finely chopped *onion*; and 1 tablespoon chopped *pimiento*. Mix well. Makes about 3½ cups.
  • **Green Goddess Dressing:** Prepare Mayonnaise as above. (*Or*, use 2 cups purchased mayonnaise.) In blender container combine Mayonnaise with ½ cup snipped *parsley*; ⅓ cup snipped *chives*; 6 *anchovy fillets*, cut up; 2 tablespoons snipped *fresh tarragon or* 2 teaspoons *dried tarragon*, crushed; and 2 tablespoons *vinegar*. Cover and blend till nearly smooth. Makes about 2⅓ cups.

Rye Bread

Rye Bread loaves also can be baked in two greased 7½x3½x2-inch loaf pans.

After brushing with water, try gently scoring the tops of the loaves diagonally at 3-inch intervals with a sharp knife. Then, bake the bread as directed in the recipe.

2¼ **to 2¾ cups all-purpose flour**
3 **packages active dry yeast**
1½ **cups water**
½ **cup molasses**
2 **tablespoons butter** *or* **margarine**
2 **tablespoons caraway seed**
2 **teaspoons salt**
½ **cup toasted wheat germ**
2¾ **cups rye flour**

Combine *2 cups* of the all-purpose flour and the yeast. Heat and stir water, molasses, butter, caraway, and salt just till warm (115° to 120°). Add to flour mixture. Beat with electric mixer 30 seconds. Beat 3 minutes at high speed. Stir in wheat germ, then rye flour and as much of the remaining all-purpose flour as you can mix in with a spoon.

On floured surface knead in enough remaining flour to make a stiff dough (8 to 10 minutes total). Shape into a ball in a greased bowl; turn once. Cover; let rise till double (about 1½ hours). Punch down; divide in half. Cover; let rest 10 minutes. Shape into 2 loaves. Place in two greased 8x4x2-inch loaf pans. Cover; let rise till nearly double (about 45 minutes). Brush with water. Bake in 350° oven about 45 minutes. Makes 2.

Whole Wheat Bread *pictured on the cover*

To avoid overbrowning, cover the *Whole Wheat Bread* with foil during the last 20 minutes of baking.

3 **to 3½ cups all-purpose flour**
1 **package active dry yeast**
1¾ **cups water**
¼ **cup packed brown sugar**
3 **tablespoons shortening**
2 **teaspoons salt**
2 **cups whole wheat flour**

Combine *2 cups* of the all-purpose flour and the yeast. Heat and stir water, brown sugar, shortening, and salt just till warm (115° to 120°). Add to flour mixture; beat with electric mixer 30 seconds, scraping bowl. Beat 3 minutes at high speed.

Stir in whole wheat flour and as much remaining all-purpose flour as you can mix in with a spoon. On a floured surface knead in enough remaining flour to make a moderately stiff dough (6 to 8 minutes total). Shape the dough into a ball in a greased bowl; turn once to grease surface. Cover; let rise till double (1 to 1½ hours).

Punch down; divide dough in half. Cover; let rest 10 minutes. Shape into loaves; place in 2 greased 8x4x2-inch loaf pans. Cover; let rise till nearly double (about 1 hour). Bake in a 375° oven about 45 minutes. Remove; cool. Makes 2 loaves.

Whole Wheat Batter Rolls *also pictured on pages 4 and 5*

Pictured clockwise:
Rye Bread, Whole Wheat Batter Rolls, Molasses Nut Bread (see recipe, page 129), Dill-Onion Bread (see recipe, page 127), and Fruit and Grain Cookies (see recipe, page 144).

2 **cups all-purpose flour**
1 **package active dry yeast**
1¼ **cups water**
2 **tablespoons butter** *or* **margarine**
1 **tablespoon honey**
1 **tablespoon molasses**
1 **teaspoon salt**
1 **teaspoon Italian seasoning**
1 **cup whole wheat flour**
   Melted butter *or* **margarine (optional)**

Combine *1½ cups* of the all-purpose flour and the yeast. Heat and stir water, butter, honey, molasses, salt, and Italian seasoning just till warm (115° to 120°). Add to flour mixture. Beat with electric mixer 30 seconds. Beat 3 minutes at high speed. Stir in whole wheat flour and remaining all-purpose flour. Cover; let rise till double (about 30 minutes). Stir batter down. Reserve ½ *cup* batter.

Spoon remaining batter into greased muffin cups, filling ⅔ full. Spoon an additional teaspoon of the reserved batter atop batter in each muffin cup. Let rise till nearly double (about 30 minutes). Bake in 375° oven about 15 minutes. Remove; cool. Brush with melted butter if desired. Makes 16.

Easy-Mix White Bread

Bread making in America began shortly after the introduction of wheat by the Spaniards in the 1500s. After observing the Indians crushing corn to make bread, the early colonists used ground wheat for their bread. Their loaves were baked in large community ovens.

5¾ **to 6¼ cups all-purpose flour**
 1 **package active dry yeast**
2¼ **cups milk**
 2 **tablespoons sugar**
 1 **tablespoon shortening**
 2 **teaspoons salt**
   Melted butter *or* margarine

In a large mixer bowl combine 2½ *cups* of the flour and the yeast. Heat milk, sugar, shortening, and salt just till warm (115° to 120°) and shortening is almost melted; stir constantly. Add to flour mixture. Beat with an electric mixer at low speed about 30 seconds, scraping sides of bowl. Beat for 3 minutes at high speed.

Stir in as much of the remaining flour as you can mix in with a spoon. Turn out onto floured surface. Knead in enough of the remaining flour to make a moderately stiff dough that is smooth and elastic (6 to 8 minutes total). Shape into a ball. Place in a greased bowl; turn once. Cover; let rise in a warm place till double (about 1¼ hours).

Punch down; turn out onto a lightly floured surface. Divide dough in half. Cover; let rest 10 minutes. Shape into loaves; place in 2 lightly greased 8x4x2-inch loaf pans. Brush loaves with melted butter or margarine. Cover; let rise in a warm place till nearly double (45 to 60 minutes). Bake in a 375° oven about 45 minutes or till done. Remove from pans; cool. Makes 2 loaves.

Caramel Rolls

 4 **to 4½ cups all-purpose flour**
 1 **package active dry yeast**
 1 **cup milk**
⅓ **cup sugar**
⅓ **cup butter *or* margarine**
 1 **teaspoon salt**
 2 **eggs**
 3 **tablespoons butter *or* margarine, melted**
½ **cup sugar**
 1 **teaspoon ground cinnamon**
⅔ **cup packed brown sugar**
¼ **cup butter *or* margarine**
 2 **tablespoons light corn syrup**
½ **cup chopped pecans**

Combine *2 cups* of the flour and the yeast. Heat milk, the ⅓ cup sugar, the ⅓ cup butter, and the salt just till warm (115° to 120°); stir constantly. Add to flour mixture; add eggs. Beat with electric mixer at low speed for 30 seconds. Beat 3 minutes at high speed. Stir in as much remaining flour as you can mix in with a spoon.

On a floured surface, knead in enough of the remaining flour to make a moderately stiff dough that is smooth and elastic (6 to 8 minutes total). Shape into a ball. Place in a greased bowl; turn once. Cover; let rise in a warm place till double (about 1 hour). Punch down; divide in half. Cover; let rest 10 minutes.

Roll *each* half into a 12x8-inch rectangle. Brush the 3 tablespoons melted butter over dough. Combine ½ cup sugar and the cinnamon; sprinkle over dough. Roll up jelly-roll style, beginning from longest side. Seal seams. Cut each into 12 pieces. In saucepan combine brown sugar, ¼ cup butter, and the corn syrup; cook and stir till butter is melted. Divide between two 9x1½-inch round baking pans. Sprinkle each pan with *half* of the pecans. Place rolls in baking pans. Cover; let rise till nearly double (about 30 minutes). Bake in a 375° oven for 20 to 25 minutes. Invert rolls onto a serving plate. Makes 24 rolls.

Dinner Rolls

Shape *Dinner Rolls* into different rolls if desired. Shapes to choose from include cloverleaves, butterhorns, Parker House rolls, or rosettes.

4 to 4½ cups all-purpose flour
1 package active dry yeast
1 cup milk
⅓ cup sugar
⅓ cup butter, margarine, *or* shortening
1 teaspoon salt
2 eggs

Combine *2 cups* of the flour and yeast. Heat milk, sugar, butter, and salt just till warm (115° to 120°) and butter is almost melted; stir constantly. Add to flour mixture; add eggs. Beat with electric mixer at low speed for 30 seconds, scraping sides of bowl. Beat 3 minutes at high speed. Stir in as much remaining flour as you can mix in with a spoon.

Turn out onto a floured surface. Knead in enough remaining flour to make a moderately stiff dough that is smooth and elastic (6 to 8 minutes total). Shape into a ball. Place in a greased bowl; turn once. Cover; let rise till double (about 1 hour).

Punch down; divide dough in half. Cover; let rest 10 minutes. Shape into desired rolls. Place in greased muffin cups or 2 to 3 inches apart on greased baking sheets. Cover; let rise till nearly double (about 30 minutes). Bake in a 375° oven for 12 to 15 minutes or till golden. Remove; cool. Makes 24 to 30 rolls.

Fruit-Filled Coffee Cake   *pictured on page 126*

Next time try a prune filling instead of the apricot when making *Fruit-Filled Coffee Cake*. To make prune filling, in a saucepan place 1 cup dried, pitted prunes and enough water to cover fruit by 1 inch. Bring mixture to boiling. Reduce heat and simmer, uncovered, for 15 to 20 minutes or till fruit is very tender. Drain off liquid. Mash fruit.

Stir in 2 tablespoons sugar and 1 tablespoon lemon juice. Add more sugar if desired; cool. Use filling as directed in the *Fruit-Filled Coffee Cake* recipe.

3 cups all-purpose flour
1 package active dry yeast
⅔ cup milk
½ cup butter *or* margarine
2 tablespoons sugar
½ teaspoon salt
1 egg
1 teaspoon vanilla *or* lemon extract
Apricot Filling
2 tablespoons butter *or* margarine, melted
Confectioners' Icing

Combine *1 cup* of the flour and the yeast. Heat together the milk, ½ cup butter, sugar, and salt just till warm (115° to 120°), stirring constantly till butter is almost melted. Add mixture to flour mixture along with egg and vanilla or lemon extract. Beat with electric mixer at low speed for 30 seconds, scraping sides of bowl. Beat 3 minutes at high speed. By hand, stir in all the remaining flour.

Place dough in a greased bowl. Cover; let rise in a warm place till double (about 1 hour). Meanwhile, prepare Apricot Filling; cool. Grease two 8x8x2-inch baking pans. Divide dough into four portions. On floured surface roll *each* portion into an 8-inch square. Place one portion of dough in each prepared pan. Brush the dough with some of the melted butter. Spoon filling over dough in pans. Place remaining portions of dough atop filling in each pan. Brush dough with some melted butter. Cover; let rise till nearly double (about 45 minutes). With finger, make indentations in the top of the dough at 1½-inch intervals if desired. Bake in a 375° oven for 15 to 20 minutes. Cool in pans on wire racks; drizzle with Confectioners' Icing. Makes 2 coffee cakes.

Apricot Filling: In saucepan place 1 cup *dried apricots* and enough water to cover fruit by 1·inch. Bring to boiling; reduce heat. Simmer, uncovered, for 15 to 20 minutes or till the fruit is very tender; drain. Mash fruit; stir in ¼ cup *sugar.* Add more sugar if desired. Cool.

Confectioners' Icing: Stir together ¾ cup sifted *powdered sugar,* ¼ teaspoon *vanilla,* and enough *milk* to make icing of drizzling consistency (about 1 tablespoon).

Dill-Onion Bread *pictured on page 122*

- **1 package active dry yeast**
- **½ cup warm water (110° to 115°)**
- **1 beaten egg**
- **½ cup cream-style cottage cheese**
- **⅓ cup finely chopped onion**
- **1 tablespoon butter *or* margarine, melted**
- **2 cups all-purpose flour**
- **½ cup toasted wheat germ**
- **⅓ cup whole bran cereal**
- **1 tablespoon sugar**
- **1 tablespoon dillseed**
- **1 teaspoon salt**

Soften yeast in warm water. Combine egg, cottage cheese, onion, and butter or margarine; mix well. In a bowl stir together flour, wheat germ, bran cereal, sugar, dillseed, and salt. Add cottage cheese and yeast mixtures, stirring well. Cover; let rise till double (about 1 hour).

Stir dough down. Knead on floured surface 1 minute. With greased hands pat into a well-greased 9x1½-inch round baking pan. Cover; let rise till nearly double (about 1 hour). Score top in diamond pattern. Bake in a 350° oven about 40 minutes. Remove from pan; cool on wire rack. Makes 1 loaf.

Waffles

It's said that the Dutch introduced the waffle to the United States. Traditionally a Dutch bride was given a waffle iron inscribed with her initials and wedding date.

To keep baked *Waffles* hot for serving, place a single layer on a wire rack placed on a baking sheet in a warm oven.

- **1¾ cups all-purpose flour**
- **1 tablespoon baking powder**
- **½ teaspoon salt**
- **2 egg yolks**
- **1¾ cups milk**
- **½ cup cooking oil *or* shortening, melted**
- **2 egg whites**

In a large mixing bowl stir together flour, baking powder, and salt. In a small mixing bowl beat egg yolks with a fork. Beat in milk and cooking oil or melted shortening. Add to flour mixture all at once. Stir mixture till blended but still slightly lumpy.

In a small mixer bowl beat egg whites till stiff peaks form. Gently fold beaten egg whites into flour-milk mixture, leaving a few fluffs of egg white. *Do not overmix.* Pour batter onto grids of a preheated, lightly greased waffle baker. Close lid quickly; do not open during baking. Use a fork to help lift the baked waffle off the grid. Makes three 9-inch waffles.

Blueberry Muffins

You can also make basic muffins from this *Blueberry Muffin* recipe. Simply omit the blueberries, the 2 tablespoons sugar, and the lemon peel. Continue as the recipe directs.

- **1¾ cups all-purpose flour**
- **¼ cup sugar**
- **2½ teaspoons baking powder**
- **¾ teaspoon salt**
- **1 beaten egg**
- **¾ cup milk**
- **⅓ cup cooking oil**
- **¾ cup fresh *or* frozen blueberries**
- **2 tablespoons sugar**
- **1 teaspoon finely shredded lemon peel**

In a large mixing bowl combine the flour, ¼ cup sugar, baking powder, and salt. Make a well in the center. Combine egg, milk, and oil. Add egg mixture all at once to flour mixture. Stir just till moistened; batter should be lumpy. Combine blueberries, the 2 tablespoons sugar, and lemon peel. Carefully fold into batter. Grease muffin cups or line with paper bake cups; fill ⅔ full. Bake in a 400° oven for 20 to 25 minutes or till golden. Remove muffins from pans; serve warm. Makes 10 to 12 muffins.

● **Cranberry Muffins:** Prepare Blueberry Muffins as above, *except* use 1 cup coarsely chopped *cranberries* combined with ¼ cup *sugar* instead of the blueberries, 2 tablespoons sugar, and lemon peel. Continue as directed.

Pictured:
Fruit-Filled Coffee Cake (see recipe, page 125), Blueberry Muffins, and Waffles.

Pancakes

Griddlecakes, flap-jacks, and flannel cakes — all are names for all-American *pancakes*. This breakfast fare, traditionally served with butter and syrup, is said to be America's version of the French crepe or the Russian blintz.

1¼ **cups all-purpose flour**
  2 **tablespoons sugar**
  2 **teaspoons baking powder**
  ½ **teaspoon salt**
  1 **beaten egg**
  1 **cup milk**
  1 **tablespoon cooking oil**

Combine flour, sugar, baking powder, and salt. Combine egg, milk, and oil; add all at once to flour mixture, stirring till blended but still slightly lumpy. Pour about ¼ *cup* batter onto a hot, lightly greased griddle for each standard-sized pancake or about *1 tablespoon* batter for each dollar-sized pancake. Cook till golden brown, turning to cook other side when pancakes have a bubbly surface and slightly dry edges. Makes about eight 4-inch pancakes or about 30 dollar-sized pancakes.

Biscuits Supreme

For Buttermilk Biscuits, prepare *Biscuits Supreme* as directed, except stir ¼ teaspoon baking soda into the flour mixture and substitute ¾ cup buttermilk for the milk.

  2 **cups all-purpose flour**
  4 **teaspoons baking powder**
  2 **teaspoons sugar**
  ½ **teaspoon cream of tartar**
  ½ **teaspoon salt**
  ½ **cup shortening**
  ⅔ **cup milk**

Combine flour, baking powder, sugar, cream of tartar, and salt. Cut in shortening till mixture resembles coarse crumbs. Make a well in the center; add milk all at once. Stir just till dough clings together. Knead gently on floured surface for 10 to 12 strokes. Roll or pat to ½-inch thickness. Cut with a 2½-inch biscuit cutter, dipping cutter in flour between cuts. Place on an ungreased baking sheet. Bake in a 450° oven for 10 to 12 minutes or till golden. Serve warm. Makes 10 to 12.

Refrigerator Bran Muffins

  3 **cups whole bran cereal**
  ½ **cup shortening**
  2 **cups buttermilk** *or* **sour milk**
  2 **beaten eggs**
2½ **cups all-purpose flour**
  1 **cup sugar**
1½ **teaspoons baking powder**
1½ **teaspoons baking soda**
  1 **teaspoon salt**

Combine bran cereal and shortening. Add 1 cup *boiling water;* stir till shortening is melted. Add buttermilk or sour milk and eggs; mix well. Combine flour, sugar, baking powder, baking soda, and salt. Add all at once to cereal mixture; stir just till moistened. Store in tightly covered container in refrigerator up to 4 weeks. To bake, line muffin cups with paper bake cups; fill ⅔ full. Bake in a 400° oven for 20 to 25 minutes. Makes 24.

Banana Date-Nut Bread

  ½ **cup pitted whole dates**
  2 **cups all-purpose flour**
  ⅔ **cup sugar**
  2 **teaspoons baking powder**
  ¼ **teaspoon baking soda**
  2 **beaten eggs**
  1 **cup mashed ripe bananas**
  ⅓ **cup cooking oil**
  ¼ **cup milk**
  1 **teaspoon vanilla**
  ½ **cup chopped walnuts**

Finely snip dates. In a mixing bowl stir together flour, sugar, baking powder, baking soda, and ½ teaspoon *salt.* Combine eggs, bananas, oil, milk, and vanilla. Add dry ingredients; stir just till moistened. Fold dates and nuts into stirred mixture.

Turn batter into a lightly greased 9x5x3-inch loaf pan. Bake in a 350° oven about 55 minutes or till wooden pick inserted in center comes out clean. Cool in pan 10 minutes; remove from pan. Cool thoroughly on wire rack. Makes 1 loaf.

Molasses Nut Bread

The molasses for which this nut bread is named had a significant influence on the economic and political history of the United States. Imported molasses was so revered by the colonists that England's tax on it was one of the causes of the American revolution.

2¼ **cups whole wheat flour**
1¾ **cups all-purpose flour**
2 **teaspoons baking soda**
1 **teaspoon salt**
2 **beaten eggs**
2 **cups buttermilk** *or* **sour milk**
½ **cup molasses**
⅓ **cup honey**
2 **teaspoons finely shredded orange** *or* **lemon peel**
1 **cup chopped walnuts**
¾ **cup raisins**

In a large mixing bowl stir together whole wheat flour, all-purpose flour, baking soda, and salt; set aside. In another bowl combine eggs, buttermilk or sour milk, molasses, honey, and orange or lemon peel; add to dry ingredients, stirring till blended. stir in nuts and raisins.

Turn batter into two greased 8x4x2-inch loaf pans. Bake in a 350° oven about 55 minutes or till wooden pick inserted near center comes out clean, covering with foil the last 15 to 20 minutes. Cool in pans 10 minutes. Remove from pans and cool thoroughly on wire racks. Makes 2 loaves.

Cherry Coffee Cake

1¼ **cups all-purpose flour**
½ **cup sugar**
1 **teaspoon baking powder**
¼ **teaspoon baking soda**
¼ **teaspoon salt**
1 **beaten egg**
½ **cup butter** *or* **margarine, melted**
½ **cup buttermilk** *or* **sour milk**
1 **teaspoon vanilla**
1 **21-ounce can cherry pie filling**
½ **teaspoon finely shredded lemon peel**
½ **cup all-purpose flour**
¼ **cup sugar**
2 **tablespoons butter** *or* **margarine, softened**

In a mixing bowl stir together the 1¼ cups flour, ½ cup sugar, baking powder, baking soda, and salt. Combine egg, ½ cup melted butter or margarine, buttermilk or sour milk, and vanilla. Add to dry ingredients, mixing well. Turn batter into a lightly greased and floured 9x9x2-inch baking pan.

Stir together cherry pie filling and lemon peel; spread filling over batter. In small mixing bowl combine ½ cup flour, ¼ cup sugar, and 2 tablespoons softened butter or margarine till mixture is crumbly. Sprinkle atop cherry filling. Bake in a 350° oven for 40 to 45 minutes or till done. Serve warm. Makes 9 servings.

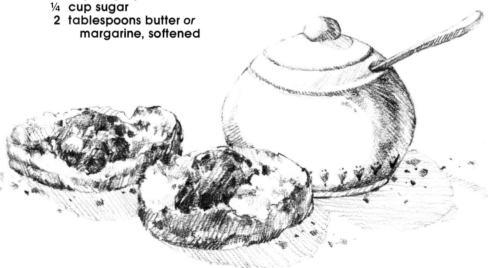

Apricot Upside-Down Cake

Americans have grown up with upside-down cakes for generations. Most of these cakes, which are inverted after baking, display a topping of pineapple rings and cherries in a buttery brown sugar glaze. *Apricot Upside-Down Cake* is a delicious variation of this popular dessert.

1   8¾-ounce can unpeeled apricot halves
2   tablespoons butter *or* margarine
½   cup packed brown sugar
4   or 5 maraschino cherries, halved
1   cup all-purpose flour
¾   cup sugar
1¼ teaspoons baking powder
½   cup milk
¼   cup shortening
1   egg
½   teaspoon vanilla

Drain apricots, reserving 2 tablespoons of the syrup. In a 9x1½-inch round baking pan melt butter. Stir in brown sugar and reserved syrup. Arrange apricot and cherry halves, cut side up, in the pan.

In a small mixer bowl stir together flour, sugar, baking powder, and ⅛ teaspoon *salt*. Add milk, shortening, egg, and vanilla. Beat with an electric mixer on low speed till combined, then on medium speed for 2 minutes. Spread batter over apricots and cherries in pan. Bake in a 350° oven for 40 to 45 minutes. Cool 5 minutes on wire rack; invert onto serving plate. Serve warm. Serves 8.

Yellow Cake

2¾ cups all-purpose flour
2½ teaspoons baking powder
1   teaspoon salt
½   cup butter *or* margarine
1¾ cups sugar
1½ teaspoons vanilla
2   eggs
1¼ cups milk

Grease and lightly flour two 8x1½-inch or 9x1½-inch round baking pans. Stir together flour, baking powder, and salt. Beat butter or margarine with electric mixer about 30 seconds. Add sugar and vanilla; beat till well combined. Add eggs, one at a time, beating 1 minute after each.

Add flour mixture and milk alternately to beaten mixture, beating after each addition. Turn into prepared pans. Bake in a 375° oven 30 to 35 minutes or till done. Cool 10 minutes on wire racks. Remove from pans; cool. Frost the cake as desired. Makes 12 servings.

● **Yellow Cupcakes:** Grease and lightly flour muffin pans or line with paper bake cups. Prepare batter for Yellow Cake as above. Fill each cup half full. Bake in a 375° oven 18 to 20 minutes or till done. Cool on a wire rack. Frost the cupcakes as desired. Makes 30.

White Layer Cake

2   cups all-purpose flour
1½ cups sugar
1   tablespoon baking powder
1   teaspoon salt
1   cup milk
½   cup shortening
2   teaspoons vanilla
4   egg whites

Grease and lightly flour two 8x1½-inch or two 9x1½-inch round baking pans. In a mixer bowl stir together flour, sugar, baking powder, and salt. Add milk, shortening, and vanilla. Beat with an electric mixer on low speed till combined, then on medium speed for 2 minutes. Add unbeaten egg whites; beat on medium speed 2 minutes more, scraping bowl frequently.

Turn into pans. Bake in a 350° oven 25 to 30 minutes or till done. Cool 10 minutes on wire racks. Remove; cool. Frost as desired. Serves 12.

● **Buttermilk White Cake:** Prepare White Layer Cake as above, *except* substitute 1 cup *buttermilk or sour milk* for the 1 cup milk, reduce the baking powder to *2 teaspoons,* and add ¼ teaspoon *baking soda.* Continue as directed.

Regal Almond Pound Cake

Pound cakes originally were made with a pound each of butter, sugar, eggs, and flour. Hand-beating the ingredients often took as long as an hour and required a strong arm.

Electric mixers have since made pound cakes easier and quicker to make. This almond-studded version possesses a texture and flavor much like old-time pound cakes.

1 cup milk
¾ cup butter *or* margarine
3 egg yolks
3 egg whites
¾ cup sliced almonds
2½ cups all-purpose flour
1 tablespoon baking powder
½ teaspoon salt
1½ cups sugar
1½ teaspoons vanilla
1 teaspoon finely shredded lemon peel
¼ teaspoon almond extract

Bring milk, butter or margarine, egg yolks, and egg whites to room temperature. Generously butter bottom and halfway up sides of a 10-inch tube pan; press the sliced almonds into butter on bottom and sides.

Combine flour, baking powder, and salt. In a large mixer bowl beat the ¾ cup butter with an electric mixer about 30 seconds. Gradually beat in sugar. Add vanilla, lemon peel, and almond extract; beat till fluffy. Add egg yolks, one at a time, beating 1 minute after each; scrape bowl often. Add flour mixture and milk alternately to beaten mixture, beating after each addition just till combined.

Thoroughly wash beaters. In a small mixer bowl beat egg whites till stiff peaks form. Fold into batter. Turn into prepared pan. Bake in a 325° oven for 60 to 70 minutes. Cool 15 minutes on a wire rack. Remove from pan; cool. Serves 12.

Angel Cake

Angel Cake was first made in 1890 by the chef of a St. Louis restaurant. The only leavening he used in his light-as-a-feather cake was egg whites that were beaten to stiff, glossy peaks.

To achieve a high, light cake, allow the egg whites to come to room temperature before beating. They will whip to a greater volume than cold egg whites right from the refrigerator.

1½ cups sifted powdered sugar
1 cup sifted cake flour *or* all-purpose flour
1½ cups egg whites (11 or 12 large)
1½ teaspoons cream of tartar
1 teaspoon vanilla
¼ teaspoon salt
1 cup sugar

Sift together powdered sugar and cake flour or all-purpose flour; repeat sifting twice. In a large mixer bowl beat egg whites, cream of tartar, vanilla, and salt with an electric mixer on medium speed till soft peaks form. Gradually add sugar, 2 tablespoons at a time, beating till stiff peaks form.

Sift about *one-fourth* of the flour mixture over whites; fold in lightly by hand. Repeat, folding in remaining flour mixture by fourths. Turn into an *ungreased* 10-inch tube pan. Bake in a 350° oven about 40 minutes or till done. Invert cake in pan; cool. Loosen cake; remove from pan. Serves 12.

Devil's Food Cake

2¼ cups all-purpose flour
½ cup unsweetened cocoa powder
1½ teaspoons baking soda
1 teaspoon salt
½ cup shortening
1 cup sugar
1 teaspoon vanilla
3 egg yolks
1⅓ cups cold water
3 egg whites
¾ cup sugar

Grease and lightly flour two 9x1½-inch round baking pans. Combine flour, cocoa powder, soda, and salt. In a large mixer bowl beat shortening with an electric mixer about 30 seconds. Add the 1 cup sugar and vanilla; beat till fluffy. Add yolks, one at a time, beating 1 minute after each. Add flour mixture and water alternately to beaten mixture, beating on low speed after each addition just till combined.

Thoroughly wash beaters. In a small mixer bowl beat egg whites till soft peaks form. Gradually add the ¾ cup sugar, beating till stiff peaks form. Fold egg white mixture into batter. Spread batter evenly in pans. Bake in a 350° oven for 30 to 35 minutes or till cakes test done. Cool 10 minutes on wire racks. Remove from pans; cool. Frost as desired. Makes 12 servings.

Choco-Nut Ripple Cake

Since cake mixes became popular in the 1940s and 50s, recipes based on cake mixes have abounded. One of these is *Choco-Nut Ripple Cake,* a moist yellow tube cake with a wave of chocolate and sunflower nuts running through the center. Use either a regular or pudding-type cake mix with this recipe.

1 **package 4-serving-size** *regular* **chocolate pudding mix**
¼ **cup all-purpose flour**
2 **tablespoons butter** *or* **margarine**
⅓ **cup sunflower nuts, coarsely chopped**
1 **package 2-layer-size yellow cake mix**
  Powdered sugar

Grease and lightly flour a 10-inch fluted tube pan. Combine pudding mix and flour. Cut in butter till mixture resembles coarse crumbs; stir in sunflower nuts. Prepare cake mix according to package directions.

Turn *one-third* of the batter into prepared pan; sprinkle with *half* of the pudding mix mixture. Add another one-third of the batter and sprinkle with remaining pudding mix mixture; top with remaining batter. Bake in a 350° oven about 45 minutes or till done. Cool 15 minutes on wire rack. Remove from pan; cool. Sprinkle with powdered sugar. Makes 12 servings.

German Chocolate Cake

1 **4-ounce package German sweet cooking chocolate**
⅓ **cup water**
1⅔ **cups all-purpose flour**
1 **teaspoon baking soda**
½ **teaspoon salt**
½ **cup butter** *or* **margarine**
1 **cup sugar**
1 **teaspoon vanilla**
3 **egg yolks**
⅔ **cup buttermilk** *or* **sour milk**
3 **stiff-beaten egg whites**
  Coconut-Pecan Frosting

Grease and lightly flour two 8x1½-inch round baking pans. Heat chocolate and water till chocolate melts; cool. Stir together flour, soda, and salt. Beat butter or margarine with an electric mixer about 30 seconds. Add sugar and vanilla; beat till fluffy. Add egg yolks, one at a time, beating 1 minute after each. Beat in chocolate mixture.

Add flour mixture and buttermilk or sour milk alternately to beaten mixture, beating after each addition. Fold in egg whites. Turn into pans. Bake in a 350° oven for 30 to 35 minutes. Cool 10 minutes. Remove from pans; cool. Fill and frost top with Coconut-Pecan Frosting. Makes 12 servings.

Coconut-Pecan Frosting: In a saucepan beat 1 *egg* slightly. Stir in one 5⅓-ounce can (⅔ cup) *evaporated milk,* ⅔ cup *sugar,* ¼ cup *butter or margarine,* and dash *salt.* Cook and stir about 12 minutes or till thickened and bubbly. Stir in 1⅓ cups flaked *coconut* and ½ cup chopped *pecans.* Cool frosting.

Carrot-Pineapple Cake

1½ **cups all-purpose flour**
1 **cup sugar**
1 **teaspoon baking powder**
1 **teaspoon ground cinnamon**
½ **teaspoon baking soda**
1 **8¼-ounce can crushed pineapple**
1 **cup finely shredded carrots (2 medium)**
⅔ **cup cooking oil**
2 **eggs**
½ **cup coconut (optional)**
1 **teaspoon vanilla**
  Cream Cheese Frosting (see recipe, page 135)

Grease and lightly flour a 9x9x2-inch baking pan. In a large mixer bowl stir together flour, sugar, baking powder, cinnamon, baking soda, and ½ teaspoon *salt.* Add *undrained* pineapple, carrots, cooking oil, eggs, coconut if desired, and vanilla. Beat with an electric mixer on low speed till combined, then on medium speed for 2 minutes. Turn into prepared pan. Bake in a 350° oven about 35 minutes or till cake tests done. Cool on wire rack. Frost with Cream Cheese Frosting. Serves 9.

Pictured:
Choco-Nut Ripple Cake and Carrot-Pineapple Cake.

Gingerbread

Early American Gingerbread, like its European relative, resembled a hard, thin cookie. It wasn't until the early 1800s that the *Gingerbread* cake like this one became popular. Soft, cake-like *Gingerbread* was one of Abraham Lincoln's favorite desserts.

½ cup shortening
1 cup molasses
2½ cups all-purpose flour
½ cup sugar
1 teaspoon baking soda
1 teaspoon ground ginger
½ teaspoon ground cinnamon
¼ teaspoon ground cloves
1 egg

Grease and lightly flour a 13x9x2-inch baking pan. In a mixing bowl pour 1 cup *boiling water* over shortening; stir to melt shortening. Stir in molasses.

Stir together flour, sugar, baking soda, ginger, cinnamon, cloves, and ½ teaspoon *salt*. Gradually stir molasses mixture into flour mixture. Add egg; beat till smooth. Pour into prepared pan. Bake in a 350° oven for 40 to 45 minutes or till cake tests done. Cool on wire rack. Makes 12 servings.

Lemon Pudding Cake

Lemon Pudding Cake is really two desserts in one. As it bakes, a cake layer forms on top with a lemon pudding-like sauce below. Serve by spooning the sauce over the cake portions in individual dessert dishes.

¾ cup sugar
¼ cup all-purpose flour
   Dash salt
3 tablespoons butter *or* margarine, melted
1½ teaspoons finely shredded lemon peel
¼ cup lemon juice
3 beaten egg yolks
1½ cups milk
3 stiff-beaten egg whites

In a large mixing bowl stir together sugar, flour, and salt. Stir in melted butter or margarine, lemon peel, and lemon juice. In a small bowl combine egg yolks and milk; stir into lemon mixture. Gently fold in stiff-beaten egg whites. Turn into an ungreased 8x8x2-inch baking pan.

Place in a larger pan on oven rack. Pour hot water into larger pan to a depth of 1 inch. Bake in a 350° oven for 35 to 40 minutes or till top is golden and springs back when touched. Serve warm or chilled in dessert dishes. Serves 6 to 8.

Cream-Filled Cake Roll

½ cup all-purpose flour
1 teaspoon baking powder
¼ teaspoon salt
4 egg yolks
½ teaspoon vanilla
⅓ cup sugar
4 egg whites
½ cup sugar
   Sifted powdered sugar
   Creamy Chocolate Filling

Grease and lightly flour a 15x10x1-inch jelly roll pan. Combine flour, baking powder, and salt. In a small mixer bowl beat egg yolks and vanilla with an electric mixer on high speed about 5 minutes or till thick and lemon-colored. Gradually add the ⅓ cup sugar, beating till sugar dissolves.

Thoroughly wash beaters. In a large mixer bowl beat egg whites till soft peaks form. Gradually add the ½ cup sugar, beating till stiff peaks form. Fold yolk mixture into egg whites. Sprinkle flour mixture over egg mixture; fold in lightly by hand. Spread batter evenly into prepared pan. Bake in a 375° oven for 12 to 15 minutes or till done.

Immediately loosen edges of cake from pan and turn out onto a towel sprinkled with sifted powdered sugar. Starting with narrow end, roll warm cake and towel together; cool on a wire rack. Unroll; spread cake with Creamy Chocolate Filling to within 1 inch of edges. Roll up cake. Chill thoroughly. Sprinkle with additional powdered sugar. Serves 10.

Creamy Chocolate Filling: Prepare 1 package 4-serving-size *regular chocolate pudding mix* according to package directions, *except* use 1½ cups *milk*. Add one 3-ounce package *cream cheese*, cut up, to hot pudding; stir till melted. Cover surface with waxed paper. Cool, then chill.

Butter Frosting

6 **tablespoons butter** *or* **margarine**
4½ **to 4¾ cups sifted powdered sugar**
¼ **cup milk**
1½ **teaspoons vanilla**

In a small mixer bowl beat butter or margarine till light and fluffy. Gradually add about *half* of the powdered sugar, beating well. Beat in the milk and vanilla. Gradually beat in the remaining powdered sugar; beat in additional milk, if necessary, to make the frosting of spreading consistency. Frosts the tops and sides of two 8- or 9-inch cake layers.
• **Chocolate Butter Frosting:** Prepare Butter Frosting as above, *except* add 2 squares (2 ounces) *unsweetened chocolate*, melted and cooled, with the vanilla.

Cream Cheese Frosting

1 **3-ounce package cream cheese**
¼ **cup butter** *or* **margarine**
1 **teaspoon vanilla**
2 **cups sifted powdered sugar**

In a mixer bowl beat together cream cheese, butter or margarine, and vanilla till light and fluffy. Gradually add the powdered sugar, beating till smooth. Frosts tops of two 9x9-inch cakes, top of one 13x9-inch cake, or about 18 cupcakes. Cover; store in the refrigerator.

White Satin Frosting

¾ **cup milk**
4 **teaspoons cornstarch**
¾ **cup shortening**
3¾ **to 4 cups sifted powdered sugar**
2 **teaspoons vanilla**
¼ **teaspoon salt**

In a small saucepan stir together milk and cornstarch. Cook and stir till thickened and bubbly; cook and stir 2 minutes more. Cover surface with waxed paper or clear plastic wrap; cool about 1 hour or till the milk mixture cools to room temperature.
In a mixer bowl beat shortening and *half* of the powdered sugar with an electric mixer till fluffy. Beat in vanilla and salt. Gradually beat in the cooled milk mixture. Beat in enough of the remaining powdered sugar till of desired consistency. Frosts tops and sides of two 8- or 9-inch layers.
• **Chocolate Satin Frosting:** Prepare White Satin Frosting as above, *except* beat in 2 squares (2 ounces) *unsweetened chocolate*, melted and cooled, with the vanilla and salt. Continue as directed.

Fluffy White Frosting

1 **cup sugar**
⅓ **cup water**
¼ **teaspoon cream of tartar**
Dash salt
2 **egg whites**
1 **teaspoon vanilla**

In a saucepan combine sugar, water, cream of tartar, and salt. Cook and stir till mixture bubbles and sugar dissolves. In a mixer bowl combine egg whites and vanilla. Add sugar syrup very slowly to unbeaten egg whites while beating constantly with electric mixer on high speed about 7 minutes or till stiff peaks form. Frosts tops and sides of two 8- or 9-inch cake layers or one 10-inch tube cake.

Apple Pie

Though it has English origins, *Apple Pie* always has been popular in America. In fact, early cook books neglected to include a recipe for *Apple Pie,* assuming every cook knew how to make this favorite.

Served with a tangy piece of cheddar cheese or a scoop of vanilla ice cream, *Apple Pie* seems certain to remain an American hallmark.

Pastry for Double-Crust Pie (see recipe, page 141)
6 **cups thinly sliced, peeled cooking apples (2 pounds)**
1 **tablespoon lemon juice (optional)**
1 **cup sugar**
2 **tablespoons all-purpose flour**
½ **to 1 teaspoon ground cinnamon**
Dash ground nutmeg
1 **tablespoon butter *or* margarine**
Sugar (optional)
Cheddar cheese slices (optional)

Prepare and roll out pastry. Line a 9-inch pie plate with *half* of the pastry. Trim to edge of plate.

If apples lack tartness, sprinkle with 1 tablespoon lemon juice if desired. Combine 1 cup sugar, flour, cinnamon, and nutmeg. (For a very juicy pie, omit the flour.) Add sugar mixture to the sliced apples; toss to coat fruit. Turn apple mixture into pastry-lined pie plate; dot with the butter or margarine.

Cut slits in top crust for steam to escape; place atop filling. Seal and flute edge. Sprinkle with sugar if desired. To prevent overbrowning, cover edge of pie with foil. Bake in a 375° oven for 25 minutes. Remove foil; bake 20 to 25 minutes more or till crust is golden. Cool pie on wire rack. Serve with cheese if desired. Makes 8 servings.

Deep-Dish Peach Pie

⅔ **cup sugar**
2 **tablespoons cornstarch**
1 **teaspoon finely shredded orange peel**
¼ **teaspoon ground nutmeg**
4 **cups sliced fresh peaches *or* frozen unsweetened sliced peaches, thawed**
2 **medium oranges, peeled and sectioned**
2 **tablespoons butter *or* margarine**
1 **cup all-purpose flour**
½ **teaspoon salt**
¼ **cup shortening *or* lard**
2 **to 3 tablespoons cold water**

In a small bowl stir together sugar, cornstarch, orange peel, and nutmeg. In a 1½-quart casserole combine the peaches and the oranges. Add the sugar mixture; stir till well coated. Dot the fruit mixture with the butter or margarine.

In a medium bowl stir together flour and salt. Cut in shortening or lard till pieces are the size of small peas. Sprinkle *1 tablespoon* of the water over part of flour mixture; gently toss with fork. Push to side of bowl. Repeat till all is moistened. Form into a ball.

On lightly floured surface flatten the dough with hands. Roll dough from the center to the edge, forming a 9-inch circle. Cut slits in pastry for steam to escape. Roll up the pastry around the rolling pin; transfer to casserole and unroll over the fruit mixture.

Trim pastry. Flute the pastry to the side of the casserole, but not over the edge. If desired, garnish top of pie with pastry cutouts made from pastry trimmings. To prevent overbrowning, cover the edge of the pastry with foil.

Place casserole on a baking sheet in oven. Bake in a 375° oven for 25 minutes. Remove foil; bake 30 to 35 minutes more or till crust is golden brown. Cool pie on wire rack. Serve warm or cool. Spoon into dessert dishes to serve. Serves 8.

Pictured clockwise:
Butterscotch Apple Dumplings (see recipe, page 138), Deep-Dish Peach Pie, and Citrus Chiffon Pie (see recipe, page 138).

Butterscotch Apple Dumplings *pictured on page 137*

**Pastry for Double-Crust Pie
(see recipe, page 141)**
6 **small tart cooking apples,
peeled and cored**
¼ **cup raisins**
1½ **cups water**
1 **cup packed brown sugar**
2 **tablespoons butter** *or*
margarine
1 **teaspoon vanilla**
Light cream

Prepare pastry. On a lightly floured surface roll pastry into a 21x14-inch rectangle. Cut into six 7-inch squares. Place one apple upright on center of each square. Fill center of each apple with some of the raisins. Moisten edges of each pastry square. Fold corners to center over apple; seal edges by pinching together. Place in a 13x9x2-inch baking pan.

In a saucepan combine water and brown sugar. Cook and stir till dissolved. Bring to boiling; stir in butter and vanilla. Pour over dumplings. Bake in a 400° oven about 35 minutes. Serve with light cream. Serves 6.

Citrus Chiffon Pie *pictured on page 137*

An Iowa family restaurant reportedly served the first chiffon pie in the 1930s. The pie soon caught on and appeared across the country.

Chiffon pies are named for their smooth and light texture that's achieved by combining either beaten egg whites or whipped cream (or both) with a gelatin mixture.

**Pastry for Single-Crust Pie
(see recipe, page 141)**
⅓ **cup sugar**
1 **envelope unflavored gelatin**
¼ **teaspoon salt**
1 **teaspoon finely shredded
orange** *or* **lemon peel
(set aside)**
⅔ **cup orange juice**
⅓ **cup lemon juice**
4 **slightly beaten egg yolks**
4 **egg whites**
⅓ **cup sugar**
½ **cup whipping cream**
Orange slice (optional)
Lemon slice (optional)

Prepare and roll out pastry. Line a 9-inch pie plate. Trim to ½ inch beyond edge. Flute edge; prick pastry. Bake in a 450° oven for 10 to 12 minutes or till golden. Cool on wire rack.

Combine ⅓ cup sugar, the gelatin, and salt. Stir in orange juice, lemon juice, and egg yolks. Cook and stir over medium heat till mixture thickens slightly. Remove from heat; stir in peel.

Chill gelatin mixture to the consistency of corn syrup, stirring occasionally. Immediately beat egg whites till soft peaks form. Gradually add ⅓ cup sugar, beating till stiff peaks form. When gelatin is the consistency of unbeaten egg whites (partially set), fold in the egg white mixture.

Whip cream till soft peaks form. Fold into gelatin mixture. If necessary, chill till mixture mounds when spooned. Turn into baked pastry shell. Chill several hours or overnight till set. Garnish with an orange and lemon slice if desired. Cover and refrigerate to store. Makes 8 servings.

Coconut Custard Pie

**Pastry for Single-Crust Pie
(see recipe, page 141)**
4 **eggs**
½ **cup sugar**
½ **teaspoon vanilla**
¼ **teaspoon salt**
2½ **cups milk**
1 **cup flaked coconut**
Ground nutmeg

Prepare and roll out pastry. Line a 9-inch pie plate. Trim to ½ inch beyond edge. Flute edge. Line pastry with foil and fill with dry beans or line with heavy-duty foil. Bake in a 450° oven 5 minutes. Remove beans and foil; cool pastry on rack.

Reduce oven temperature to 350°. For filling, in a mixing bowl beat eggs slightly with a rotary beater or fork. Stir in sugar, vanilla, and salt. Stir in milk; mix well. Stir in coconut.

Place pie shell on oven rack; pour filling into partially baked shell. Sprinkle with nutmeg. Cover edge of pie with foil. Bake in a 350° oven 20 minutes. Remove foil; bake about 20 minutes more or till knife inserted near center comes out clean. Cool. Cover; refrigerate to store. Serves 8.

Lemon Meringue Pie

Thoroughly cool cream pies such as *Lemon Meringue Pie* and *Vanilla Cream Pie* before serving. Otherwise, the filling will be too soft to hold a cut edge.

Slicing meringue-topped pies can be tricky because the meringue tends to stick to the knife edge. To prevent this, dip the knife in water before cutting each slice.

Pastry for Single-Crust Pie (see recipe, page 141)
- 1½ cups sugar
- 3 tablespoons cornstarch
- 3 tablespoons all-purpose flour
- Dash salt
- 1½ cups water
- 3 egg yolks
- 2 tablespoons butter *or* margarine
- ½ teaspoon finely shredded lemon peel
- ⅓ cup lemon juice
- Meringue

Prepare and roll out pastry. Line a 9-inch pie plate. Trim pastry to ½ inch beyond edge. Flute edge; prick pastry. Bake in a 450° oven for 10 to 12 minutes or till golden. Cool.

In a saucepan combine sugar, cornstarch, flour, and salt. Gradually stir in water. Cook and stir over medium-high heat till thickened and bubbly. Reduce heat; cook and stir 2 minutes more. Remove from heat.

Beat egg yolks slightly. Stir about *1 cup* of the hot mixture into yolks. Return mixture to saucepan; bring to a gentle boil, stirring constantly. Cook and stir 2 minutes more. Remove from heat. Stir in butter and lemon peel. Gradually stir in lemon juice, mixing well. Pour into baked pastry shell.

Make Meringue. Spread over hot filling; seal to edge. Bake pie in a 350° oven for 12 to 15 minutes or till golden. Cool on wire rack. Cover; refrigerate to store. Makes 8 servings.

Meringue: In a small mixer bowl beat 3 *egg whites,* ½ teaspoon *vanilla,* and ¼ teaspoon *cream of tartar* with an electric mixer on medium speed about 1 minute or till soft peaks form. Gradually add 6 tablespoons *sugar,* 1 tablespoon at a time, beating on high speed about 4 minutes or till the mixture forms stiff, glossy peaks and the sugar dissolves.

Vanilla Cream Pie

Pastry for Single-Crust Pie (see recipe, page 141)
- 1 cup sugar
- ½ cup all-purpose flour *or* ¼ cup cornstarch
- ¼ teaspoon salt
- 3 cups milk
- 4 egg yolks
- 3 tablespoons butter *or* margarine
- 1½ teaspoons vanilla
- Meringue (see recipe above)

Prepare and roll out pastry. Line a 9-inch pie plate. Trim pastry to ½ inch beyond edge. Flute edge; prick pastry. Bake in a 450° oven for 10 to 12 minutes or till golden. Cool on wire rack.

In a saucepan combine sugar, flour or cornstarch, and salt. Gradually stir in milk. Cook and stir over medium heat till thickened and bubbly. Cook and stir 2 minutes more. Remove from heat.

Beat egg yolks slightly. Stir about *1 cup* of the hot mixture into yolks. Return mixture to saucepan; bring to a gentle boil, stirring constantly. Cook and stir 2 minutes more. Remove from heat. Stir in butter and vanilla. Pour into baked pastry shell.

Make Meringue. Spread over hot filling; seal to edge. Bake in a 350° oven for 12 to 15 minutes or till golden. Cool on wire rack. Cover; refrigerate to store. Makes 8 servings.

- **Chocolate Chip-Nut Pie:** Prepare Vanilla Cream Pie as above, *except* reduce the sugar to ¾ *cup* and stir in ½ cup *semisweet chocolate pieces* with the vanilla. Sprinkle ⅓ cup chopped *pecans* over Meringue and bake as directed.

- **Banana Cream Pie:** Prepare Vanilla Cream Pie as above, *except* slice 3 *bananas* into the bottom of the baked pastry shell. Pour hot filling over bananas. Continue as directed.

French Silk Pie

To ensure a creamy smooth texture for this sinfully rich pie, use butter, not margarine to make the filling.

When testing the recipe in the Better Homes and Gardens Test Kitchen, we discovered that some brands of margarine produce a sticky, nonfluffy filling. For this reason, we recommend using only butter in this recipe.

Pastry for Single-Crust Pie (see recipe, page 141)
- 1 **cup sugar**
- ¾ **cup butter (not margarine)**
- 3 **squares (3 ounces) unsweetened chocolate, melted and cooled**
- 1½ **teaspoons vanilla**
- 3 **eggs**
  Unsweetened whipped cream (optional)
  Chocolate curls (optional)

Prepare and roll out pastry. Line a 9-inch pie plate. Trim pastry to ½ inch beyond edge. Flute edge; prick pastry. Bake in a 450° oven for 10 to 12 minutes or till golden. Cool on wire rack.

In a small mixer bowl beat together sugar and butter about 4 minutes or till light. Beat in cooled chocolate and vanilla. Add eggs, one at a time, beating with an electric mixer on medium speed for 2 minutes after each addition, scraping sides of bowl constantly. Turn into baked pastry shell. Chill several hours or overnight till set. Garnish with whipped cream and chocolate curls if desired. Cover and refrigerate to store. Makes 10 servings.

• **Mint French Silk Pie:** Prepare French Silk Pie as above, *except* decrease vanilla to ¼ *teaspoon* and beat in ¼ teaspoon *peppermint extract* or 2 tablespoons *crème de menthe or peppermint schnapps* with the chocolate and vanilla.

Grasshopper Pie

Chocolate Wafer Crust (see recipe, page 49)
- 6½ **cups tiny marshmallows**
- ¼ **cup milk**
- ¼ **cup green crème de menthe**
- 2 **tablespoons white crème de cacao**
- 2 **cups whipping cream**
  Unsweetened whipped cream
  Chocolate curls

Prepare Chocolate Wafer Crust. For filling, in a large saucepan combine marshmallows and milk. Cook over low heat, stirring constantly, till marshmallows are melted. Remove from heat. Cool mixture, stirring every 5 minutes.

Combine crème de menthe and crème de cacao; stir into marshmallow mixture. Whip 2 cups whipping cream till soft peaks form; fold in marshmallow mixture. Turn mixture into chilled wafer crust. Freeze several hours or overnight till firm. Before serving, garnish pie with additional unsweetened whipped cream and chocolate curls. Serves 10.

Graham Cracker Crust

- 18 **graham cracker squares**
- ¼ **cup sugar**
- 6 **tablespoons butter *or* margarine, melted**

Place graham crackers in a plastic bag or between 2 sheets of plastic wrap or waxed paper. Crush into fine crumbs. (Or, crush crackers into fine crumbs in a blender.) Measure 1¼ cups crumbs.

In a mixing bowl combine crumbs and sugar. Stir in melted butter or margarine; toss to thoroughly combine. Turn the crumb mixture into a 9-inch pie plate. Press onto the bottom and sides to form a firm, even crust. Refrigerate about 1 hour or till firm. (Or, bake in a 375° oven for 6 to 9 minutes or till edges are brown. Cool on a wire rack.)

Pastry for Single-Crust Pie

Pies are second only to ice cream on America's list of favorite desserts. They've been popular since our country's beginning when they were eaten for breakfast as well as at other meals.

A tender, flaky crust is crucial to a good pie. For best results, don't overmix the ingredients, and handle the rolled-out pastry gently.

1¼ **cups all-purpose flour**
½ **teaspoon salt**
⅓ **cup shortening *or* lard**
3 **to 4 tablespoons cold water**

In a mixing bowl stir together flour and salt. Cut in shortening or lard till pieces are the size of small peas. Sprinkle *1 tablespoon* of the water over part of the mixture; gently toss with a fork. Push to side of bowl. Repeat till all is moistened. Form dough into a ball.

On a lightly floured surface flatten dough with hands. Roll dough from center to edge, forming a circle about 12 inches in diameter. Wrap pastry around rolling pin. Unroll onto a 9-inch pie plate.

Ease pastry into pie plate, being careful not to stretch pastry. Trim to ½ inch beyond edge of pie plate; fold under extra pastry. Make a fluted, rope-shaped, or scalloped edge. Do not prick pastry. Bake as directed in individual recipe.

• **Baked Pastry Shell:** Prepare Pastry for Single-Crust Pie as above, *except* prick bottom and sides with the tines of a fork. Bake in a 450° oven for 10 to 12 minutes or till golden. Cool on a wire rack.

• **Pastry for Double-Crust Pie:** Prepare Pastry for Single-Crust Pie as above, *except* use 2 cups all-purpose *flour,* 1 teaspoon *salt,* ⅔ cup *shortening or lard,* and 6 to 7 tablespoons *cold water.* Divide dough in half. Roll out *half* of dough as above. Fit into pie plate. Trim pastry even with rim.

For top crust, roll out remaining dough. Cut slits for steam to escape. Place desired pie filling in pie shell. Top with pastry for top crust. Trim top crust ½ inch beyond edge of pie plate. Fold extra pastry under bottom crust; flute edge. Bake as directed in individual recipe.

Wheaten Snickerdoodles

Snickerdoodles started turning up in American cook books in the middle 1800s. They are known by their crinkled tops and light coating of cinnamon-sugar.

Wheaten Snicker-doodles flirt with tradition by using whole wheat flour instead of all-purpose flour.

1½ **cups whole wheat flour**
 ½ **teaspoon baking soda**
 ½ **teaspoon cream of tartar**
 ½ **cup butter** *or* **margarine**
 ¾ **cup packed brown sugar**
 1 **egg**
 1 **teaspoon vanilla**
 2 **tablespoons sugar**
 ½ **teaspoon ground cinnamon**

Stir together flour, soda, cream of tartar, and ¼ teaspoon *salt*. In a mixer bowl beat butter for 30 seconds. Add brown sugar; beat till fluffy. Add egg and vanilla; beat well. Add flour mixture to beaten mixture and beat till well blended.

Shape into 1-inch balls; roll in a mixture of the sugar and cinnamon. Place 2 inches apart on ungreased cookie sheet; flatten slightly. Bake in a 375° oven 8 to 10 minutes or till done. Remove to a wire rack; cool. Makes about 30.

Honey Peanut Butter Cookies

2¼ **cups all-purpose flour**
 ½ **teaspoon baking soda**
 ½ **teaspoon salt**
 ½ **cup shortening**
 ½ **cup peanut butter**
 ½ **cup packed brown sugar**
 1 **egg**
 ½ **cup honey**

Stir together flour, baking soda, and salt. In a mixer bowl beat together shortening, peanut butter, and brown sugar till fluffy. Add egg and honey; beat well. Add flour mixture to beaten mixture; beat till well blended. Cover and chill 1 hour.

Using 1 tablespoon of dough for each, shape into balls. Place on greased cookie sheet. Flatten with lightly floured fork. Bake in a 350° oven about 10 minutes. Cool 1 minute; remove. Cool. Makes 42.

Chocolate Crinkles

2 **cups all-purpose flour**
 2 **teaspoons baking powder**
1½ **cups sugar**
 ½ **cup cooking oil**
 4 **squares (4 ounces)**
   unsweetened chocolate,
   melted and cooled
 2 **teaspoons vanilla**
 3 **eggs**
   Sifted powdered sugar

Stir together flour and baking powder. In a mixer bowl combine sugar, oil, cooled chocolate, and vanilla. Beat in eggs. Add flour mixture to chocolate mixture; beat well. Cover and chill.

Using 1 tablespoon dough for each, shape into balls; roll in powdered sugar. Place on a greased cookie sheet. Bake in a 375° oven for 10 to 12 minutes or till done. While cookies are warm, roll again in powdered sugar if desired. Cool. Makes about 48.

Macaroon Drops

2 **egg whites**
 1 **teaspoon vanilla**
   Dash salt
 ½ **cup sugar**
 2 **tablespoons all-purpose flour**
 2 **cups flaked coconut**

Beat whites, vanilla, and salt till soft peaks form. Gradually add sugar, beating till stiff peaks form. Fold in flour, then coconut. Drop from a teaspoon 1½ inches apart onto greased cookie sheet. Bake in a 325° oven about 20 minutes. Remove; cool. Makes 24.

Pictured clockwise:
Raisin-Filled Granola Bars (see recipe, page 145), Wheaten Snickerdoodles, Refrigerator Nut Slices (see recipe, page 145), Honey Peanut Butter Cookies, and Chocolate Crinkles.

Chocolate Chip Cookies *pictured on pages 4 and 5*

In 1940 Ruth Wakefield, who ran the Toll House Inn in Massachusetts, cut up a bar of chocolate, folded it into cookie dough, and baked the original Toll House chocolate chip cookie.

When a machine was invented to mold chocolate into chips, America's love affair with *Chocolate Chip Cookies* deepened. Today they are an integral part of Americana.

2½ cups all-purpose flour
1 teaspoon baking soda
½ cup butter *or* margarine
½ cup shortening
1 cup packed brown sugar
½ cup sugar
2 eggs
1½ teaspoons vanilla
1 12-ounce package (2 cups) semisweet chocolate pieces
1 cup chopped walnuts *or* pecans

Stir together flour, baking soda, and ½ teaspoon *salt*. Beat butter or margarine and shortening with an electric mixer on medium speed for 30 seconds. Add brown sugar and sugar; beat till fluffy. Add eggs and vanilla; beat well.

Add flour mixture to beaten mixture; beat till well blended. Stir in chocolate pieces and nuts. Drop from a teaspoon 2 inches apart onto an ungreased cookie sheet. Bake in a 375° oven for 8 to 10 minutes or till done. Remove to wire rack; cool. Makes about 72.

Oatmeal Drop Cookies

1¼ cups all-purpose flour
½ teaspoon baking soda
¼ cup butter *or* margarine
¼ cup shortening
⅓ cup sugar
⅓ cup packed brown sugar
1 egg
1 teaspoon vanilla
⅓ cup buttermilk *or* sour milk
1¼ cups quick-cooking rolled oats
½ cup raisins *or* semisweet chocolate pieces
½ cup chopped walnuts *or* pecans (optional)

Stir together flour, baking soda, and ¼ teaspoon *salt*. In a mixer bowl beat butter and shortening with electric mixer for 30 seconds. Add sugar and brown sugar; beat till fluffy. Add egg and vanilla; beat well.

Add flour mixture and buttermilk alternately to beaten mixture; beat till well blended. Stir in oats, raisins or chocolate pieces, and nuts if desired. Drop from a teaspoon 2 inches apart onto a lightly greased cookie sheet. Bake in a 375° oven for 10 to 12 minutes or till done. Remove; cool. Makes 48.

• **Chocolate-Oatmeal Drop Cookies:** Prepare Oatmeal Drop Cookies as above, *except* beat in 2 squares (2 ounces) *unsweetened chocolate*, melted and cooled, after beating in egg and vanilla, and increase the buttermilk to ½ *cup*.

Fruit and Grain Cookies *pictured on page 122*

1 cup whole wheat flour
¼ cup toasted wheat germ
¼ cup nonfat dry milk powder
¼ teaspoon baking powder
¼ teaspoon baking soda
½ cup butter *or* margarine
½ cup peanut butter
1 egg
¾ cup honey
1 teaspoon vanilla
1 cup raisins
1 cup dried apricots, snipped
¾ cup quick-cooking rolled oats
½ cup chopped walnuts
⅓ cup unsalted sunflower nuts
⅓ cup shredded coconut

Stir together the whole wheat flour, wheat germ, milk powder, baking powder, baking soda, and ½ teaspoon *salt*. In a large mixer bowl beat butter or margarine and peanut butter for 30 seconds. Add the egg, honey, and vanilla; beat well. Add flour mixture to beaten mixture and beat till well blended.

Stir together raisins, apricots, oats, walnuts, sunflower nuts, and coconut; add to beaten mixture. Mix well. Drop from a teaspoon 2 inches apart onto an ungreased cookie sheet. Bake in a 350° oven for 10 to 11 minutes or till done. Cool about 1 minute before removing to a wire rack. Cool thoroughly. Makes about 60.

Refrigerator Nut Slices *pictured on page 143*

2¼ **cups all-purpose flour**
½ **teaspoon baking powder**
¼ **teaspoon salt**
1 **cup butter *or* margarine**
1 **cup sugar**
1 **egg**
1 **teaspoon vanilla**
½ **cup finely chopped pecans**

Combine flour, baking powder, and salt. In a mixer bowl beat butter for 30 seconds. Add sugar and beat till fluffy. Add egg and vanilla; beat well. Add flour mixture to beaten mixture; beat till well blended. Stir in pecans. Cover; chill 30 minutes. Shape dough into two 7-inch-long rolls. Wrap in waxed paper or clear plastic wrap. Chill several hours or overnight.

Cut into ¼-inch slices. Place 1 inch apart on ungreased cookie sheet. Bake in a 375° oven 10 to 12 minutes or till light brown. Cool about 1 minute; remove to wire rack. Cool. Makes about 60.

• **Chip-Chocolate Slices:** Prepare the Refrigerator Nut Slices as above, *except* stir 2 squares (2 ounces) *semisweet chocolate*, grated, and ½ teaspoon finely shredded *orange peel* in with the pecans. Continue as directed.

• **Caramel-Nut Slices:** Prepare Refrigerator Nut Slices as above, *except* add ¾ teaspoon ground *cinnamon* to flour mixture. Reduce the sugar to ½ *cup* and add ½ cup packed *brown sugar.* Continue as directed.

Cocoa Brownies

Americans have had a liking for brownies since the 1920s. Some believe the first batch of brownies was actually a fallen cake.

There are generally two types of brownies — the chewy, fudgy variety and the kind with a cakelike texture such as these moist *Cocoa Brownies.*

1 **cup all-purpose flour**
⅓ **cup unsweetened cocoa powder**
½ **teaspoon baking powder**
¼ **teaspoon salt**
½ **cup butter *or* margarine**
1 **cup sugar**
2 **eggs**
1 **teaspoon vanilla**
⅓ **cup water**
½ **cup chopped walnuts**
Powdered sugar

Lightly grease a 13x9x2-inch baking pan. Combine flour, cocoa powder, baking powder, and salt. Beat butter or margarine with an electric mixer for 30 seconds. Add sugar; beat till fluffy. Add eggs and vanilla; beat well. Stir in water.

Add flour mixture to beaten mixture; mix well. Stir in nuts. Turn batter into prepared pan. Bake in a 350° oven for 20 to 25 minutes or till done. Cool on wire rack. Cut into bars. Sprinkle with powdered sugar. Makes 36.

Raisin-Filled Granola Bars *pictured on page 143*

½ **cup sugar**
1 **tablespoon cornstarch**
2 **cups raisins**
1 **cup water**
2 **tablespoons lemon juice**
2 **cups all-purpose flour**
½ **teaspoon baking soda**
¾ **cup butter *or* margarine**
1 **cup packed brown sugar**
1½ **cups granola**
2 **tablespoons water**

Grease and lightly flour a 13x9x2-inch baking pan. In a saucepan combine sugar and cornstarch; stir in raisins and 1 cup water. Cook and stir over medium heat till thickened and bubbly. Remove from heat. Stir in lemon juice; cool.

Combine flour and baking soda. Beat butter for 30 seconds. Add brown sugar; beat till fluffy. Add flour mixture to beaten mixture; beat till well blended. Stir in granola and 2 tablespoons water.

Pat *half* of the granola mixture into prepared baking pan; spread with raisin mixture. Sprinkle with remaining granola mixture. Lightly press with hand. Bake in a 350° oven for 30 to 35 minutes or till done. Cut into bars while warm. Cool thoroughly. Makes 32.

Peach Berry Cobbler

Cobbler — a deep-dish dessert of sweetened fruit bubbling beneath a rich biscuit crust — is an American original.

Peach Berry Cobbler can be made with sliced fresh nectarines, pears, or apples instead of the peaches. Whatever fruit you use, serve this dessert warm with light cream or vanilla ice cream.

⅓ **cup packed brown sugar**
1 **tablespoon cornstarch**
1 **tablespoon butter**
1 **tablespoon lemon juice**
2 **cups sliced fresh peaches**
1 **cup fresh blueberries**
1 **cup all-purpose flour**
½ **cup sugar**
1½ **teaspoons baking powder**
¼ **cup butter**
½ **cup milk**
2 **tablespoons sugar**
¼ **teaspoon ground nutmeg**

In a medium saucepan combine brown sugar and cornstarch; stir in ½ cup *water.* Cook and stir till thickened and bubbly. Add 1 tablespoon butter and lemon juice. Stir in peaches and blueberries; heat through. Keep warm.

For topper, combine flour, ½ cup sugar, baking powder, and ¼ teaspoon *salt.* Cut in ¼ cup butter. Add milk all at once. Stir just till moistened.

Turn hot fruit mixture into an 8x1½-inch round baking dish. Spoon topper over fruit. Mix 2 tablespoons sugar and the nutmeg; sprinkle over topper. Bake in a 350° oven for 30 to 35 minutes or till done. Makes 6 servings.

Banana Bread Pudding

In the past, bread puddings were an ideal way to use up stale bread. Though freezer storage and the increased shelf life have made stale bread a less abundant commodity, bread puddings still rate as a popular dessert.

If there's no dry bread in the house to make *Banana Bread Pudding,* dry soft bread quickly in the oven. Place the bread slices on an oven rack in a 300° oven. Bake about 5 minutes or till the bread is dry but not brown.

2 **small bananas, sliced**
1 **tablespoon lemon juice**
4 **slices dry white bread**
2 **tablespoons butter *or* margarine, softened**
½ **cup sugar**
1 **teaspoon ground cinnamon**
½ **teaspoon ground nutmeg**
4 **beaten eggs**
2 **cups milk**
1 **teaspoon vanilla**

Toss banana slices with the lemon juice. Spread bread slices with the butter. Cut into ½-inch cubes. Arrange *half* of the bread cubes in a 10x6x2-inch baking dish; top with *half* of the banana slices. Repeat with remaining bread and banana slices.

Combine sugar, cinnamon, and nutmeg; set aside 2 tablespoons for topping. Combine eggs, milk, vanilla, and remaining sugar-spice mixture. Pour over bread and bananas. Sprinkle reserved 2 tablespoons sugar-spice mixture over top.

Place in a larger pan on oven rack. Pour hot water into larger pan to a depth of 1 inch. Bake in a 350° oven 50 to 55 minutes or till knife inserted near center comes out clean. Serve warm or cool. Serves 8.

• **Raisin Bread Pudding:** Prepare Banana Bread Pudding as above, *except* substitute ½ cup *raisins* for the bananas. Omit the lemon juice. Continue as directed.

Coconut Crunch Torte

1 **cup flaked coconut**
½ **cup crushed graham crackers (7 squares) *or* crushed rich round crackers (12)**
⅓ **cup chopped walnuts**
4 **egg whites**
1 **teaspoon vanilla**
1 **cup sugar**
 Frozen whipped dessert topping, thawed, *or* vanilla ice cream

In a small bowl combine coconut, crushed crackers, and walnuts. In a large mixer bowl beat egg whites, vanilla, and ½ teaspoon *salt* till soft peaks form. Add sugar, 1 tablespoon at a time, beating till stiff peaks form. Fold in coconut mixture. Spread in a well-greased 9-inch pie plate.

Bake in a 350° oven for 30 to 35 minutes or till light brown. Cool on wire rack. To serve, cut into wedges; top with whipped topping or ice cream. Garnish with additional nuts if desired. Makes 6 to 8 servings.

Pictured:
Peach Berry Cobbler, Cream Puffs filled with ice cream (see recipe, page 148), and Hard Candy (see recipe, page 151).

Cheesecake

Cheesecakes date back to ancient times when Greeks and Romans served them as festival food.

Americans have always loved *Cheesecake* and its variations. George Washington was no exception. He was so fond of the rich, creamy dessert that Mrs. Washington felt compelled to include several recipes in her cook book.

1½ **cups crushed graham crackers (21 squares)**
6 **tablespoons butter** *or* **margarine, melted**
3 **8-ounce packages cream cheese, softened**
½ **teaspoon finely shredded lemon peel**
½ **teaspoon vanilla**
1 **cup sugar**
2 **tablespoons all-purpose flour**
¼ **teaspoon salt**
2 **eggs**
1 **egg yolk**
¼ **cup milk**
1 **8-ounce carton dairy sour cream**
2 **tablespoons sugar**
1 **teaspoon vanilla**

Stir together crushed crackers and butter or margarine. Press into bottom and about 1½ inches up sides of an 8- or 9-inch springform pan.

In a large mixer bowl beat together softened cream cheese, lemon peel, and the ½ teaspoon vanilla with an electric mixer till fluffy. Stir together the 1 cup sugar, the flour, and salt; gradually beat into cream cheese mixture.

Add the eggs and egg yolk all at once, beating on low speed just till blended. Stir in milk. Turn into prepared crust. Bake in a 450° oven for 10 minutes. Reduce oven temperature to 300°; bake for 50 to 55 minutes more or till the center appears set and a knife inserted near the center comes out clean.

Stir together sour cream, the 2 tablespoons sugar, and the 1 teaspoon vanilla. Spread evenly over hot cheesecake. Return to the 300° oven for 5 minutes. Remove pan from oven. Cool on wire rack about 30 minutes; remove sides of pan. Cool cheesecake, then chill thoroughly. Serves 16.

Cream Puffs   *pictured on page 147*

½ **cup butter** *or* **margarine**
1 **cup water**
1 **cup all-purpose flour**
¼ **teaspoon salt**
4 **eggs**
 Whipped cream, pudding, or ice cream
 Fudge Sauce (see recipe, page 153) (optional)

In a medium saucepan melt butter or margarine. Add water; bring to boiling. Add flour and salt all at once; stir vigorously. Cook and stir till mixture forms a ball that doesn't separate. Remove from heat; cool about 5 minutes.

Add the eggs, one at a time, beating after each addition with a wooden spoon for 1 to 2 minutes or till smooth. Drop batter by heaping tablespoonfuls 3 inches apart onto a greased baking sheet.

Bake in a 400° oven about 30 minutes or till golden brown and puffy. Remove from oven; split, removing any soft dough inside. Cool on a wire rack. Fill with whipped cream, pudding, or ice cream. Top filled cream puffs with Fudge Sauce if desired. Makes about 10.

● **Eclairs:** Prepare dough for Cream Puffs as above. Spoon some of the dough into a pastry tube fitted with a number 10 or larger tip. Slowly pipe strips of dough through the tube onto a greased baking sheet, making each eclair about 4 inches long, ¾ inch wide, and ½ inch high. Bake in a 400° oven for 30 minutes or till golden brown and puffy. Continue as above. Makes 12 to 14.

Lemon Cheesecake Squares

The weaning of America from old-time iceboxes to iceless refrigerators brought a new era of convenient cooking to the kitchen. It made possible refrigerator desserts such as *Lemon Cheesecake Squares* and *Layered Pudding Dessert*, which can be made ahead and chilled until serving time.

2 **cups crushed graham crackers (28 squares)**
6 **tablespoons butter *or* margarine, melted**
1 **3-ounce package lemon-flavored gelatin**
¾ **cup sugar**
1 **8-ounce package cream cheese, softened**
½ **teaspoon finely shredded lemon peel**
2 **tablespoons lemon juice**
1 **teaspoon vanilla**
1 **13-ounce can (1⅔ cups) evaporated milk, chilled icy cold**

Stir together crushed crackers and melted butter or margarine; reserve ⅓ cup of the mixture. Press remaining into the bottom of a 13x9x2-inch baking pan. If desired, bake crust in a 375° oven for 6 to 9 minutes. Cool

Dissolve gelatin in ¾ cup *boiling water*. Chill till syrupy. Meanwhile, in a small mixer bowl gradually beat sugar into cream cheese. Add lemon peel, lemon juice, and vanilla; beat till fluffy. Beat in gelatin mixture.

In a large mixer bowl beat evaporated milk till soft peaks form. Fold cream cheese mixture into whipped milk. Turn mixture into prepared crust. Sprinkle reserved cracker mixture atop. Chill at least 4 hours or overnight. Serves 12 to 16.

Layered Pudding Dessert

½ **cup butter *or* margarine**
1 **cup all-purpose flour**
1 **cup finely chopped peanuts**
1 **8-ounce package cream cheese, softened**
1 **cup sifted powdered sugar**
1 **4-ounce container frozen whipped dessert topping, thawed**
2 **packages 4-serving-size *instant* pistachio pudding mix**
3 **cups milk**
Grated chocolate

Cut butter into flour till mixture resembles coarse crumbs; stir in ¾ *cup* of the peanuts. Press evenly into bottom of a 13x9x2-inch baking dish. Bake in a 350° oven 20 minutes; cool. Chill 30 minutes.

Meanwhile, in a small mixer bowl beat cream cheese with electric mixer on low speed till fluffy; beat in powdered sugar. Fold in *half* of the thawed whipped topping. Spread over crust.

In a mixing bowl combine pudding mixes and milk; beat with rotary beater 2 minutes. Spoon atop cream cheese layer. Chill 5 minutes. Spread remaining whipped topping over all. Top with remaining peanuts and chocolate. Cover; chill. Serves 16.

● **Mocha Layered Dessert:** Prepare Layered Pudding Dessert as above, *except* substitute 2 packages 4-serving-size *instant chocolate fudge pudding mix* for the pistachio pudding mix, and dissolve 2 teaspoons *instant coffee crystals* in the milk. Continue as directed.

Sherbet Cream Squares

1½ **cups finely crushed chocolate wafers (30)**
6 **tablespoons butter *or* margarine, melted**
1 **1½-ounce envelope dessert topping mix**
1 **quart vanilla ice cream**
1 **pint orange sherbet**
3 **tablespoons orange liqueur**

Combine chocolate wafers and melted butter; reserve ¼ cup of the mixture. Press *half* of the remaining mixture into bottom of a 9x9x2-inch pan.

Prepare dessert topping mix according to package directions. In a chilled mixing bowl stir ice cream with wooden spoon just till softened; stir in sherbet and liqueur. Fold in whipped topping. Turn *half* of the ice cream mixture into pan; sprinkle with remaining half of the wafer mixture. Spoon remaining ice cream mixture atop. Sprinkle with reserved ¼ cup wafer mixture. Cover; freeze. Serves 12.

Pumpkin Ginger Freeze *pictured on page 152*

36 gingersnaps
1 16-ounce can pumpkin
½ cup sugar
1 teaspoon ground ginger
1 teaspoon ground cinnamon
¼ teaspoon ground nutmeg
1 cup chopped pecans, toasted
½ gallon vanilla ice cream
1 8-ounce container frozen whipped dessert topping, thawed

In the bottom of a 13x9x2-inch pan arrange *half* of the gingersnaps; set aside. In a mixing bowl stir together pumpkin, sugar, ginger, cinnamon, and nutmeg. Stir in ¾ *cup* of the pecans.

In a chilled large mixing bowl stir ice cream with a wooden spoon just till softened. Quickly fold in pumpkin mixture. Spoon *half* of the ice cream mixture over gingersnaps in pan. Cover with remaining gingersnaps; top with remaining ice cream mixture. Spread whipped topping over ice cream mixture. Cover; freeze at least 5 hours. To serve, cut into squares; garnish with remaining pecans. Serves 16.

Any-Fruit Sherbet

Although sherbets can be served as an appetizer or to cleanse the palate between courses, they are usually reserved for dessert. Because it is light and tart, *Any-Fruit Sherbet* is especially refreshing after a hearty or spicy meal.

½ to ¾ cup sugar
1 envelope unflavored gelatin
Dash salt
½ cup water
2 cups Fresh Fruit Puree
1 13-ounce can (1⅔ cups) evaporated milk
2 egg whites
¼ cup sugar

In a saucepan combine the ½ to ¾ cup sugar (depending on sweetness of fruit), gelatin, and salt. Add water; heat and stir till gelatin dissolves. Stir in desired Fresh Fruit Puree and evaporated milk. Turn into a 9x9x2-inch pan. Cover; freeze firm.

In a small mixer bowl beat egg whites till soft peaks form. Gradually add the ¼ cup sugar, beating till stiff peaks form. Break frozen mixture into chunks; turn into a chilled large mixer bowl. Beat with electric mixer till fluffy. Fold in whites. Return to pan. Cover; freeze firm. If necessary, let stand a few minutes before serving. Makes 1½ quarts.

Fresh Fruit Puree: In blender container or food processor bowl place 3 to 4 cups of one or a combination of the following: peeled and cut *apricots, avocados, bananas, kiwi, melons, nectarines, papayas, peaches, pears, pineapple, or plums;* pitted dark sweet *cherries; or berries.* Cover and blend to make 2 cups puree.

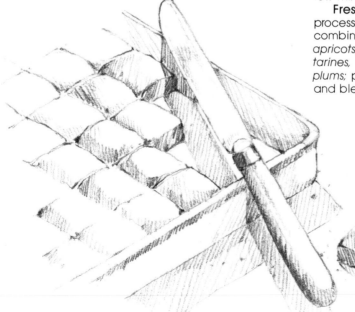

Four-Fruit Freeze

1 **cup mashed bananas (2 medium)**
1 **8-ounce can crushed pineapple (juice pack)**
½ **teaspoon finely shredded orange peel**
⅓ **cup orange juice**
¼ **cup sugar**
1 **tablespoon lemon juice**

In a mixing bowl combine mashed bananas, *undrained* crushed pineapple, orange peel, orange juice, sugar, and lemon juice; stir to mix thoroughly. Turn mixture into a small loaf pan; cover and freeze 6 hours or overnight. Let stand at room temperature 5 to 10 minutes before serving. Spoon into sherbet dishes. Makes 6 servings.

Hard Candy   *pictured on page 147*

To make both red and green *Hard Candy,* make two batches, one using red food coloring and oil of cinnamon, and another using green food coloring and oil of wintergreen.

Homemade *Hard Candy* is great for gift-giving. Pack the candies in decorative tins or boxes for an extra special touch.

2 **cups sugar**
½ **cup water**
½ **cup light corn syrup**
Dash salt
Few drops red *or* **green food coloring**
6 **to 8 drops oil of cinnamon** *or* **oil of wintergreen**

In a heavy 1-quart saucepan combine the sugar, water, corn syrup, and salt. Cook and stir till sugar dissolves and mixture boils. Cook, without stirring, over medium heat till candy thermometer registers 290° (soft-crack stage). Mixture should boil gently over entire surface.

Stir in food coloring and oil of cinnamon or wintergreen. (Use red coloring with cinnamon and green with wintergreen.) Pour into a buttered 8x8x2-inch baking pan. Let stand at room temperature a few minutes or till a film forms over top.

With knife, press a line across candy ¾ inch from edge without breaking through film on surface. Repeat around other 3 sides of pan, intersecting lines at corners to form squares. (If lines do not hold shape, candy is not cool enough.) Continue marking lines ¾ inch apart toward center. While waiting for the center to cool enough, retrace lines, pressing deeper but not breaking film. Cool. Turn out; break into pieces. Makes 100.

Easy Walnut Toffee

If a candy thermometer is not available, use the cold water test to determine when to stop cooking the candy.

To test for the soft-crack stage, remove saucepan from heat. Drop a little hot syrup into very cold water. The syrup should separate into threads that are not brittle. If this stage has not been reached, return saucepan to heat and retest every 2 to 3 minutes.

½ **cup butter** *or* **margarine**
¾ **cup packed brown sugar**
½ **cup semisweet chocolate pieces**
½ **cup chopped walnuts**

In a 1½-quart saucepan melt butter or margarine. Add brown sugar. Cook, stirring often, over medium heat till candy thermometer registers 290° (soft-crack stage). Remove from heat and spread mixture into a buttered 8x8x2-inch pan. Let stand at room temperature 3 minutes to firm surface. Sprinkle chocolate pieces atop toffee. Let stand for 1 to 2 minutes.

When chocolate is softened, spread evenly over toffee; sprinkle walnuts atop. Refrigerate about 45 minutes or till thoroughly chilled. To serve, break into pieces. Makes about 1 pound.

Caramel-Chocolate Fondue

1 14-ounce can Eagle Brand
   sweetened condensed milk
1 12-ounce jar caramel topping
1 6-ounce package (1 cup)
   semisweet chocolate pieces
   Apples, strawberries, *or*
   bananas, cut into
   bite-sized pieces

In a medium saucepan combine sweetened condensed milk, caramel topping, and chocolate pieces. Cook and stir over low heat till chocolate is melted. Transfer to fondue pot; place over fondue burner. To serve, dip bite-sized fruit in sauce. Makes 3 cups.

Fudge Sauce

Americans love a dish of plain ice cream. But who can resist their favorite homemade sauce ladled on top? Given here are some of America's favorites.

¾ cup sugar
3 tablespoons unsweetened
   cocoa powder
1 13-ounce can (1⅔ cups)
   evaporated milk
1 teaspoon vanilla

In a medium saucepan stir together sugar and cocoa. Add evaporated milk; stir to blend. Bring to a full rolling boil, stirring constantly. Boil 8 to 10 minutes, stirring frequently. Remove from heat; stir in vanilla. Serve warm or cool. Makes 1½ cups.

Honey Fruit Sauce

¼ cup orange juice
2 tablespoons honey
2 tablespoons orange liqueur
2 teaspoons cornstarch
1 8¼-ounce can crushed
   pineapple
2 oranges, peeled and
   sectioned
1 cup pitted tart red cherries
   or pitted dark sweet
   cherries
¼ cup flaked coconut (optional)

In a medium saucepan stir together orange juice, honey, orange liqueur, and cornstarch. Drain pineapple, reserving syrup. Add reserved syrup to orange juice mixture in saucepan. Cook and stir till mixture is thickened and bubbly. Cook and stir 2 minutes more.

To saucepan add pineapple, orange sections, cherries, and flaked coconut if desired. Cook till heated through. Serve warm over ice cream or cake slices. Makes about 2½ cups.

Caramel Pecan Sauce

Pictured clockwise:
Fudge Sauce, Honey Fruit Sauce, Caramel Pecan Sauce, and Pumpkin Ginger Freeze (see recipe, page 150).

¼ cup packed brown sugar
1 tablespoon cornstarch
¼ teaspoon salt
⅓ cup light cream
2 tablespoons light corn syrup
¼ cup coarsely chopped pecans
1 tablespoon butter *or*
   margarine
1 tablespoon rum *or* brandy

In a heavy saucepan stir together brown sugar, cornstarch, and salt. Stir in ¼ cup *water*. Stir in light cream and corn syrup. Cook, stirring constantly, till thickened and bubbly (mixture may appear curdled during cooking). Stir in the coarsely chopped pecans, the butter or margarine, and rum or brandy. Remove from heat. Cover; cool to room temperature. Serve over ice cream. Makes about 1 cup.

Shrimp Cocktail *pictured on page 157*

A hundred years ago, shrimp were available only to those Americans who lived near the Gulf and Pacific coasts. Now, modern methods of freezing both raw and cooked shrimp have made it possible for Americans in every state to enjoy seafood specialties like *Shrimp Cocktail.*

When cooking shrimp, keep in mind that overcooking shrinks and toughens them. The secret to perfectly cooked shrimp is cooking just till the shrimp become firm and turn pink.

1 pound fresh *or* frozen shelled shrimp, cooked, drained, and chilled
Lettuce
Seafood Cocktail Sauce (see recipe below)
Lemon wedges

Arrange cooked and chilled shrimp in lettuce-lined cocktail cups or glasses. Spoon some Seafood Cocktail Sauce into *each* cup or glass. Garnish with lemon wedges. Makes 4 servings.

Seafood Cocktail Sauce

¾ cup chili sauce
2 tablespoons lemon juice
1 tablespoon prepared horseradish
2 teaspoons Worcestershire sauce
½ teaspoon finely chopped onion
Few dashes bottled hot pepper sauce

In a small bowl stir together the chili sauce, lemon juice, horseradish, Worcestershire sauce, onion, and hot pepper sauce. Mix well; cover and refrigerate for several hours. Serve with fish or seafood. Makes about 1 cup.

Piquant Deviled Eggs

6 hard-cooked eggs
¼ cup mayonnaise *or* salad dressing
5 small pimiento-stuffed olives, finely chopped
2 tablespoons finely chopped dill pickle
1 teaspoon prepared mustard
Paprika (optional)

Halve hard-cooked eggs lengthwise; remove yolks. Mash yolks with a fork. Stir in mayonnaise or salad dressing, chopped olives, chopped dill pickle, and mustard. Stuff egg whites with yolk mixture. Chill. Sprinkle with paprika if desired. Makes 12 servings.

Cocktail Meatballs in Barbecue Sauce

1 beaten egg
¼ cup milk
1 cup soft bread crumbs
2 tablespoons finely chopped onion
1 pound ground beef
1 12-ounce bottle chili sauce
2 tablespoons vinegar
1 tablespoon brown sugar
½ teaspoon celery seed
Several dashes bottled hot pepper sauce
¼ cup water
2 teaspoons cornstarch

In a mixing bowl combine egg and milk; stir in bread crumbs, onion, and ½ teaspoon *salt.* Add ground beef; mix well. Shape into ¾-inch meatballs. Place in a 15x10x1-inch baking pan. Bake meatballs in a 375° oven about 20 minutes or till done. Drain off fat.

Meanwhile, in a large saucepan combine chili sauce, vinegar, brown sugar, celery seed, and hot pepper sauce; heat to boiling. Combine water and cornstarch; stir into chili sauce mixture. Cook and stir till thickened and bubbly. Cook and stir 2 minutes more. Add meatballs; heat through. Serve warm with wooden picks. Makes about 36.

Pigs in a Blanket

In some older cook books, hors d'oeuvres called *Pigs in a Blanket* were oysters wrapped in bacon strips and broiled. The more recent use of the phrase refers to miniature biscuit-wrapped franks or sausages commonly served with a catsup-based dipping sauce.

Serve *Pigs in a Blanket* with one or more of the dipping sauces. Refrigerate any leftover sauce and use as a zesty topping for hamburgers or franks.

 1 **package (10) refrigerated biscuits**
20 **cocktail wieners** *or* **small smoked sausage links**
   Cocktail Dipping Sauce, Onion-Mustard Sauce, *or* **Horseradish Sauce**

Cut biscuits in half crosswise. Flatten each half into a 2-inch circle. Wrap each around a wiener or sausage link. Place, seam side down, on a greased baking sheet. Bake in a 400° oven for 8 to 10 minutes or till biscuits are golden. Serve warm with desired dipping sauce. Makes 20 appetizers.

Cocktail Dipping Sauce: In a small saucepan combine ½ cup *catsup*, 2 teaspoons *brown sugar*, ½ teaspoon *dry mustard*, and a dash *bottled hot pepper sauce*. Heat and stir till warm. Makes ½ cup.

Onion-Mustard Sauce: Combine 2 tablespoons *milk* and 4 teaspoons *regular onion soup mix*; let stand 5 minutes. Stir onion soup mixture and 1 tablespoon *prepared mustard* into ½ cup *dairy sour cream*. Serve warm or chilled. (To serve warm, heat through but *do not boil.*) Makes ⅔ cup.

Horseradish Sauce: Stir together one 4-ounce container *whipped cream cheese*, 2 tablespoons *prepared horseradish*, 2 tablespoons *milk*, and ¼ teaspoon *paprika*. Serve chilled. Makes ¾ cup.

Braunschweiger Ball

1 **pound braunschweiger** *or* **liverwurst, broken up**
1 **8-ounce package cream cheese, softened**
2 **tablespoons milk**
1 **tablespoon grated onion**
1 **teaspoon chili powder**
¼ **teaspoon garlic salt**
1 **tablespoon milk**
  Few dashes bottled hot pepper sauce
  Assorted crackers

In a small mixer bowl beat together braunschweiger or liverwurst, *half* of the cream cheese, the 2 tablespoons milk, grated onion, chili powder, and garlic salt till smooth. Chill slightly.

Shape braunschweiger mixture into a ball; place on serving plate. Beat together the remaining cream cheese, the 1 tablespoon milk, and the hot pepper sauce. Spread over braunschweiger mixture; refrigerate till firm. Sprinkle with snipped parsley if desired. Serve with crackers. Makes 1.

Four-Cheese Ball

1 **cup shredded Swiss cheese**
1 **cup shredded American cheese**
1 **3-ounce package cream cheese**
¼ **cup mayonnaise**
2 **tablespoons chopped pimiento**
1 **teaspoon Worcestershire sauce**
½ **teaspoon onion powder**
¼ **teaspoon bottled hot pepper sauce**
½ **cup crushed potato chips**
1½ **teaspoons grated Parmesan cheese**
  Assorted crackers *or* **fresh fruit**

Bring cheeses to room temperature. In a small mixer bowl beat together cream cheese and mayonnaise; beat in Swiss cheese and American cheese. Add pimiento, Worcestershire sauce, onion powder, and hot pepper sauce. Chill slightly. Shape into a ball. Combine potato chips and Parmesan cheese; press over outside of ball. Chill till firm. Serve with crackers or fruit. Makes 1.

Salmon Party Spread

For an eye-catching appetizer, mold *Salmon Party Spread* into decorative shapes, as pictured at right. After mixing, turn the salmon spread into a 2½-cup mold or several smaller molds. Cover and refrigerate for 6 hours or overnight. Unmold onto a serving platter and garnish with fresh dill or the nut-parsley mixture in the recipe.

1 15½-ounce can salmon, drained
1 8-ounce package cream cheese, softened
1 tablespoon lemon juice
1 teaspoon grated onion
1 teaspoon prepared horseradish
½ cup chopped pecans
2 tablespoons snipped parsley
   Assorted crackers

Flake salmon, discarding skin and bones. In a mixing bowl stir together cream cheese, lemon juice, grated onion, and horseradish. Add salmon; mix well. Chill thoroughly. Form salmon mixture into an 8-inch-long log. Combine pecans and parsley; roll log in nut mixture. Chill. Serve with assorted crackers. Makes 1.

Herb Curry Dip

1 cup mayonnaise
1 cup dairy sour cream
1 tablespoon snipped parsley
2 teaspoons lemon juice
1 to 1½ teaspoons curry powder
¾ teaspoon dried basil, crushed
½ teaspoon dried oregano. crushed
½ teaspoon dried thyme, crushed
½ teaspoon Worcestershire sauce
   Assorted fresh vegetable dippers or potato chips

In a mixing bowl combine mayonnaise, sour cream, parsley, lemon juice, curry powder, basil, oregano, thyme, and Worcestershire sauce; mix thoroughly. Cover; refrigerate till serving time. Serve with fresh vegetable dippers or potato chips. Makes 2 cups.

Spiced Granola

Though granola was developed as a breakfast cereal, creative nibblers also enjoy it sprinkled on peanut butter sandwiches, yogurt, ice cream, or just as a crunchy snack.

Honey-sweetened *Spiced Granola* is accented with just enough allspice to let you know it's there.

2 cups quick-cooking rolled oats
⅔ cup shredded coconut
½ cup wheat germ
½ cup peanut halves
¼ cup cooking oil
¼ cup honey
¼ teaspoon ground allspice
1 cup raisins

In a large bowl combine the oats, coconut, wheat germ, and peanuts. Combine oil, honey, allspice, and ¼ cup *water.* Pour honey mixture over oat mixture; toss to coat well.

Spread mixture in 2 ungreased 15x10x1-inch baking pans. Bake in a 300° oven about 25 minutes or till light brown, stirring once. Cool slightly in pans on wire racks. Add raisins. Cool. Store in a tightly covered container. Makes 4½ cups.

Cereal Party Snack

2 cups small pretzels
2 cups corn puff cereal
1 3-ounce can chow mein noodles
⅓ cup butter, melted
1 tablespoon Worcestershire sauce
⅛ teaspoon onion powder
⅛ teaspoon garlic powder

In a 13x9x2-inch baking pan combine pretzels, cereal, and noodles. Combine butter, Worcestershire, onion powder, and garlic powder; drizzle over cereal mixture, tossing to coat well. Bake in a 300° oven 45 minutes; stir twice. Makes 6½ cups.

Pictured clockwise:
Shrimp Cocktail (see recipe, page 154), Salmon Party Spread, Herb Curry Dip, and Cereal Party Snack.

Hot Chocolate

1 **cup water**
⅓ **cup sugar**
2 **squares (2 ounces) unsweetened chocolate**
  Dash salt
4 **cups milk**
  **Whipped cream *or*
marshmallows (optional)**

In a saucepan combine water, sugar, chocolate, and salt. Cook and stir over medium-low heat till chocolate melts. Gradually stir in milk; heat just till boiling. *Do not boil.* Remove from heat; beat with a rotary beater till frothy. Serve in cups or mugs. Top with a dollop of whipped cream or a few marshmallows if desired. Makes 6 (6-ounce) servings.

Vanilla Milk Shake   *chocolate variation pictured on pages 96 and 161*

Though the electric blender performs numerous chopping and mixing tasks in the kitchen, it was introduced in 1938 solely as a beverage maker. The swift action of the blender blades makes shakes, malts, and nogs with a creamy, smooth consistency.

1 **cup milk**
1 **pint vanilla ice cream
(2 cups)**

Place milk in a blender container; add ice cream. Cover; blend till smooth. Pour into glasses. Serve immediately. Makes 2 (8-ounce) servings.
  • **Chocolate Milk Shake:** Prepare Vanilla Milk Shake as above, *except* add ¼ cup *chocolate-flavored syrup* with the milk.
  • **Strawberry Milk Shake:** Prepare Vanilla Milk Shake as above, *except* add one 10-ounce package frozen *strawberries or raspberries,* broken up, with the milk.
  Recipe note: For a malted milk shake, prepare any of the shake recipes as above, *except* add 2 tablespoons *instant malted milk powder* with the milk.

Fruit Nog Pick-Me-Up

1 **8-ounce carton flavored
yogurt (any flavor)**
1 **cup milk**
1 **cup fresh *or* frozen unsweetened blueberries,
raspberries, strawberries,
or peach slices**
1 **egg**
2 **teaspoons sugar (optional)**
¼ **teaspoon vanilla *or*
almond extract**
2 **to 3 ice cubes**

In a blender container place yogurt, milk, fruit, egg, sugar if desired, and vanilla or almond extract; cover and blend at high speed till mixture is frothy.
  Add ice cubes, one at a time, through hole in lid of blender or with lid ajar, blending till smooth after each addition. Pour into glasses; garnish with fruit if desired. Serve immediately. Makes 4 (6-ounce) servings.

Sherbet-Soda Punch

1 **46-ounce can pineapple-
orange juice, chilled**
1 **28-ounce bottle ginger ale,
chilled**
1 **pint orange sherbet, lemon
sherbet, *or* vanilla
ice cream**

For each serving, pour ½ *cup* of the pineapple-orange juice in a 10-ounce glass; add about ¼ *cup* of the ginger ale and stir gently. Top each with a scoop of sherbet or ice cream. Makes 12 (10-ounce) servings.

Tomato Sipper

Serve mildly herbed *Tomato Sipper* as a light appetizer or as an any-time refreshing beverage.

This drink also can be served hot. Simply stir together in a medium saucepan all the ingredients except the celery stalks and heat through. Serve the hot *Tomato Sipper* in mugs and garnish with lemon slices instead of the celery stalks.

1 **teaspoon instant chicken bouillon granules**
1 **cup boiling water**
3 **cups tomato juice**
2 **tablespoons lemon juice**
1 **teaspoon sugar**
1 **teaspoon Worcestershire sauce**
  Dash celery seed
¼ **teaspoon dried basil, crushed**
8 **stalks celery with leaves**

Dissolve bouillon granules in the boiling water. In a pitcher combine tomato juice, lemon juice, sugar, Worcestershire sauce, celery seed, basil, and bouillon mixture. Cover and chill. To serve, pour into glasses. Garnish each serving with a stalk of celery. Makes 8 (4-ounce) servings.

Berry Punch   *pictured on page 161*

1 **3-ounce package strawberry- or raspberry-flavored gelatin**
½ **cup sugar**
2 **cups boiling water**
2½ **cups cold water**
1 **10-ounce package frozen strawberries or raspberries**
1 **6-ounce can frozen lemonade concentrate**
  Ice cubes
1 **28-ounce bottle lemon-lime carbonated beverage, chilled**
  Orange, lemon, and lime slices (optional)

Stir together gelatin and sugar. Add the 2 cups boiling water; stir till gelatin is dissolved. Stir in the 2½ cups cold water, frozen strawberries or raspberries, and frozen lemonade concentrate; stir till berries and concentrate are thawed. Pour mixture over ice cubes in punch bowl. Gently stir in the lemon-lime carbonated beverage. Float orange, lemon, and lime slices in the punch if desired. Makes 20 (4-ounce) servings.

Spiced Sun Tea

Solar energy aids the steeping process in *Spiced Sun Tea*. But you don't need the sun to brew sun tea. To make the tea without the sun, simply prepare as directed, except let it stand at room temperature till of desired strength.

3 **quarts cold water**
3 **inches stick cinnamon**
1 **teaspoon whole cloves**
8 **tea bags**

Pour the water into a 4-quart jar. For spice bag, place cinnamon and cloves in cheesecloth and tie. Add spice bag and tea bags to jar. (Use more tea bags if stronger tea is desired.) Cover; let stand in full sun about 8 hours or till of desired strength. Remove spice bag and tea bags. Cover; refrigerate. Makes 3 quarts.

Recipe note: To make Spiced Sun Tea in two 2-quart jars, divide spices evenly between 2 cheesecloth bags. Add 1½ quarts cold water, 1 spice bag, and 4 tea bags to each jar.

Frozen Daiquiri

1 **6-ounce can frozen limeade concentrate**
1 **6-ounce can frozen lemonade concentrate**
1 **juice can (¾ cup) light rum**
1 **juice can (¾ cup) water**
1 **16-ounce bottle lemon-lime carbonated beverage**
Lime slices (optional)

Combine limeade concentrate, lemonade concentrate, rum, and water; gently stir in carbonated beverage. Pour into a 9x9x2-inch pan. Freeze till firm. To serve, spoon mixture into cocktail glasses. If desired, garnish each serving with a lime slice. Store remaining mixture in a covered container in the freezer. Makes 4 (10-ounce) servings.

Wine Spritzer

Spruce up a *Wine Spritzer* by serving it over ice cubes that have a small piece of fruit frozen in the center. To make fruited ice cubes, place a small strawberry or lemon twist in each compartment of an ice cube tray. Add water and freeze into cubes.

Lemon twist
Ice cubes
4 **ounces dry white *or* dry red wine, chilled (½ cup)**
2 **ounces carbonated water, chilled (¼ cup)**

In a tall glass place the lemon twist. Fill the glass with ice cubes. Pour in the chilled dry white or dry red wine. Gently stir in the chilled carbonated water. Makes 1 (6-ounce) serving.

Hot Spiced Wine

4 **to 6 inches stick cinnamon, broken**
1 **teaspoon whole cloves**
1 **medium orange, halved**
2 **lemon slices**
1 **1.06-liter bottle dry white wine**
¼ **cup sugar**

For spice bag, place cinnamon and cloves in cheesecloth and tie. In a large saucepan combine orange halves, lemon slices, wine, sugar, and spice bag. Bring mixture almost to boiling; reduce heat. Cover and simmer 15 minutes. Remove orange, lemon, and spice bag. Serve hot. Makes 8 (4-ounce) servings.

Dessert Coffee

½ **cup hot strong coffee**
Desired coffee flavoring (see choices below)
Whipped cream
Ground cinnamon *or* ground nutmeg

In a coffee cup or mug combine hot coffee and desired flavoring. Dollop with whipped cream; sprinkle with spice. Makes 1 (6-ounce) serving.
 • **Café Israel:** Stir 2 tablespoons *chocolate-flavored syrup* and 2 tablespoons *orange liqueur* into coffee.
 • **Café Columbian:** Stir 2 tablespoons *coffee liqueur* and 1 tablespoon *chocolate-flavored syrup* into coffee.
 • **Irish Coffee:** Stir 1 tablespoon *Irish whiskey* and 2 teaspoons *sugar* into coffee.
 • **Café Almond:** Stir 2 tablespoons *Amaretto* into coffee.

Pictured clockwise from front:
Chocolate Milk Shake (see recipe, page 158), Wine Spritzer, Berry Punch (see recipe, page 159), Dessert Coffee, and Frozen Daiquiri.

AMERICA CELEBRATES

American celebrations are times of tradition. Family and friends congregate to share a meal and good times.

Food is noteworthy during these occasions and often reflects national favorites or family customs. The recipes that follow are a selection of these holiday foods.

Thanksgiving is an American holiday observed on the fourth Thursday of November. Many families celebrate with such food as roast turkey and stuffing, cranberry sauce, and pumpkin pie.

This holiday marks the time of the first Thanksgiving when Pilgrims and Indians

gathered to give thanks for surviving a horrendous winter. In 1863, President Abraham Lincoln proclaimed it a national holiday.

A festive mood continues into the Christmas and New Year's holidays. Parties often precede this season with food and drink complementing the holiday merrymaking. Ethnic specialties are an important part of our traditional holiday foods.

Spring and summer bring the celebrations for Easter, Memorial Day, weddings, graduations, and the Fourth of July. Because many of these occasions fall during warm weather, they are often celebrated with outdoor parties, backyard barbecues, picnics, fried chicken, ice cream, and cold drinks.

Fall holds its own special occasions. It's a time for state fairs, harvest festivals, and Halloween. Frankfurters are just one of the familiar foods that appear at fall

fairs and festivals. As evening temperatures gradually become more brisk, steaming hot drinks and fall foods abound.

Recipes pictured: *Buttermilk Doughnuts* (see recipe, page 182); *Lemonade, Strawberry Shortcake,* and *Roasted Corn on the Cob* (see recipes, page 180); and *Basic Grilled Burgers* (see recipe, page 177).

Roast Turkey with Stuffing *pictured on page 167*

If Ben Franklin had had his way, the turkey would be our national emblem instead of the eagle. Franklin considered the eagle "a bird of bad moral character" and the turkey "a much more respectable bird . . . a true native of America." Wild turkeys were abundant when the Pilgrims arrived and most likely were served at the first Thanksgiving. Today, roast turkey is the main attraction at many holiday dinners.

1 **10-pound turkey**
  Sage Stuffing, Oyster Stuffing,
  ***or* Chestnut Stuffing**
  (see recipes below) *or*
  Corn Bread Sausage Stuffing
  (see recipe, page 165)
  Cooking oil
  Fresh fruit (optional)

Rinse turkey and pat dry with paper toweling. Rub inside of cavities with salt, if desired. Spoon some of the desired stuffing loosely into neck cavity; pull the neck skin to the back of the turkey and fasten securely with a small skewer. Lightly spoon remaining stuffing into body cavity. If opening has a band of skin across tail, tuck drumsticks under band; if not, use string to tie legs securely to tail. Twist wing tips under back.

Place turkey, breast side up, on a rack in a shallow roasting pan. Brush skin of turkey with cooking oil. Insert a meat thermometer in center of inside thigh muscle, making sure the bulb of the thermometer does not touch bone.

Roast, uncovered, in a 325° oven for 4 to 4½ hours or till meat thermometer registers 185° and drumstick moves easily in socket. When turkey is two-thirds done, cut band of skin or string between legs so thighs will cook evenly. Let stand 15 minutes before carving. Serve on a platter garnished with fresh fruit if desired. Makes 10 to 12 servings.

Sage Stuffing

Bread stuffings always have been an American favorite. New Englanders boast *Oyster Stuffing* and Southerners are partial to *Corn Bread Sausage Stuffing. Sage Stuffing* is popular nationwide.

The origin of *Chestnut Stuffing* is unknown, but historians say it was a holiday tradition served at George Washington's table.

1 **cup finely chopped celery**
1 **medium onion, chopped**
  (½ cup)
½ **cup butter *or* margarine**
1 **teaspoon poultry seasoning**
  ***or* ground sage**
½ **teaspoon salt**
⅛ **teaspoon pepper**
8 **cups dry bread cubes**
¾ **to 1 cup chicken broth *or***
  water

In a saucepan cook celery and onion in butter or margarine till tender but not brown. Remove from heat; stir in poultry seasoning or sage, salt, and pepper. Place the dry bread cubes in a large mixing bowl. Add the celery mixture. Drizzle with enough broth or water to moisten, tossing lightly. Use to stuff one 10-pound turkey. Serves 10 to 12.

● **Oyster Stuffing:** Prepare Sage Stuffing as directed above, *except* add 1 pint shucked *oysters*, drained and chopped, *or* two 8-ounce cans whole *oysters*, drained and chopped, with the seasonings. Reserve the drained oyster liquid if desired, and substitute it for part of the chicken broth or water. Continue as directed above.

● **Chestnut Stuffing:** Prepare Sage Stuffing as directed above, *except* add 1 pound fresh *chestnuts*, roasted and coarsely chopped, *or* 12 ounces canned unsweetened *chestnuts*, coarsely chopped, with the seasonings. (To roast the fresh chestnuts, use a sharp knife to slash an X into each chestnut. Place on a baking sheet; bake in a 400° oven for 15 minutes. Cool and peel.) Continue as directed above.

Corn Bread Sausage Stuffing *pictured on page 167*

1 **cup all-purpose flour**
1 **cup yellow cornmeal**
¼ **cup sugar**
4 **teaspoons baking powder**
½ **teaspoon salt**
2 **slightly beaten eggs**
1 **cup milk**
¼ **cup bacon drippings *or* cooking oil**
1 **pound bulk pork sausage**
1 **medium onion, chopped (½ cup)**
½ **cup chopped green pepper**
½ **cup chopped celery**
¼ **cup snipped parsley**
2 **teaspoons poultry seasoning**
1 **to 1¼ cups chicken broth *or* water**

For corn bread, stir together flour, cornmeal, sugar, baking powder, and salt. Combine eggs, milk, and bacon drippings or cooking oil. Add to dry mixture; stir just till combined. Turn mixture into a greased 9x9x2-inch baking pan. Bake in a 425° oven for 20 to 25 minutes. Cool. Crumble enough corn bread to make 6 cups.

In a skillet cook sausage, onion, green pepper, and celery till sausage is brown and vegetables are tender. Drain off fat. In a mixing bowl combine corn bread crumbs, parsley, poultry seasoning, and sausage mixture. Add enough of the chicken broth or water to moisten. Toss lightly to mix. Use to stuff one 10-pound turkey. (Any stuffing that does not fit in bird can be baked in a small casserole, covered, in a 325° oven about 30 minutes.) Makes 16 servings.

Scalloped Corn

Corn was a vital staple of the American settlers' diet. When times were hard, it was common for them to eat some form of corn three times a day, either fresh, dried, or ground into cornmeal.

1 **beaten egg**
1 **cup milk**
1 **cup coarsely crushed saltine crackers (22 crackers)**
1 **17-ounce can cream-style corn**
¼ **cup finely chopped onion**
3 **tablespoons chopped pimiento**
1 **tablespoon butter *or* margarine, melted**

Combine egg, milk, ⅔ *cup* of the crushed crackers, ¼ teaspoon *salt*, and dash *pepper*. Stir in corn, onion, and pimiento; mix well. Turn into a 1-quart casserole. Toss melted butter or margarine with the remaining crushed crackers; sprinkle atop corn mixture. Bake, uncovered, in a 350° oven about 1 hour or till a knife inserted near center comes out clean. Makes 6 servings.

Candied Sweet Potatoes

Americans have combined cooked sweet potatoes, brown sugar, and marshmallow since before the Revolutionary War.

Yams are a common substitute for sweet potatoes. Actually yams are a variety of sweet potato with copper skin and orange flesh.

8 **medium sweet potatoes**
⅓ **cup packed brown sugar**
¼ **cup butter *or* margarine**
½ **teaspoon salt**
¾ **cup tiny marshmallows**

Scrub potatoes; cut off woody portions and ends. Cook, covered, in enough boiling salted water to cover for 30 to 35 minutes or just till tender. Drain, peel, and cut into slices ½ inch thick.

In a 1½-quart casserole layer *half each* of the potatoes, brown sugar, butter, and salt. Repeat layering. Bake, uncovered, in a 375° oven for 30 to 40 minutes or till glazed. Sprinkle marshmallows atop. Bake about 5 minutes more or till light brown. Makes 6 servings.

● **Skillet Candied Sweet Potatoes:** Use ingredients for Candied Sweet Potatoes as listed above, *except* omit the marshmallows. Cook and slice potatoes as above. Melt butter in a 12-inch skillet. Stir in brown sugar, salt, and ¼ cup *water.* Add potatoes. Cook, uncovered, over medium heat for 10 to 15 minutes or till glazed, basting and turning gently 2 to 3 times.

Cranberry Sauce

"Craneberries," as the first American settlers called them, were named for their pale pink blossoms resembling the head and neck of a crane. Coincidentally, cranes were often seen eating the fruit while wading in the marshy bogs where the berries grew.

The best ripeness test for cranberries is their ability to bounce. Judging ripeness by color can be tricky because varieties differ in their degree of redness.

1½ **cups sugar**
1¼ **cups water**
1 **12-ounce package (3 cups) cranberries**

In a large saucepan combine sugar and water. Bring to boiling, stirring constantly. Boil, uncovered, 3 minutes. Add cranberries; return to boiling. Cook over high heat 8 minutes or till skins pop. Serve warm or chilled. (For molded sauce, after mixture returns to boiling, cook 10 minutes or till drop of sauce gels on cold plate. Turn into 3-cup mold. Chill till firm. Unmold.) Makes 2½ cups.

Cranberry Relish

2 **medium oranges**
4 **cups fresh cranberries (1 pound)**
2 **cups sugar**
¼ **cup finely chopped walnuts**

With vegetable peeler, remove orange portion of the peel of *one* orange; set aside. Completely peel and section both oranges. Using a food grinder with coarse blade or food processor with steel blade, grind reserved peel, orange sections, and cranberries. Stir in sugar and walnuts. Cover and refrigerate till chilled. Makes 3½ cups.

Creamed Onions

24 **whole pearl onions, peeled (1 pound),** *or* **3 medium onions, cut into wedges**
3 **tablespoons butter**
3 **tablespoons all-purpose flour Dash ground nutmeg**
1½ **cups light cream** *or* **milk**
2 **tablespoons snipped parsley**

In a covered saucepan cook onions in boiling salted water for 8 to 10 minutes or till tender. Drain well and set aside. In a saucepan melt butter; stir in flour, nutmeg, ½ teaspoon *salt,* and dash *pepper.* Add cream or milk all at once. Cook and stir till thickened and bubbly. Cook and stir 1 minute more. Stir in onions and parsley; heat through. Makes 6 to 8 servings.

Pumpkin Pie

Pumpkin Pie was inspired by the abundance of pumpkin and the colonists' memories of English custard pie. Molasses sweetened the first pumpkin pies, but refined sugar is more popular today.

Pastry for Single-Crust Pie (see recipe, page 141)
1 **16-ounce can pumpkin**
¾ **cup sugar**
1 **teaspoon ground cinnamon**
½ **teaspoon ground ginger**
½ **teaspoon ground nutmeg**
3 **eggs**
1 **5⅓-ounce can (⅔ cup) evaporated milk**
½ **cup milk Whipped cream (optional) Chopped nuts (optional)**

Prepare and roll out pastry. Line a 9-inch pie plate. Trim pastry to 1 inch beyond plate edge. Fold under, forming stand-up rim. Snip at ¼-inch intervals. Press snipped pastry strips to rim in opposite directions. Combine pumpkin, sugar, spices, and ½ teaspoon *salt.* With fork, beat in eggs. Add evaporated milk and milk; mix well.

Place pie shell on oven rack; pour in pumpkin mixture. Cover pie edge with foil. Bake in a 375° oven 25 minutes; remove foil. Bake 25 to 30 minutes more or till knife inserted near center comes out clean. Cool. Top with whipped cream and nuts, if desired. Cover; chill to store. Serves 8.

Pictured clockwise:
Roast Turkey with Corn Bread Sausage Stuffing (see recipes, pages 164 and 165), Cranberry Relish, and Pumpkin Pie.

Roast Beef with Yorkshire Pudding

Yorkshire Pudding originally was baked in a dripping pan beneath the roast. The juices that fell from the roast seasoned the pudding as it baked to a golden puff below.

1 **4-pound beef rib roast**
4 **eggs**
2 **cups milk**
2 **cups all-purpose flour**
1 **teaspoon salt**

Place meat, fat side up, in a 15½x10½x2-inch baking pan. Sprinkle with a little salt and pepper. Insert a meat thermometer. Roast meat in a 325° oven to desired doneness. Allow 2¼ hours for rare or till thermometer registers 140°; 3 hours for medium (160°); or 3¼ hours for well-done (170°). Remove meat from pan. Cover with foil; keep warm.

Reserve ¼ *cup* drippings in roasting pan. (Or, pour 2 tablespoons of drippings into each of two 8x1½-inch round baking pans.) Set aside. Increase oven temperature to 400°. Beat eggs on low speed of electric mixer for ½ minute. Add milk; beat 15 seconds. Add flour and the 1 teaspoon salt; beat 2 minutes or till smooth. Pour batter over drippings in pan(s). Bake in a 400° oven for 35 to 40 minutes for roasting pan or for 30 to 35 minutes for round baking pans. Cut into squares or wedges to serve. Serve at once with roast. Makes 10 servings.

Oyster Stew

Serving *Oyster Stew* on Christmas Eve is an American tradition that has remained a favorite for generations. It was popularized by the custom of serving fish for the last meal of the Advent fast.

1 **pint shucked oysters**
¾ **teaspoon salt**
2 **cups milk**
1 **cup light cream**
   Dash bottled hot pepper sauce (optional)
   Paprika
   Butter *or* margarine

In a saucepan combine *undrained* oysters and salt. Cook over medium heat about 5 minutes or till edges of oysters curl. Stir in milk, cream, and pepper sauce if desired. Heat through. Season to taste. Sprinkle *each* serving with paprika and top with a pat of butter. Serves 4.

● **Vegetable-Oyster Stew:** Prepare Oyster Stew as directed above, *except* in a small saucepan cook ½ cup finely chopped *carrots* and ½ cup finely chopped *celery* in 2 tablespoons *butter*, covered, for 10 to 15 minutes or till vegetables are tender but not brown. Stir vegetable mixture and 1 teaspoon *Worcestershire sauce* into oyster-milk mixture. Heat through.

Hopping John

Many Southerners eat *Hopping John* on New Year's Day for good luck. The origin of its name is uncertain. Some say children were to hop once around the table before eating. Others say it refers to the custom of inviting a guest to eat by saying, "Hop in, John."

1 **cup dry black-eyed peas (6 ounces)**
6 **cups water**
6 **slices bacon, cut up, *or* 4 ounces salt pork, diced**
4 **cups water**
¾ **cup chopped onion**
1 **stalk celery, chopped (½ cup)**
1½ **teaspoons salt**
½ **to ¾ teaspoon ground red pepper**
1 **cup long grain rice**

Rinse dry peas. In a large saucepan or Dutch oven combine peas and the 6 cups water. Bring to boiling. Reduce heat; simmer for 2 minutes. Remove from heat. Cover; let stand 1 hour. (Or, soak peas overnight in a covered pan.) Drain peas and rinse.

In same saucepan cook bacon or salt pork till crisp. Drain off fat, reserving about 3 tablespoons. Add the peas, 4 cups water, onion, celery, salt, and red pepper. Bring to boiling. Cover. Reduce heat; simmer 30 minutes. Add uncooked rice. Cover and simmer about 20 minutes more or till peas and rice are tender, stirring occasionally. Makes 8 servings.

24-Hour Fruit Salad

This salad is perfect for a holiday dinner. Make it the day before, then refrigerate and forget it until you are ready to serve the meal.

1 20-ounce can pineapple chunks
3 slightly beaten egg yolks
2 tablespoons sugar
2 tablespoons vinegar
1 tablespoon butter *or* margarine
   Dash salt
1 16-ounce can pitted light sweet cherries, drained
3 oranges, peeled and sectioned
2 cups tiny marshmallows
1 cup whipping cream

Drain pineapple; reserve 2 tablespoons syrup. To make custard, in a heavy small saucepan combine reserved pineapple syrup, egg yolks, sugar, vinegar, butter or margarine, and salt. Cook and stir over low heat about 6 minutes or till mixture thickens slightly and coats a metal spoon. Cool to room temperature.

In a large bowl combine pineapple chunks, cherries, orange sections, and marshmallows. Pour custard over fruit mixture; stir gently. Beat the whipping cream till soft peaks form. Fold whipped cream into fruit mixture. Turn into a serving bowl. Cover and refrigerate 24 hours or overnight. Makes 10 to 12 servings.

Pennsylvania Dutch Christmas Loaves

4½ to 5 cups all-purpose flour
1 package active dry yeast
1¼ cups milk
¾ cup sugar
½ cup butter *or* margarine
1 teaspoon salt
1 egg
¾ cup raisins
½ cup currants
⅓ cup finely chopped candied citron
   Powdered Sugar Glaze
½ cup finely chopped blanched almonds

In a large mixer bowl combine *2 cups* of the flour and the yeast. In a saucepan heat the 1¼ cups milk, sugar, butter or margarine, and salt just till warm (115° to 120°) and butter is almost melted. Stir into flour mixture; add egg. Beat at low speed of electric mixer for ½ minute, scraping sides of bowl. Beat 3 minutes at high speed. Add raisins, currants, and chopped candied citron; mix well. By hand stir in enough of the remaining flour to make a moderately soft dough.

Turn out onto a lightly floured surface; knead till smooth and elastic (5 to 8 minutes total). Place dough in a lightly greased bowl; turn once to grease surface. Cover; let rise in a warm place till double (about 1½ hours).

Punch down dough; turn out onto lightly floured surface. Divide into 4 equal portions. Shape each into a 6-inch round loaf. Place on two greased baking sheets 3 inches apart. Cover; let rise again till nearly double (about 1 hour).

Bake in a 375° oven for 20 to 30 minutes or till loaves sound hollow when lightly tapped. Cool on a wire rack. Drizzle with Powdered Sugar Glaze; sprinkle almonds atop. Makes 4 loaves.

Powdered Sugar Glaze: Stir together 1 cup sifted *powdered sugar,* ¼ teaspoon *vanilla,* and 1 to 2 tablespoons *milk* to make the glaze of drizzling consistency.

Dark Fruitcake

When American fruit-cake, or "great cake," became popular in the South, cooks were known to compete for the blackest cake. Some even browned the flour before mixing to darken the color.

3 cups all-purpose flour
2 teaspoons baking powder
2 teaspoons ground cinnamon
1 teaspoon salt
½ teaspoon ground nutmeg
½ teaspoon ground allspice
½ teaspoon ground cloves
16 ounces diced mixed candied fruits and peels (2½ cups)
1 15-ounce package (3 cups) raisins
1 8-ounce package (1⅓ cups) pitted whole dates, snipped
8 ounces whole red or green candied cherries (1⅓ cups)
1 cup slivered almonds
1 cup pecan halves
½ cup chopped candied pineapple
4 eggs
1¾ cups packed brown sugar
1 cup orange juice
¾ cup butter or margarine, melted and cooled
¼ cup molasses
   Wine, brandy, or fruit juice

Grease three 8x4x2-inch loaf pans or two 10x3½x2½-inch loaf pans. Line bottom and sides of pans with brown paper to prevent overbrowning; grease paper. In a large mixing bowl stir together flour, baking powder, cinnamon, salt, nutmeg, allspice, and cloves. Add fruits and peels, raisins, dates, cherries, almonds, pecans, and pineapple; mix till well coated.

In a medium mixing bowl beat eggs till foamy. Add brown sugar, orange juice, butter or margarine, and molasses; beat till blended. Stir into fruit mixture. Turn batter into pans, filling each about ¾ full. Bake in a 300° oven about 2 hours or till cakes test done. (Cover all pans loosely with foil after 1 hour of baking to prevent overbrowning.) Place cakes in pans on wire racks; cool thoroughly. Remove from pans.

Wrap in cheesecloth moistened with wine, brandy, or fruit juices. Overwrap with foil or clear plastic wrap, or place in an airtight container. Store at least 1 week in refrigerator. (Store 3 to 4 weeks for a blended and mellow flavor.) Remoisten cheesecloth as needed if cakes are stored longer than 1 week. Makes 40 servings.

Cranberry-Nut Bread

3 medium oranges
1 beaten egg
2 tablespoons cooking oil
2 cups all-purpose flour
¾ cup sugar
1½ teaspoons baking powder
1 teaspoon salt
½ teaspoon baking soda
1 cup coarsely chopped fresh or frozen cranberries
½ cup chopped walnuts
1 cup sifted powdered sugar

Finely shred peel from 1 orange; reserve peel. Squeeze juice from all oranges. Measure ¾ cup of the juice; set aside remaining orange juice.

In a mixing bowl combine egg, cooking oil, the ¾ cup orange juice, and 1 teaspoon of the shredded orange peel. In another mixing bowl stir together flour, sugar, baking powder, salt, and baking soda. Add orange juice mixture to flour mixture; stir just till dry ingredients are moistened. Fold in chopped cranberries and walnuts.

Turn batter into one lightly greased 8x4x2-inch loaf pan or three 6x3x2-inch loaf pans. Bake in a 350° oven for 50 to 60 minutes for large pan (bake 30 to 40 minutes for smaller pans) or till a wooden pick inserted near center comes out clean. Cool bread 10 minutes in pan on wire rack; remove from pan. Cool thoroughly.

For glaze, in a small bowl stir 1 tablespoon of the reserved orange juice into powdered sugar. Stir in more orange juice to make of drizzling consistency. Drizzle glaze atop cooled loaves; garnish with remaining shredded orange peel. Makes 1 large or 3 small loaves.

Mince-Apple Pie

Mince pie is the Christmas pie of Little Jack Horner fame. Its original oblong shape and lattice crust symbolized the Bethlehem manger filled with hay. The apples stood for growth, and the spices represented gifts the Wise Men brought to the Christ child.

Pastry for Double-Crust Pie (see recipe, page 141)
3 **cups thinly sliced, peeled cooking apples (about 1 pound)**
1 **28-ounce jar (2⅔ cups) prepared mincemeat**
2 **tablespoons lemon juice**
Milk
Sugar
Hard Sauce (see recipe, page 173)

Prepare and roll out pastry. Line a 9-inch pie plate with *half* of the pastry. Trim pastry to edge of pie plate. In a mixing bowl combine sliced apples, mincemeat, and lemon juice. Pour mixture into pastry-lined pie plate.

Cut slits in top crust; place atop filling. Seal and flute edge. Brush with milk and sprinkle with a little sugar. To prevent overbrowning, cover edge of pie with foil. Bake in a 375° oven for 25 minutes. Remove foil; bake about 25 minutes more or till crust is golden. Cool on wire rack before serving. Serve with Hard Sauce. Makes 8 servings.

Rolled Ginger Cookies *pictured on page 172*

Use this recipe to make and cut out ginger-bread men. After baking add a festive touch by decorating each with frosting, colored sugars, and small candies.

5 **cups all-purpose flour**
2 **teaspoons ground ginger**
1½ **teaspoons baking soda**
1 **teaspoon ground cinnamon**
1 **teaspoon ground cloves**
½ **teaspoon salt**
1 **cup shortening**
1 **cup sugar**
1 **egg**
1 **cup molasses**
2 **tablespoons vinegar**

Stir together flour, ginger, baking soda, cinnamon, cloves, and salt. In a large mixer bowl beat shortening for 30 seconds. Add sugar; beat till fluffy. Add egg, molasses, and vinegar; beat well. Add flour mixture to beaten mixture, beating well. Cover; chill 3 hours or overnight.

Divide dough into thirds. On a lightly floured surface, roll dough, one-third at a time, to ⅛-inch thickness. (Keep remainder chilled.) Cut into desired shapes. Place 1 inch apart on greased cookie sheet. Bake in a 375° oven for 5 to 6 minutes. Cool 1 minute; remove to a wire rack. Cool thoroughly. Makes 60 cookies.

Apees

These Pennsylvania Christmas favorites are said to be named after Ann Page, a 19th century Philadelphia cook. Her initials were imprinted on the top of each cookie.

1 **cup butter** *or* **margarine**
1 **cup sugar**
1 **egg**
½ **cup dairy sour cream**
1 **teaspoon vanilla**
2 **cups all-purpose flour**

Beat butter 30 seconds. Add sugar; beat till fluffy. Add egg, sour cream, and vanilla; beat well. Stir in flour. Drop from teaspoon 2 inches apart onto an ungreased cookie sheet. Bake in a 375° oven 8 to 10 minutes (cookies should be pale). Makes 60.

Recipe note: If desired, wrap dough and chill well. Roll half at a time on a lightly floured surface to ¼-inch thickness. Cut with a 2-inch round cutter. Keep remaining dough chilled till needed. Bake as above.

Pressed Cookies

3½ **cups all-purpose flour**
1 **teaspoon baking powder**
1½ **cups butter** *or* **margarine**
1 **cup sugar**
1 **egg**
1 **teaspoon vanilla**
½ **teaspoon almond extract (optional)**

Stir together flour and baking powder. Beat butter or margarine for 30 seconds. Add sugar and beat till fluffy. Add egg, vanilla, and almond extract if desired; beat well. Gradually add dry ingredients to beaten mixture, beating till well blended. *Do not chill.* Force dough through a cookie press onto an ungreased cookie sheet. If desired, decorate with colored sugars or small candies. Bake in a 400° oven for 7 to 8 minutes. Remove; cool. Makes about 60.

Plum Pudding

Originally from England, *Plum Pudding* has become a Christmas tradition in America. It was first served with the meats of the holiday feast and gradually developed into the sweet steamed pudding served today.

Pictured clockwise: *Peanut Brittle (see recipe, page 174), Pressed Cookies, Rolled Ginger Cookies (see recipe, page 171), Eggnog (see recipe, page 175), Fudge (see recipe, page 174), and Candied Citrus Peel (see recipe, page 175).*

3 **slices bread, torn into pieces**
1 **5⅓-ounce can (⅔ cup) evaporated milk**
2 **ounces beef suet, ground**
¾ **cup packed brown sugar**
1 **beaten egg**
¼ **cup orange juice**
½ **teaspoon vanilla**
1½ **cups raisins**
¾ **cup pitted whole dates, snipped**
½ **cup diced mixed candied fruits and peels**
⅓ **cup chopped walnuts**
¾ **cup all-purpose flour**
1½ **teaspoons ground cinnamon**
¾ **teaspoon baking soda**
¾ **teaspoon ground cloves**
¾ **teaspoon ground mace**
¼ **teaspoon salt**
Hard Sauce

Soak torn bread in evaporated milk about 3 minutes or till softened; beat lightly to break up. Stir in ground suet, brown sugar, egg, orange juice, and vanilla. Add raisins, snipped dates, candied fruits and peels, and chopped nuts.

Stir together flour, cinnamon, baking soda, cloves, mace, and salt. Add to fruit mixture; stir till combined. Turn mixture into a well-greased 3-pound shortening can or 6½-cup tower mold. Cover with foil, pressing foil tightly against rim of the can or mold. Place on a rack in a deep kettle; add boiling water to a depth of 1 inch. Cover kettle; boil gently (bubbles break surface) and steam 4 hours or till done. Add more boiling water if necessary. Cool 10 minutes; unmold. Serve warm with Hard Sauce. Serves 8 to 10.

Hard Sauce: In a small mixer bowl beat together 2 cups sifted *powdered sugar* and ½ cup softened *butter* or *margarine*. Beat in 1 teaspoon *vanilla*. Spread in 7½x3½x2-inch loaf pan. Chill till firm. Cut into pieces to serve. Makes 1⅓ cups.

Peanut Brittle   *pictured on page 172*

For a brown sugar variation of *Peanut Brittle,* prepare *Peanut Brittle* as the recipe directs, but use only 1 cup sugar and add 1 cup packed brown sugar. Cook over medium heat, stirring constantly, to 275° and till syrup turns a deep golden color (mixture should boil gently over entire surface). Add peanuts; cook, stirring often, to 295° and till syrup is a dark golden color. Continue as the recipe directs.

2 cups sugar
1 cup light corn syrup
½ cup water
¼ cup butter *or* margarine
½ teaspoon salt
3 cups raw *or* roasted shelled peanuts
1½ teaspoons baking soda

Butter the sides of a heavy 3-quart saucepan. In it combine sugar, corn syrup, water, butter or margarine, and salt. Cook and stir till sugar dissolves and mixture comes to boiling. Cook, stirring occasionally, to 275° (soft-crack stage) and till syrup turns a golden color (mixture should boil gently over entire surface). Add peanuts and continue cooking, stirring often, to 295° and till syrup is a clear golden color. Remove from heat. Quickly stir in baking soda. Immediately pour hot mixture into two buttered 15x10x1-inch pans or baking sheets. If desired, use two forks to lift and pull candy as it cools to stretch it thin. Cool; break into pieces. Makes about 2¼ pounds.

Fudge   *pictured on page 172*

4 cups sugar
2 5⅓-ounce cans (1⅓ cups) evaporated milk
1 cup butter *or* margarine
1 12-ounce package (2 cups) semisweet chocolate pieces
1 7-ounce jar marshmallow creme
1 cup chopped walnuts
1 teaspoon vanilla

Butter the sides of a heavy 3-quart saucepan. In it combine sugar, evaporated milk, and butter or margarine. Cook and stir over medium heat till mixture comes to boiling. Cook to 236° (soft-ball stage), stirring frequently (mixture should boil over entire surface). Remove from heat. Add the chocolate pieces, marshmallow creme, walnuts, and vanilla; stir till blended and chocolate is melted. Turn into a buttered 9x9x2-inch or 13x9x2-inch pan. Score into squares while warm; cut when firm. If fudge is soft, chill. Makes about 3½ pounds.

Divinity

If it's a humid day when you make *Divinity,* you'll have to beat longer to enable the candy mixture to hold its shape before dropping it onto the waxed paper.

For an easy variation, try adding ½ cup chopped candied cherries or chopped walnuts after the 4 or 5 minutes beating time. Then continue as the *Divinity* recipe directs.

For easier shaping, spread *Divinity* in a buttered 10x6x2-inch dish. Let candy cool, then cut into squares.

2½ **cups sugar**
 ½ **cup light corn syrup**
 ½ **cup water**
 ¼ **teaspoon salt**
  2 **egg whites**
  1 **teaspoon vanilla**

In heavy 2-quart saucepan combine sugar, corn syrup, water, and salt. Cook and stir till sugar dissolves and mixture comes to boiling. Cook over medium heat to 260° (hard-ball stage), without stirring (mixture should boil gently over entire surface). As temperature nears 250°, beat egg whites to stiff peaks. Gradually pour hot syrup in a thin stream over egg whites, beating at high speed of electric mixer. Add vanilla; beat 4 to 5 minutes more or till mixture holds its shape. Drop from a teaspoon onto waxed paper. Makes about 36 pieces.

Candied Citrus Peel *pictured on page 172*

  4 **medium grapefruit** *or*
    6 medium oranges
  2 **cups sugar**
 ½ **cup water**
    Sugar

Cut the peel of grapefruit or oranges into 6 to 8 sections; carefully remove from pulp (reserve pulp for another use). Remove white membrane from peel; discard membrane. Cut peel into strips ½ inch wide (should yield about 2 cups).

In saucepan place peel and enough cold water to cover; heat to boiling. Boil 5 minutes. Drain. In same saucepan combine peel, 2 cups sugar, and the ½ cup water. Heat and stir till sugar dissolves. Boil gently about 20 minutes or till peel is translucent. Drain well; roll in additional sugar. Dry on wire rack. Makes 2 cups.

Eggnog *pictured on page 172*

For a nonalcoholic eggnog, prepare *Eggnog* as directed, but omit the rum and bourbon and increase the milk to 3 cups.

  6 **egg yolks**
 ¼ **cup sugar**
  2 **cups milk**
 ½ **cup light rum**
 ½ **cup bourbon**
  1 **teaspoon vanilla**
 ¼ **teaspoon salt**
  1 **cup whipping cream**
  6 **egg whites**
 ¼ **cup sugar**
    Ground nutmeg

Beat egg yolks till blended. Gradually add ¼ cup sugar, beating till thick and lemon-colored. Stir in milk. Stir in rum, bourbon, vanilla, and salt. Refrigerate 4 to 6 hours or till chilled.

Whip cream; set aside. Wash beaters well. In a large mixer bowl beat egg whites till soft peaks form. Gradually add ¼ cup sugar, beating to stiff peaks. Fold yolk mixture and whipped cream into egg whites. Sprinkle nutmeg atop each serving. Serve immediately. Makes 15 (4-ounce) servings.

Hot Buttered Rum

  3 **tablespoons rum**
  2 **to 3 teaspoons brown sugar**
    Dash ground nutmeg
  1 **teaspoon butter** *or* **margarine**

In a warmed 10-ounce mug combine rum, brown sugar, and nutmeg. Add boiling *water* to fill mug ¾ full. Float butter atop. Makes 1 serving.

AMERICA CELEBRATES

Easter

Glazed Ham

The tradition of serving ham at Easter dates back to the 19th century when ham fairs were held before Good Friday in the Notre Dame plaza of Paris.

Ham is an American favorite that's easy to serve at large gatherings. For example, the *Glazed Ham* serves 20 to 25 and leftover ham is easily incorporated into other menus.

 1 **10- to 14-pound fully cooked whole ham**
 1 **10-ounce jar cherry preserves**
 ¼ **cup red wine vinegar**
 2 **tablespoons light corn syrup**
 ¼ **teaspoon ground cinnamon**
 ¼ **teaspoon ground nutmeg**
 ¼ **teaspoon ground cloves**
 ⅓ **cup toasted slivered almonds**
 3 **tablespoons water**

Place the whole ham on a rack in a shallow baking pan. Insert a meat thermometer. Bake, uncovered, in a 325° oven till the thermometer registers 140° (for 2 to 3 hours).

Meanwhile, for glaze, in a saucepan combine the preserves, vinegar, corn syrup, cinnamon, nutmeg, and cloves. Cook and stir till boiling. Reduce heat; simmer 2 minutes. Stir in the almonds. Reserve ¾ cup of the glaze.

About 15 minutes before the ham is done, spoon some of the remaining glaze over ham, basting occasionally. Remove from oven; place on a heated serving platter. Stir the water into reserved ¾ cup glaze; heat and pass glaze mixture. Makes 20 to 25 servings.

Hot Cross Buns

3½ **to 4 cups all-purpose flour**
 2 **packages active dry yeast**
 1 **teaspoon ground cinnamon**
 ¾ **cup milk**
 ½ **cup cooking oil**
 ⅓ **cup sugar**
 ¾ **teaspoon salt**
 3 **eggs**
 ⅔ **cup dried currants**
 1 **slightly beaten egg white**
1½ **cups sifted powdered sugar**
 ¼ **teaspoon vanilla**
    Dash salt

In a large mixer bowl combine *1½ cups* of the flour, the yeast, and cinnamon. In a saucepan heat milk, oil, sugar, and ¾ teaspoon salt just till warm (115° to 120°); stir constantly. Add to flour mixture; add eggs. Beat at low speed of electric mixer for ½ minute, scraping sides of bowl constantly. Beat 3 minutes at high speed. Stir in currants and as much of the remaining flour as you can mix in with a spoon. Turn dough out onto a lightly floured surface. Knead in enough of the remaining flour to make a moderately soft dough that is smooth and elastic (3 to 5 minutes total). Shape into a ball. Place in a lightly greased bowl; turn once to grease surface. Cover; let rise in a warm place till double (about 1½ hours).

Punch down; turn out onto a lightly floured surface. Cover; let rest 10 minutes. Divide dough into 18 pieces; form each piece into a smooth ball. Place on a greased baking sheet 1½ inches apart. Cover; let rise till nearly double (30 to 45 minutes). With a sharp knife cut a shallow cross in each; brush tops with some of the slightly beaten egg white (reserve remaining egg white). Bake the buns in a 375° oven for 12 to 15 minutes or till a golden brown. Cool slightly.

Meanwhile, combine the powdered sugar, vanilla, dash salt, and the reserved portion of beaten egg white. Add additional milk, if necessary, to make of piping consistency. Pipe crosses on tops of buns. Makes 18.

Country-Style Barbecued Ribs

Barbecues on the Fourth of July probably became popular because it was more pleasant to cook outdoors than indoors on a hot summer day. Although the Southwest is best known for its barbecues, grilling is an all-American cooking technique.

Steaks, ribs, and hamburger are just a few of the meats that lend themselves to this style of cooking.

- **4 pounds pork country-style ribs**
- **1 cup chopped onion**
- **1 clove garlic, minced**
- **¼ cup cooking oil**
- **1 8-ounce can tomato sauce**
- **½ cup water**
- **¼ cup packed brown sugar**
- **¼ cup lemon juice**
- **2 tablespoons Worcestershire sauce**
- **2 tablespoons prepared mustard**
- **1 teaspoon celery seed**
- **1 teaspoon salt**
- **¼ teaspoon pepper**

Cook ribs, covered, in enough boiling salted water to cover for 45 to 60 minutes or till tender. Drain. For sauce, cook onion and garlic in cooking oil till tender. Stir in tomato sauce, ½ cup water, brown sugar, lemon juice, Worcestershire sauce, mustard, celery seed, salt, and pepper. Simmer, uncovered, 15 minutes, stirring once or twice. Grill ribs over *slow* coals about 45 minutes or till done, turning every 15 minutes. Brush with sauce during the last 15 minutes and just before serving. Serves 6.

Easy Barbecue Sauce

- **1 14-ounce bottle hot-style catsup**
- **3 tablespoons vinegar**
- **2 teaspoons celery seed**
- **⅛ teaspoon garlic powder**

Combine hot-style catsup, vinegar, celery seed, and garlic powder. Use to baste hamburgers, beef, or chicken during the last 10 minutes of grilling. Makes about 1½ cups sauce.

Basic Grilled Burgers *pictured on pages 163 and 178*

The hamburger is said to be named after the city of Hamburg, West Germany. However, American ingenuity is credited with placing the meat patty in a bun to create this national sandwich favorite.

- **1 pound ground beef**
- **½ teaspoon salt**
- **Dash pepper**
- **Hamburger buns**

Mix beef, salt, and pepper. Form into four 4-inch patties. Grill over *medium-hot* coals for 5 to 6 minutes; turn and grill 4 to 5 minutes more. Serve on hamburger buns. If desired, serve with lettuce, sliced onion, sliced tomato, and pickles. Makes 4 servings.

Recipe note: For an easy variation, add any of the following ingredients to the basic ground meat mixture: 2 tablespoons chopped *green onion;* 2 tablespoons drained *sweet pickle relish;* 2 tablespoons chopped *pimiento-stuffed olives;* 1 tablespoon prepared *horseradish;* or ¼ teaspoon *minced dried garlic.*

Oven-Fried Chicken

What's more American than fried chicken? You can choose from the Southern variation of *Southern Fried Chicken with Cream Gravy* (see recipe, page 34), or the more basic *Oven-Fried Chicken* and *Skillet-Fried Chicken.*

Summer picnic coolers often are filled with chilled fried chicken. And for those who like late evening snacks or easy lunches, leftover fried chicken is good right from the refrigerator.

3 **cups corn flakes** *or* ½ **cup fine dry bread crumbs**
1 **2½- to 3-pound broiler-fryer chicken, cut up**
¼ **cup butter** *or* **margarine, melted**

For the crumb mixture, crush corn flakes finely enough to make 1 cup crumbs or use the ½ cup bread crumbs; set aside.

Rinse chicken pieces; pat dry with paper toweling. Season chicken with salt and pepper. Brush *each* piece with melted butter or margarine. Place crushed corn flakes or bread crumbs on a sheet of waxed paper; roll chicken in crumbs to coat. Arrange chicken, skin side up and so pieces don't touch, in a shallow baking pan. Bake in a 375° oven about 50 minutes or till tender. *Do not turn.* (Chicken is done when it is easily pierced with a fork. Test the thigh or breast at a point near the bone, because these parts require the most cooking time.) Makes 6 servings.

Skillet-Fried Chicken

1 **2½- to 3-pound broiler-fryer chicken, cut up**
¼ **cup all-purpose flour**
1½ **teaspoons salt**
1 **teaspoon paprika**
¼ **teaspoon pepper**
2 **tablespoons cooking oil** *or* **shortening**

Rinse chicken pieces; pat dry with paper toweling. In a plastic or paper bag combine flour, salt, paprika, and pepper. Add a few chicken pieces at a time; shake to coat.

In a 12-inch skillet heat oil or shortening. Add chicken, placing meaty pieces toward center of skillet. Cook, uncovered, over medium heat for 10 to 15 minutes, turning to brown evenly. Reduce heat; cover tightly. Cook 30 minutes. Uncover; cook 10 to 15 minutes more. Chicken is done when it is easily pierced with a fork. Drain chicken pieces on paper toweling. Makes 6 servings.

Creamy Potato Salad

6 **medium potatoes (2 pounds)**
1 **cup thinly sliced celery**
1 **medium onion, finely chopped (½ cup)**
⅓ **cup chopped sweet pickle**
1¼ **cups mayonnaise** *or* **salad dressing**
2 **teaspoons sugar**
2 **teaspoons celery seed**
2 **teaspoons vinegar**
2 **teaspoons prepared mustard**
1½ **teaspoons salt**
2 **hard-cooked eggs, coarsely chopped**

In a saucepan cook potatoes, covered, in boiling salted water for 25 to 30 minutes or till tender; drain well. Peel and cube potatoes. Transfer to a large bowl. Add celery, onion, and sweet pickle. Combine mayonnaise or salad dressing, sugar, celery seed, vinegar, prepared mustard, and salt. Add mayonnaise mixture to potatoes. Toss lightly to coat potato mixture. Carefully fold in the chopped eggs. Cover and refrigerate till thoroughly chilled. Makes 8 servings.

Pictured clockwise:
Lemonade, Strawberry Shortcake, Roasted Corn on the Cob (see recipes, page 180), and Basic Grilled Burgers (see recipe, page 177).

Roasted Corn on the Cob *pictured on pages 163 and 178*

**1 cup butter *or* margarine,
 softened**
½ teaspoon salt
**½ teaspoon dried rosemary,
 crushed**
**½ teaspoon dried marjoram,
 crushed**
6 fresh ears of corn

Beat together butter or margarine and salt till fluffy. Beat in rosemary and marjoram. Let stand at room temperature 1 hour. Turn back husks of corn; remove silks with stiff brush. (Or, remove husks entirely if desired.)

Place each ear on a piece of heavy-duty foil. Spread *each* with about *2 tablespoons* of the butter mixture. Lay husks back in position. Wrap corn securely with foil. Roast ears directly on *medium-hot* coals for 15 to 20 minutes, turning frequently. (Or, on covered grill with an elevated rack, roast corn 15 to 20 minutes.) Makes 6 servings.

Picnic Coleslaw

**1 small head cabbage, cored
 and chopped (5 cups)**
¼ cup chopped onion
¼ cup chopped green pepper
¼ cup chopped pimiento
½ cup sugar
⅓ cup vinegar
1 teaspoon celery seed
½ teaspoon dry mustard

In large bowl combine cabbage, onion, green pepper, and pimiento. Combine the sugar, vinegar, celery seed, dry mustard, ¼ cup *water*, and ½ teaspoon *salt;* stir till sugar dissolves. Pour over cabbage mixture. Toss well. Cover and refrigerate several hours or overnight. Makes 5 cups.

Strawberry Shortcake *pictured on pages 4 and 5, 163, and 178*

Strawberries get their name from the way they originally were sent to market — strung on straw. The berries are at their best in early summer, making *Strawberry Shortcake* a popular 4th of July dessert.

**6 cups fresh strawberries,
 sliced**
¼ cup sugar
2 cups all-purpose flour
2 tablespoons sugar
1 tablespoon baking powder
½ cup butter *or* margarine
1 beaten egg
⅔ cup milk
**3 tablespoons butter *or*
 margarine, softened
 (optional)**
1 cup whipping cream
2 tablespoons sugar

Combine strawberries and ¼ cup sugar; set aside. For shortcake, combine flour, 2 tablespoons sugar, baking powder, and ½ teaspoon *salt.* Cut in the ½ cup butter till mixture resembles coarse crumbs. Combine beaten egg and milk; add all at once to dry ingredients and stir just to moisten. Spread dough in a greased 8x1½-inch round baking pan, building up edges slightly. Bake in a 450° oven for 15 to 18 minutes or till done.

Cool 10 minutes on wire rack. Remove from pan. Split into 2 layers; lift top off carefully. If desired, spread bottom layer with the 3 tablespoons butter. Whip cream with 2 tablespoons sugar just to soft peaks. Spoon berries and whipped cream between layers and over top. Serve shortcake warm. Makes 8 servings.

Lemonade *pictured on pages 4 and 5, 163, and 178*

1 cup sugar
1 cup lemon juice
 Ice cubes

For lemonade, combine sugar, lemon juice, and 5 cups *water;* stir to dissolve sugar. Serve over ice. Garnish with lemon slices if desired. Makes 6 (8-ounce) servings.

Corn Dogs

If any food symbolizes American celebrations, it's the hot dog. It's said that Harry Stevens, the owner of a refreshment concession at the New York Polo Grounds, introduced the food at a ball game in the early 1900s. His vendors sold the frankfurters in the stands by yelling, "Get your red hot dachshund sausages."

Cartoonist Tad Dorgan heard the vendors' cry and was inspired to create a cartoon character that was a talking sausage he named "hot dog."

Although the cartoon character faded, the name has stuck. Now hot dogs are part of the scene at many American celebrations such as fairs, festivals, carnivals, and sporting events. *Corn Dogs, Coney Islands,* and *Bacon-Wrapped Franks* are variations that have become popular.

1 cup all-purpose flour
⅔ cup yellow cornmeal
2 tablespoons sugar
1½ teaspoons baking powder
1 teaspoon salt
½ teaspoon dry mustard
2 tablespoons shortening
1 beaten egg
¾ cup milk
1 pound frankfurters (8 to 10)
Cooking oil for deep-fat frying

In a bowl combine flour, cornmeal, sugar, baking powder, salt, and dry mustard. Cut in 2 tablespoons shortening till mixture resembles fine crumbs. Combine egg and milk. Add to dry ingredients; mix well. Insert a wooden skewer into the end of each frankfurter. Pour oil into skillet to a depth of 1 inch; heat to 375°.

Coat franks with batter. (If batter is too thick, add 1 to 2 tablespoons additional milk.) Arrange coated franks 3 at a time in hot oil; turn franks with tongs after 10 seconds to prevent batter from sliding off. Cook 3 minutes, turning again halfway through cooking time. Serve hot with catsup and mustard if desired. Makes 4 or 5 servings.

Coney Islands

½ pound ground beef
1 medium onion, chopped (½ cup)
¼ cup chopped green pepper
1 8-ounce can tomato sauce
½ cup water
½ teaspoon chili powder
½ teaspoon paprika
¼ teaspoon salt
⅛ teaspoon ground red pepper (optional)
6 frankfurters
6 frankfurter buns, warmed

In a skillet cook ground beef, onion, and green pepper till meat is brown. Drain. Add tomato sauce, water, chili powder, paprika, salt, and ground red pepper if desired. Simmer 15 minutes. In a saucepan cover frankfurters with cold water; bring to boiling. Simmer 5 minutes. To serve, place franks in buns and top each with ground beef mixture. Makes 6 servings.

Bacon-Wrapped Franks   *pictured on page 183*

8 slices bacon
8 frankfurters *or* fully cooked bratwursts
2 tablespoons prepared mustard
2 tablespoons finely chopped onion
2 slices American, Swiss, brick, *or* Muenster cheese
Bottled barbecue sauce
8 frankfurter buns, split and toasted

Partially cook bacon. Drain; set aside. Slit frankfurters or bratwursts lengthwise, cutting almost to ends and only ¾ of the way through. Spread inside of each frank or bratwurst with mustard; add some of the onion. Cut each slice of cheese into 4 strips. Lay 1 strip of cheese inside each frank or bratwurst. Wrap each frank with a strip of bacon; secure with wooden picks.

Grill over *hot* coals for 10 to 12 minutes or till bacon cooks crisp on all sides, brushing with barbecue sauce and turning frequently. Remove picks. Serve frankfurters or bratwursts in toasted buns. Makes 4 servings.

181

Buttermilk Doughnuts *also pictured on page 163*

According to legend, a sea captain is credited with cutting the hole in the doughnut sometime during the 19th century. He complained to his cook about the doughy center and asked that it be cut out. The cook liked the faster method of cooking and the captain enjoyed the holed doughnut.

Doughnuts are an American coffee-dunking favorite and are good on a brisk fall day with plenty of hot apple cider.

3¼ cups all-purpose flour
1 teaspoon baking soda
½ teaspoon baking powder
½ teaspoon ground nutmeg
⅛ teaspoon salt
2 slightly beaten eggs
½ cup sugar
2 tablespoons butter *or* margarine, melted
1 cup buttermilk *or* sour milk
Shortening *or* cooking oil for deep-fat frying

Stir together flour, baking soda, baking powder, nutmeg, and salt; set aside. In a large mixer bowl beat eggs and sugar till thick and lemon-colored. Stir in melted butter or margarine. Add flour mixture and buttermilk or sour milk alternately to egg mixture, beating after each addition just till combined. Cover; refrigerate 2 hours.

Turn dough out onto a lightly floured surface. Roll to ½-inch thickness; cut with a floured 2½-inch doughnut cutter. Fry in deep, hot fat (375°) about 1 minute per side or till golden, turning once. Drain on paper toweling. While warm, sprinkle with additional sugar if desired. Makes 18.

Soft Pretzels

4 to 4½ cups all-purpose flour
1 package active dry yeast
1½ cups milk
¼ cup sugar
2 tablespoons cooking oil
1½ teaspoons salt
3 tablespoons salt
2 quarts boiling water
1 slightly beaten egg white
1 tablespoon water
Coarse salt *or* sesame seed

Combine *2 cups* of the flour and the yeast. Heat milk, sugar, oil, and 1½ teaspoons salt just till warm (115° to 120°), stirring constantly. Add to flour mixture. Beat with electric mixer ½ minute, scraping bowl. Beat 3 minutes at high speed. Stir in as much of remaining flour as you can mix in with a spoon. Turn out onto a floured surface. Knead in enough of remaining flour to make a moderately stiff dough that is smooth and elastic (6 to 8 minutes total). Shape into ball. Place in greased bowl; turn once. Cover; let rise in a warm place till double (about 1½ hours).

Punch down; turn out onto floured surface. Cover; let rest 10 minutes. Roll into a 12x8-inch rectangle. Cut into sixteen 12x½-inch strips. Roll each into a rope.

Shape one rope of dough into a circle, overlapping about 4 inches from each end; leave ends free. Take one end of dough in each hand and twist at the point where dough overlaps. Carefully lift ends across to the opposite edge of the circle. Tuck ends under edge for pretzel shape; moisten and press to seal. Repeat with remaining dough. Let rise, uncovered, 20 minutes.

Dissolve 3 tablespoons salt in the 2 quarts boiling water. Lower 3 or 4 pretzels at a time into boiling water; boil 2 minutes, turning once. Remove to paper toweling; let stand a few seconds, then place ½ inch apart on a well-greased baking sheet. Brush with a mixture of egg white and 1 tablespoon water. Sprinkle with coarse salt or sesame seed. Bake in a 350° oven 25 to 30 minutes or till golden. Makes 16.

Pictured clockwise:
Buttermilk Doughnuts, Bacon-Wrapped Franks (see recipe, page 181), Caramel Apples, and Hot Spiced Cider (see recipes, page 184).

Saltwater Taffy

The Boardwalk of Atlantic City, New Jersey, is known for its saltwater taffy, which is said to be made with ocean water.

Homemade taffy was the basis of a popular form of entertainment — the taffy pull — from the late 18th century into the 20th century.

2 **cups sugar**
1 **cup light corn syrup**
1 **cup water**
1½ **teaspoons salt**
2 **tablespoons butter** *or* **margarine**
¼ **teaspoon oil of peppermint (optional)**
7 **drops green food coloring (optional)**

Butter the sides of a 2-quart saucepan. In it combine sugar, corn syrup, water, and salt. Cook over medium heat, stirring constantly, till sugar is dissolved. Continue cooking to 265° (hard-ball stage), without stirring (mixture should boil gently over entire surface).

Remove from heat; stir in butter or margarine. Stir in flavoring and food coloring if desired. Pour into a buttered 15x10x1-inch pan. Cool about 20 minutes or till easily handled. Butter hands and pull candy till difficult to pull. Cut into fourths; pull each fourth into a long strand about ½ inch thick. With buttered scissors snip taffy into bite-size pieces. Wrap each in clear plastic wrap. Store overnight. Makes 1½ pounds.

Hot Spiced Cider   *pictured on page 183*

8 **cups apple cider** *or* **apple juice**
½ **cup packed brown sugar**
  Dash ground nutmeg
6 **inches stick cinnamon**
1 **teaspoon whole allspice**
1 **teaspoon whole cloves**
8 **thin orange wedges** *or* **slices**
8 **whole cloves**

In a large saucepan combine apple cider or apple juice, brown sugar, and nutmeg. For spice bag, place cinnamon, allspice, and the 1 teaspoon cloves in cheesecloth and tie; add to cider mixture. Bring to boiling. Cover; reduce heat and simmer 10 minutes. Remove spice bag and discard. Serve the hot cider in mugs with a clove-studded orange wedge or slice in each mug. Makes 8 (8-ounce) servings.

Caramel Apples   *pictured on page 183*

12 **to 14 small tart apples**
12 **to 14 wooden skewers**
½ **cup butter** *or* **margarine**
2 **cups packed brown sugar**
1 **cup light corn syrup**
  Dash salt
1 **14½-ounce can Eagle Brand sweetened condensed milk**
1 **teaspoon vanilla**
1 **cup chopped peanuts (optional)**

Wash and dry apples; remove stems. Insert skewers in stem end of apples. In a heavy 3-quart saucepan melt the butter or margarine. Stir in brown sugar, corn syrup, and salt; mix well. Bring to boiling, stirring constantly. Stir in sweetened condensed milk. Cook to 245° (firm-ball stage), stirring constantly (mixture should boil gently over entire surface). Remove from heat; stir in vanilla.

Dip one apple into caramel mixture, turning to coat. Scrape excess caramel from bottom of apple. Immediately dip bottom half of apple in peanuts, if desired. Place on buttered baking sheet. Repeat with remaining apples. Cool. Makes 12 to 14 caramel apples.

Popcorn Balls

Store unpopped popcorn in an airtight container so the kernels will retain their moisture. Popcorn that dries out doesn't pop well.

It's not necessary to store popcorn in the refrigerator. The unpopped kernels keep just as well at room temperature.

20 **cups popped popcorn (about 1 cup unpopped)**
2 **cups sugar**
1 **cup water**
½ **cup light corn syrup**
1 **teaspoon vinegar**
½ **teaspoon salt**
1 **teaspoon vanilla**

Remove unpopped kernels from popped corn. Put popcorn in a large roasting pan; keep warm in a 300° oven. Butter the sides of a 2-quart saucepan. In it combine sugar, water, corn syrup, vinegar, and salt. Cook sugar mixture to 270° (soft-crack stage), stirring frequently (mixture should boil gently over entire surface).

Remove from heat; stir in vanilla. Slowly pour over hot popcorn. Stir just till mixed. Butter hands; using a buttered cup, scoop up popcorn mixture. Shape with hands into 2½- to 3-inch balls. Cool on waxed paper. Makes 13 to 15 balls.

Caramel Corn

8 **cups popped popcorn (about ⅓ cup)**
¾ **cup packed brown sugar**
6 **tablespoons butter** or **margarine**
3 **tablespoons light corn syrup**
¼ **teaspoon salt**
¼ **teaspoon baking soda**
¼ **teaspoon vanilla**

Remove all unpopped kernels from popped corn. Put popcorn in a 17x12x2-inch baking pan. In a 1½-quart saucepan combine brown sugar, the butter or margarine, corn syrup, and salt. Cook and stir over medium heat till butter melts and mixture boils. Cook, without stirring, for 5 minutes more.

Remove from heat. Stir in soda and vanilla. Pour over popcorn; gently stir to coat. Bake in a 300° oven 15 minutes; stir. Bake 5 to 10 minutes more. Cool in a large bowl. Makes 8 cups.

Glazed Nuts

1½ **cups raw peanuts, blanched whole almonds, cashews,** or **pecan halves**
½ **cup sugar**
2 **tablespoons butter** or **margarine**
 Salt

In a heavy 8-inch skillet stir together the nuts, the sugar, and butter or margarine. Cook over medium heat, stirring constantly, for 6 to 8 minutes or till sugar is melted and golden in color and nuts are toasted.

Spread nuts on a buttered baking sheet or on aluminum foil; separate into clusters. Sprinkle lightly with salt. Cool. Makes about ½ pound.

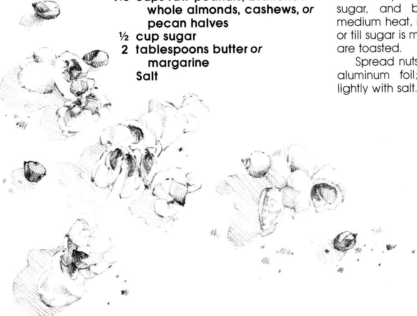

Index

A-B

Abalone Steaks 85
Anadama Bread 22
Angel Cake 131
Any-Fruit Sherbet 150
Apees 173
Appetizers (see also, Snacks)
  Braunschweiger Ball 155
  Ceviche 81
  Chili con Queso 81
  Cocktail Meatballs in
    Barbecue Sauce 154
  Four-Cheese Ball 155
  Guacamole 81
  Herb Curry Dip 156
  Lomi Lomi Salmon 95
  Pigs in a Blanket 155
  Piquant Deviled Eggs 154
  Salmon Party Spread 156
  Shrimp Cocktail 154
  Tomato Sipper 159
Apples
  Apple Cake 62
  Apple Jonathan 64
  Apple Pandowdy 28
  Apple Pie 136
  Apple-Stuffed Rib Roast 103
  Butterscotch Apple Dumplings . 138
  Caramel Apples 184
  Mince-Apple Pie 171
  Ozark Pudding 62
  Waldorf Salad 21
Apricot-Pineapple Pie 95
Apricot Upside-Down Cake 130
Artichokes with Citrus Butter
  Sauce 89
Avocado-Grapefruit Salad 76
Bacon-Wrapped Franks 181
Baked Beans, Boston 18
Baked Pastry Shell 141
Baked Stuffed Whitefish 58
Bananas
  Banana Bread Pudding 146
  Banana Cream Pie 139
  Banana Date-Nut Bread 128
  Bananas Foster 50
Barley-Stuffed Trout 88
Basic Beef Stew 98
Basic Grilled Burgers 177
Basque Potatoes 89

Beans (see also, Green Beans)
  Bean and Cheese Burritos 72
  Black Bean Soup 39
  Boston Baked Beans 18
  Chimichangas 72
  Garbanzo Salad 76
  Lentil Casserole 89
  Marinated Three-Bean Salad . . 119
  Red Beans and Rice 32
  Refried Beans 74
  Spicy Bacon-Bean Pot 119
Beaten Biscuits 43
Beef
  Basic Beef Stew 98
  Beef Burritos 72
  Beef Pot Roast 54
  Beef Teriyaki with Pineapple . . . 84
  Chicken Fried Steak with
    Cream Gravy 55
  Chimichangas 72
  Corned Beef Hash 99
  Cornish Beef Pasties 54
  Grillades and Grits 32
  Herbed Meat-Vegetable
    Kabobs 98
  Kentucky Burgoo 33
  New England Boiled Dinner . . . 10
  Old-Fashioned Fresh
    Vegetable-Beef Soup 99
  Philadelphia Pepper Pot 10
  Plymouth Succotash 12
  Red Flannel Hash 10
  Reubens 99
  Roast Beef Hash 99
  Roast Beef with Yorkshire
    Pudding 168
  Snapper Soup 17
  Steak Sandwiches 98
  Texas-Style Chili 71
Beef, Ground
  Basic Grilled Burgers 177
  Cocktail Meatballs in
    Barbecue Sauce 154
  Coney Islands 181
  Lasagna 103
  Picadillo 69
  Sausage Sandwiches 105
  Sloppy Joes 101
  Spaghetti and Meat Sauce . . . 104
  Stuffed Burgers 101
  Stuffed Cabbage Rolls 55
  Stuffed Peppers 100
  Tacos 68
  Taco Salad 100
  Tamale Pie 68

Beets, Harvard 18
Beignets 44
Berry Punch 159
Beverages, Alcoholic
   Café Almond 160
   Café Brûlot 51
   Café Columbian 160
   Café Israel 160
   California Cooler 95
   Dessert Coffee 160
   Eggnog 175
   Fish House Punch 29
   Frozen Daiquiri 160
   Hot Buttered Rum 175
   Hot Spiced Wine 160
   Irish Coffee 160
   Mai Tai 95
   Mint Julep 51
   Ramos Gin Fizz 51
   Wine Spritzer 160
   Yard of Flannel 29
Beverages, Nonalcoholic
   Berry Punch 159
   Chocolate Milk Shake 158
   Fruit Nog Pick-Me-Up 158
   Hot Chocolate 158
   Hot Spiced Cider 184
   Lemonade 180
   New Mexican Chocolate 80
   New Orleans Cafe au Lait 51
   Sherbet-Soda Punch 158
   Spiced Sun Tea 159
   Strawberry Milk Shake 158
   Tomato Sipper 159
   Vanilla Milk Shake 158
Biscuits Supreme 128
Black Bean Soup 39
Black Bottom Pie 49
Blueberries
   Blueberry Muffins 127
   Blueberry Grunt 28
   Blueberry Sourdough Pancakes 91
Blue Corn Bread 77
Boiled Lobster 15
Boston Baked Beans 18
Boston Brown Bread 23
Bran Muffins, Refrigerator 128
Braunschweiger Ball 155
Breads, Quick
   Banana Date-Nut Bread 128
   Beaten Biscuits 43
   Biscuits Supreme 128
   Blueberry Muffins 127
   Blueberry Sourdough Pancakes 91
   Blue Corn Bread 77
   Boston Brown Bread 23

Breads, Quick *(continued)*
   Buñuelos 79
   Buttermilk Doughnuts 182
   Cherry Coffee Cake 129
   Corn Sticks 43
   Corn Tortillas 76
   Cranberry Muffins 127
   Cranberry-Nut Bread 170
   Fig Bread 93
   Flour Tortillas 77
   Funnel Cakes 23
   Honey-Wheat Muffins 61
   Les Oreilles de Cochon 46
   Molasses Nut Bread 129
   Orange-Nut Bread 61
   Pancakes 128
   Pumpkin Bread 23
   Refrigerator Bran Muffins 128
   Southern Corn Bread 43
   Spoon Bread 42
   Waffles 127
Breads, Yeast
   Anadama Bread 22
   Beignets 44
   Caramel Rolls 124
   Dill-Onion Bread 127
   Dinner Rolls 125
   Easy-Mix White Bread 124
   Fruit-Filled Coffee Cake 125
   Hot Cross Buns 176
   Moravian Sugar Cake 44
   Pain Perdu 42
   Parker House Rolls 22
   Pennsylvania Dutch Christmas
     Loaves 169
   Pueblo Bread 77
   Rye Bread 123
   Soft Pretzels 182
   Sourdough Bread 91
   Swedish Limpa 61
   Whole Wheat Batter Rolls 123
   Whole Wheat Bread 123
Broccoli-Stuffed Cornish Hens 109
Broiled Scrod with Lemon Butter . . 14
Brown Sugar-Rhubarb Pie 65
Buñuelos 79
Burritos, Bean and Cheese 72
Burritos, Beef 72
Butter Frosting 135
Buttermilk Doughnuts 182
Buttermilk White Cake 130
Butterscotch Apple Dumplings . . .138

C

Caesar Salad 90
Café Almond 160
Café Brûlot 51
Café Columbian 160
Café Israel 160
Cakes
   Angel Cake 131
   Apple Cake 62
   Apricot Upside-Down Cake . . .130
   Buttermilk White Cake 130
   Carrot-Pineapple Cake 133
   Choco-Nut Ripple Cake 133
   Coconut Cake 46
   Cream-Filled Cake Roll 134
   Dark Fruitcake 170
   Devil's Food Cake 131
   German Chocolate Cake 133
   Gingerbread 134
   Grapefruit Chiffon Loaf Cake . . 94
   Hartford Election Cake 26
   Lane Cake 45
   Lemon Pudding Cake 134
   Lord Baltimore Cake 24
   Mother Ann's Birthday Cake . . . 26
   Prune Cake 94
   Regal Almond Pound Cake . . .131
   White Layer Cake 130
   Yellow Cake 130
   Yellow Cupcakes 130
California Cooler 95
Candied Citrus Peel 175
Candied Sweet Potatoes 165
Candies
   Candied Citrus Peel 175
   Divinity 175
   Easy Walnut Toffee 151
   Fudge 174
   Hard Candy 151
   Peanut Brittle 174
   Pralines 50
   Saltwater Taffy 184
Caramel Apples 184
Caramel-Chocolate Fondue 153
Caramel Corn 185
Caramel-Nut Slices 145
Caramel Pecan Sauce 153
Caramel Rolls 124
Carrot-Pineapple Cake 133
Carrots, Glazed 120
Catfish, Country Fried 58
Cereal Party Snack 156
Ceviche 81

Cheese
  Bean and Cheese Burritos 72
  Braunschweiger Ball 155
  Chef's Salad 105
  Cheesecake 148
  Cheesy Green Bean Casserole . 115
  Cheesy Scalloped Potatoes . . .118
  Chiles Rellenos 74
  Chili con Queso 81
  Four-Cheese Ball 155
  Lasagna 103
  Macaroni and Cheese 111
  Pizza 104
  Potato Cheese Soup 118
  Shallot Soufflé with
    Mushroom Sauce 113
  Sourdough Cheese Puff 111
  Submarine Sandwiches 105
Chef's Salad 105
Cherry Coffee Cake 129
Cherry Pie 64
Chess Tarts 48
Chestnut Stuffing 164
Chicken
  Chef's Salad 105
  Chicken Andouille Gumbo 34
  Chicken Fricassee 106
  Chicken Pies 106
  Chicken Salad 108
  Chicken Stoltzfus 12
  Chicken Tetrazzini 106
  Chop Suey 84
  Elegant Chicken a la King 108
  Kentucky Burgoo 33
  Oven-Fried Chicken 179
  Plymouth Succotash 12
  Skillet-Fried Chicken 179
  Sour Cream Chicken
    Enchiladas 72
  Southern Fried Chicken with
    Cream Gravy 34
  Stuffed Sopaipillas 69
  Submarine Sandwiches 105
Chicken Fried Steak with
    Cream Gravy 55
Chiles Rellenos 74
Chili con Queso 81
Chili, Texas-Style 71
Chimichangas 72
Chip-Chocolate Slices 145
Chocolate
  Chocolate Butter Frosting 135
  Chocolate Chip Cookies 144
  Chocolate Chip-Nut Pie 139
  Chocolate Crinkles 142
  Chocolate Milkshake 158

Chocolate (continued)
  Chocolate-Oatmeal Drop
    Cookies 144
  Chocolate Satin Frosting 135
  Choco-Nut Ripple Cake 133
  Chocolate Wafer Crust 140
Chop Suey 84
Cioppino 86
Citrus Chiffon Pie 138
Clams
  Manhattan Clam Chowder 17
  New England Clam Chowder . 17
  Steamed Clams 16
Cocktail Meatballs in Barbecue
    Sauce 154
Cocoa Brownies 145
Coconut
  Coconut Cake 46
  Coconut Crunch Torte 146
  Coconut Custard Pie 138
Codfish Balls 14
Coleslaw, Picnic 180
Coney Islands 181
Cookies
  Apees 173
  Caramel-Nut Slices 145
  Chip-Chocolate Slices 145
  Chocolate Chip Cookies 144
  Chocolate Crinkles 142
  Chocolate-Oatmeal Drop
    Cookies 144
  Cocoa Brownies 145
  Fruit and Grain Cookies 144
  Honey Peanut Butter Cookies . .142
  Indian Feast Day Cookies 79
  Joe Froggers 24
  Macaroon Drops 142
  Oatmeal Drop Cookies 144
  Pressed Cookies 173
  Raisin-Filled Granola Bars 145
  Refrigerator Nut Slices 145
  Rolled Ginger Cookies 171
  Short'nin' Bread 48
  Walnut Bars 62
  Wheaten Snickerdoodles 142
Corn
  Corn Oysters 20
  Corn Relish 60
  Corn-Stuffed Pork Chops 56
  Roasted Corn on the Cob 180
Corn Bread
  Blue Corn Bread 77
  Corn Bread Sausage Stuffing . .165
  Southern Corn Bread 43

Corn Dogs 181
Corned Beef Hash 99
Cornish Beef Pasties 54
Cornish Hens, Broccoli-Stuffed . . .109
Cornmeal Dumplings 56
Corn Sticks 43
Corn Tortillas 76
Country Fried Catfish 58
Country-Style Barbecued Ribs . . .177
Courtbouillon 36
Crab Cakes 16
Crab Louis 86
Cranberries
  Cranberry Catsup 90
  Cranberry Muffins 127
  Cranberry-Nut Bread 170
  Cranberry Relish 166
  Cranberry Sauce 166
Crawfish Étouffée 38
Cream Cheese Frosting 135
Creamed Onions 166
Cream-Filled Cake Roll 134
Cream Puffs 148
Creamy Potato Salad 179
Cucumber Salad 21

D

Daiquiri, Frozen 160
Dark Fruitcake 170
Deep-Dish Peach Pie 136
Dessert Coffee 160
Desserts (see also Cakes,
    Candies, Pies, and Cookies)
  Any-Fruit Sherbet 150
  Apple Jonathan 64
  Apple Pandowdy 28
  Banana Bread Pudding 146
  Bananas Foster 50
  Blueberry Grunt 28
  Buñuelos 79
  Butterscotch Apple Dumplings . 138
  Caramel Apples 184
  Caramel-Chocolate Fondue . .153
  Cheesecake 148
  Coconut Crunch Torte 146
  Cream Puffs 148
  Eclairs 148
  Flan 79
  Four-Fruit Freeze 151
  Fruit Cobbler 65
  Indian Pudding 28
  Layered Pudding Dessert 149

188

Desserts *(continued)*
    Lemon Cheesecake Squares . . 149
    Mocha Layered Dessert 149
    Ozark Pudding 62
    Peach Berry Cobbler 146
    Philadelphia Ice Cream 29
    Plum Pudding 173
    Pumpkin Ginger Freeze 150
    Raisin Bread Pudding 146
    Sherbet Cream Squares 149
    Strawberry Shortcake 180
Devil's Food Cake 131
Dill-Onion Bread 127
Dinner Rolls 125
Dirty Rice 41
Divinity 175
Dutch Fried Green Tomatoes 20

E-G

Easy Barbecue Sauce 177
Easy-Mix White Bread 124
Easy Walnut Toffee 151
Eclairs 148
Eggnog 175
Eggplant Soufflé 42
Eggs
    Egg Salad Sandwiches 114
    Eggs Benedict 113
    Eggs Florentine 114
    Huevos Rancheros 73
    Piquant Deviled Eggs 154
    Shallot Soufflé with Mushroom
        Sauce 113
    Sourdough Cheese Puff 111
Elegant Chicken a la King 108
Enchiladas, Sour Cream Chicken   72
Fig Bread 93
Fish
    Baked Stuffed Whitefish 58
    Barley-Stuffed Trout 88
    Broiled Scrod with Lemon
        Butter 14
    Ceviche 81
    Cioppino 86
    Codfish Balls 14
    Country Fried Catfish 58
    Courtbouillon 36
    Fish and Chips 110
    Grilled Salmon Steaks 88
    Lomi Lomi Salmon 95
    Oven-Fried Fish 109
    Poached Salmon with
        Egg Sauce 14
    Pompano en Papillote 36

Fish *(continued)*
    Salmon Party Spread 156
    Salmon Patties 110
    Tuna-Noodle Casserole 111
    Tuna Salad 108
Fish House Punch 29
Flan 79
Flour Tortillas 77
Fluffy White Frosting 135
Four-Cheese Ball 155
Four-Fruit Freeze 151
Frankfurters
    Bacon-Wrapped Franks 181
    Coney Islands 181
    Corn Dogs 181
French-Fried Onion Rings 116
French Fries 116
French Onion Soup 116
French Silk Pie 140
Fresh Fruit Salad 93
Fried Frog Legs 39
Fried Peach Pies 48
Frog Legs, Fried 39
Frostings
    Butter Frosting 135
    Chocolate Butter Frosting 135
    Chocolate Satin Frosting 135
    Coconut-Pecan Frosting 133
    Cream Cheese Frosting 135
    Fluffy White Frosting 135
    White Satin Frosting 135
Frozen Daiquiri 160
Fruit
    Any-Fruit Sherbet 150
    Apricot-Pineapple Pie 95
    Apricot Upside-Down Cake . . . 130
    Avocado-Grapefruit Salad 76
    Banana Bread Pudding 146
    Banana Cream Pie 139
    Banana Date-Nut Bread 128
    Beef Teriyaki with Pineapple . . . 84
    Berry Punch 159
    Blueberry Muffins 127
    Candied Citrus Peel 175
    Carrot-Pineapple Cake 133
    Cherry Coffee Cake 129
    Cherry Pie 64
    Citrus Chiffon Pie 138
    Cranberry Catsup 90
    Cranberry Muffins 127
    Cranberry-Nut Bread 170
    Cranberry Relish 166
    Cranberry Sauce 166
    Dark Fruitcake 170
    Deep-Dish Peach Pie 136
    Fig Bread 93

Fruit *(continued)*
    Four-Fruit Freeze 151
    Fresh Fruit Salad 93
    Fruit and Grain Cookies 144
    Fruit Cobbler 65
    Fruit-Filled Coffee Cake 125
    Fruit-Filled Empanadas 80
    Fruit Nog Pick-Me-Up 158
    Grapefruit Chiffon Loaf Cake . . 94
    Honey Fruit Sauce 153
    Lemon Meringue Pie 139
    Peach-Berry Cobbler 146
    Plum Pudding 173
    Prune Cake 94
    Raisin Bread Pudding 146
    Raisin-Filled Granola Bars 145
    Strawberry Milk Shake 158
    Strawberry Shortcake 180
    24-Hour Fruit Salad 169
Fudge 174
Fudge Sauce 153
Funnel Cakes 23
Game
    Grilled Elk Burgers 85
    Marinated Venison Chops 85
    Pheasant with Wild Rice 58
Garbanzo Salad 76
Garlic Vinaigrette 121
German Chocolate Cake 133
Gingerbread 134
Glazed Carrots 120
Glazed Ham 176
Glazed Nuts 185
Glazed Sweet Potatoes 41
Graham Cracker Crust 140
Granola, Spiced 156
Grapefruit Chiffon Loaf Cake 94
Grasshopper Pie 140
Green Beans
    Cheesy Green Bean Casserole 115
    Green Bean Casserole 115
    Green Beans Amadine 115
    Green Beans Chow Mein 115
    Sour Cream Green Bean
        Casserole 115
Green Chili Sauce 73
Green Goddess Dressing 121
Grillades and Grits 32
Grilled Elk Burgers 85
Grilled Salmon Steaks 88
Guacamole 81
Gumbo, Chicken Andouille 34
Gumbo, Seafood 37

H-R

Ham
    Chef's Salad 105
    Glazed Ham 176
    Ham with Red-Eye Gravy 34
    Submarine Sandwiches 105
Hard Candy 151
Hartford Election Cake 26
Harvard Beets 18
Hashed Brown Potatoes 116
Herb Curry Dip 156
Herbed Fresh Tomato Soup 120
Herbed Meat-Vegetable Kabobs   98
Herbed Vinaigrette 121
Honey
    Honey Fruit Sauce 153
    Honey Peanut Butter Cookies .. 142
    Honey-Wheat Muffins 61
Hopping John 168
Hot Buttered Rum 175
Hot Chocolate 158
Hot Cross Buns 176
Hot Spiced Cider 184
Hot Spiced Wine 160
Huevos Rancheros 73
Ice Cream, Philadelphia 29
Indian Feast Day Cookies 79
Indian Pudding 28
Irish Coffee 160
Jambalaya, Shrimp 37
Joe Froggers 24
Kentucky Burgoo 33
Key Lime Pie 50
Lane Cake 45
Lasagna 103
Layered Pudding Dessert 149
Lemons
    Lemonade 180
    Lemon Cheesecake Squares .. 149
    Lemon Meringue Pie 139
    Lemon Pudding Cake 134
Lentil Casserole 89
Les Oreilles de Cochon 46
Lobster, Boiled 15
Lobster Newburg 15
Lomi Lomi Salmon 95
Lord Baltimore Cake 24
Macadamia Nut Pie 93
Macaroni and Cheese 111
Macaroon Drops 142
Mai Tai 95
Manhattan Clam Chowder 17

Maple Custard Pie 27
Maple Syrup Acorn Squash 18
Marinated Three-Bean Salad 119
Marinated Venison Chops 85
Mayonnaise 121
Meatballs in Barbecue Sauce,
    Cocktail 154
Mince-Apple Pie 171
Mint French Silk Pie 140
Mint Julep 51
Mocha Layered Dessert 149
Molasses Nut Bread 129
Moravian Sugar Cake 44
Mormon Split Pea Soup 84
Mother Ann's Birthday Cake 26
New England Boiled Dinner 10
New England Clam Chowder 17
New Mexican Chocolate 80
New Orleans Café au Lait 51
New Orleans Muffuletta 33
New Potatoes and Peas 119
Oatmeal Drop Cookies 144
Okra Pickles 41
Old-Fashioned Fresh Vegetable-
    Beef Soup 99
Orange-Nut Bread 61
Oven-Fried Chicken 179
Oven-Fried Fish 109
Oyster Stew 168
Oyster Stuffing 164
Ozark Pudding 62
Pain Perdu 42
Pancakes 128
Pancakes, Blueberry Sourdough . 91
Parker House Rolls 22
Pastry for Double-Crust Pie 141
Pastry for Single-Crust Pie 141
Peach-Berry Cobbler 146
Peanut Brittle 174
Peanut Butter Cookies, Honey .. 142
Peanut Butter Sandwiches 114
Peanut Soup 39
Pennsylvania Dutch Christmas
    Loaves 169
Pheasant with Wild Rice 58
Philadelphia Ice Cream 29
Philadelphia Pepper Pot 10
Picadillo 69
Picnic Coleslaw 180
Piecrusts
    Baked Pastry Shell 141
    Chocolate Wafer Crust 49
    Gingersnap-Graham Crust 49
    Graham Cracker Crust 140
    Pastry for Double-Crust Pie 141
    Pastry for Single-Crust Pie 141

Pies
    Apple Pie 136
    Apricot-Pineapple Pie 95
    Banana Cream Pie 139
    Black Bottom Pie 49
    Brown Sugar-Rhubarb Pie 65
    Cherry Pie 64
    Chess Tarts 48
    Chocolate Chip-Nut Pie 139
    Citrus Chiffon Pie 138
    Coconut Custard Pie 138
    Deep-Dish Peach Pie 136
    French Silk Pie 140
    Fried Peach Pies 48
    Fruit-Filled Empanadas 80
    Grasshopper Pie 140
    Key Lime Pie 50
    Lemon Meringue Pie 139
    Macadamia Nut Pie 93
    Maple Custard Pie 27
    Mince-Apple Pie 171
    Mint French Silk Pie 140
    Pumpkin Pie 166
    Shoofly Pie 27
    Vanilla Cream Pie 139
Pigs in a Blanket 155
Piquant Deviled Eggs 154
Pizza 104
Plum Pudding 173
Plymouth Succotash 12
Poached Salmon with Egg Sauce   14
Pompano en Papillote 36
Popcorn Balls 185
Pork
    Apple-Stuffed Rib Roast 103
    Chop Suey 84
    Corn-Stuffed Pork Chops 56
    Country-Style Barbecued Ribs . 177
    Eggs Benedict 113
    Hopping John 168
    Mormon Split Pea Soup 84
    Picadillo 69
    Pork Stew with Cornmeal
        Dumplings 56
    Posole 71
    Red Beans and Rice 32
    Sausage and Kraut 55
    Schnitz un Knepp 11
    Scrapple 11
    Stuffed Cabbage Rolls 55
Posole 71
Potatoes
    Basque Potatoes 89
    Cheesy Scalloped Potatoes .. 118
    Creamy Potato Salad 179

Potatoes (continued)
French Fries 116
Hashed Brown Potatoes 116
New Potatoes and Peas 119
Potato Cheese Soup 118
Potato Pancakes with Pizazz . . .118
Potatoes Au Gratin 115
Scalloped Potatoes 118
Scootin' 'Long the Shore 20
Seattle Clam Hash 88
Twice-Baked Potatoes 59
Pralines 50
Pressed Cookies 173
Prune Cake 94
Pueblo Bread 77
Pumpkin
Pumpkin Bread 23
Pumpkin-Ginger Freeze 150
Pumpkin Pie 166
Pumpkin Soup 20
Raisin Bread Pudding 146
Raisin-Filled Granola Bars 145
Ramos Gin Fizz 51
Red Beans and Rice 32
Red Chili Sauce 68
Red Flannel Hash 10
Refried Beans 74
Refrigerator Bran Muffins 128
Refrigerator Nut Slices 145
Regal Almond Pound Cake 131
Rhubarb Pie, Brown Sugar- 65
Roast Beef Hash 99
Roast Beef with Yorkshire
Pudding 168
Roasted Corn on the Cob 180
Roast Turkey with Stuffing 164
Rolled Ginger Cookies 171
Rye Bread 123

S

Sage Stuffing 164
Salad Dressings
Garlic Vinaigrette 121
Green Goddess Dressing 121
Herbed Vinaigrette 121
Mayonnaise 121
Thousand Island Dressing 121
Vinaigrette 121
Salads, Main-Dish
Chef's Salad 105
Chicken Salad 108
Crab Louis 86
Taco Salad 100
Tuna Salad 108

Salads, Side-Dish
Avocado-Grapefruit Salad 76
Caesar Salad 90
Creamy Potato Salad 179
Cucumber Salad 21
Fresh Fruit Salad 93
Garbanzo Salad 76
Marinated Three-Bean Salad . .119
Picnic Coleslaw 180
Spinach, Bacon, and
Mushroom Salad 121
24-Hour Fruit Salad 169
Waldorf Salad 121
Wilted Salad 60
Salmon
Grilled Salmon Steaks 88
Lomi Lomi Salmon 95
Poached Salmon with Egg
Sauce 14
Salmon Party Spread 156
Salmon Patties 110
Saltwater Taffy 184
Sandwiches
Bacon-Wrapped Franks 181
Basic Grilled Burgers 177
Coney Islands 181
Egg Salad Sandwiches 114
Grilled Elk Burgers 85
New Orleans Muffuletta 33
Peanut Butter Sandwiches 114
Reubens 99
Sausage Sandwiches 105
Sloppy Joes 101
Steak Sandwiches 98
Stuffed Burgers 101
Submarine Sandwiches 105
Sauces
Caramel Pecan Sauce 153
Cranberry Catsup 90
Cranberry Sauce 166
Easy Barbecue Sauce 177
Fudge Sauce 153
Green Chili Sauce 73
Guacamole 81
Honey Fruit Sauce 153
Mayonnaise 121
Red Chili Sauce 68
Seafood Cocktail Sauce 154
Tartar Sauce 109
Sausage
Bacon-Wrapped Franks 181
Chicken Andouille Gumbo 34
Corn Bread Sausage Stuffing . .165
Lasagna 103
New Orleans Muffuletta 33

Sausage (continued)
Pigs in a Blanket 155
Pizza 104
Red Beans and Rice 32
Sausage and Kraut 55
Sausage Sandwiches 105
Spaghetti and Meat Sauce 104
Stuffed Sopaipillas 69
Submarine Sandwiches 105
Tacos 68
Sautéed Bay Scallops 15
Scalloped Corn 165
Scalloped Potatoes 118
Scalloped Tomatoes 60
Schnitz un Knepp 11
Scootin' 'Long the Shore 20
Scrapple 11
Seafood
Abalone Steaks 85
Boiled Lobster 15
Cioppino 86
Crab Cakes 16
Crab Louis 86
Crawfish Étouffée 38
Lobster Newburg 15
Manhattan Clam Chowder 17
New England Clam Chowder . 17
Oyster Stew 168
Oyster Stuffing 164
Pompano en Papillote 36
Sautéed Bay Scallops 15
Seafood Gumbo 37
Seattle Clam Hash 88
Shrimp Cocktail 154
Shrimp Creole 38
Shrimp Jambalaya 37
Steamed Clams 16
Vegetable-Oyster Stew 168
Seafood Cocktail Sauce 154
Seattle Clam Hash 88
Shaker Spinach with Rosemary . . 21
Shallot Soufflé with Mushroom
Sauce .113
Sherbet Cream Squares 149
Sherbet-Soda Punch 158
Shoofly Pie 27
Short'nin' Bread 48
Shrimp
Pompano en Papillote 36
Shrimp Cocktail 154
Shrimp Creole 38
Shrimp Jambalaya 37
Skillet Candied Sweet Potatoes . .165
Skillet-Fried Chicken 179
Sloppy Joes 101

Snacks (see also, Appetizers)
  Caramel Corn 185
  Cereal Party Snack 156
  Glazed Nuts 185
  Popcorn Balls 185
  Spiced Granola 156
  Tostaditas 76
Snapper Soup 17
Soft Pretzels 182
Soups and Stews
  Basic Beef Stew 98
  Black Bean Soup 39
  Chicken Andouille Gumbo 34
  Chicken Stoltzfus 12
  Cioppino 86
  Courtbouillon 36
  French Onion Soup 116
  Herbed Fresh Tomato Soup 120
  Kentucky Burgoo 33
  Manhattan Clam Chowder 17
  Mormon Split Pea Soup 84
  New England Clam Chowder   17
  Old-Fashioned Fresh
    Vegetable-Beef Soup 99
  Oyster Stew 168
  Peanut Soup 39
  Philadelphia Pepper Pot 10
  Pork Stew with Cornmeal
    Dumplings 56
  Posole 71
  Potato Cheese Soup 118
  Pumpkin Soup 20
  Seafood Gumbo 37
  Snapper Soup 17
  Turkey Frame Soup 108
  Vegetable-Oyster Stew 168
Sour Cream Chicken Enchiladas . 72
Sour Cream Green Bean
  Casserole 115
Sourdough
  Blueberry Sourdough Pancakes 91
  Sourdough Bread 91
  Sourdough Cheese Puff 111
  Sourdough Starter 91
Southern Corn Bread 43
Southern Fried Chicken with
  Cream Gravy 34
Spaghetti and Meat Sauce 104
Spanish Rice 120
Spiced Granola 156
Spiced Sun Tea 159
Spicy Bacon-Bean Pot 119
Spinach, Bacon, and Mushroom
  Salad 121
Spinach with Rosemary, Shaker . . 21

Spoon Bread 42
Squash, Maple Syrup Acorn 18
Steak Sandwiches 98
Steamed Clams 16
Stews (see Soups and Stews)
Strawberry Milk Shake 158
Strawberry Shortcake 180
Stuffed Burgers 101
Stuffed Cabbage Rolls 55
Stuffed Peppers 100
Stuffed Sopaipillas 69
Stuffings
  Chestnut Stuffing 164
  Corn Bread Sausage Stuffing . .165
  Oyster Stuffing 164
  Sage Stuffing 164
Submarine Sandwiches 105
Summer Vegetables 74
Swedish Limpa 61
Sweet Potatoes
  Candied Sweet Potatoes 165
  Glazed Sweet Potatoes 41
  Skillet Candied Sweet
    Potatoes 165

T-Z

Tacos 68
Taco Salad 100
Tamale Pie 68
Tartar Sauce 109
Texas-Style Chili 71
Thousand Island Dressing 121
Tomato Sipper 159
Tomato Soup, Herbed Fresh 120
Tortillas, Corn 76
Tortillas, Flour 77
Tostaditas 76
Tuna Noodle Casserole 111
Tuna Salad 108
Turkey Frame Soup 108
Turkey with Stuffing, Roast 164
24-Hour Fruit Salad 169
Twice-Baked Potatoes 59
Vanilla Cream Pie 139
Vanilla Milk Shake 158
Vegetable-Oyster Stew 168
Vegetables (see also, Potatoes)
  Artichokes with Citrus Butter
    Sauce 89
  Black Bean Soup 39
  Boston Baked Beans 18
  Candied Sweet Potatoes 165
  Cheesy Green Bean Casserole 115
  Chiles Rellenos 74

Vegetables (continued)
  Corn Oysters 20
  Corn Relish 60
  Creamed Onions 166
  Dutch Fried Green Tomatoes . . 20
  Eggplant Soufflé 42
  French-Fried Onion Rings 116
  French Onion Soup 116
  Glazed Carrots 120
  Glazed Sweet Potatoes 41
  Green Bean Casserole 115
  Green Beans Amandine 115
  Green Beans Chow Mein 115
  Harvard Beets 18
  Herbed Fresh Tomato Soup 120
  Lentil Casserole 89
  Maple Syrup Acorn Squash 18
  New Potatoes and Peas 119
  Okra Pickles 41
  Refried Beans 74
  Roasted Corn on the Cob 180
  Scalloped Corn 165
  Scalloped Tomatoes 60
  Shaker Spinach with Rosemary   21
  Skillet Candied Sweet
    Potatoes 165
  Sour Cream Green Bean
    Casserole 115
  Spanish Rice 120
  Spicy Bacon-Bean Pot 119
  Spinach, Bacon, and
    Mushroom Salad 121
  Summer Vegetables 74
  Whipped Rutabaga Puff 59
Venison Chops, Marinated 85
Waffles 127
Waldorf Salad 21
Walnut Bars 62
Wheaten Snickerdoodles 142
Whipped Rutabaga Puff 59
White Layer Cake 130
White Satin Frosting 135
Whole Wheat Batter Rolls 123
Whole Wheat Bread 123
Wilted Salad 60
Wine Spritzer 160
Yard of Flannel 29
Yellow Cake 130
Yellow Cupcakes 130